TROPICAL GARDEN STYLE
WITH **HARDY PLANTS**

A L A N H E M S L E Y

GUILD OF MASTER CRAFTSMAN
PUBLICATIONS LTD

First published 2002 by

Guild of Master Craftsman Publications Ltd

Castle Place, 166 High Street, Lewes, East Sussex BN7 1XU

Reprinted 2003

ISBN 1 86108 237 1

A catalogue record for this book is available from the British Library.

Editor: David Arscott

Book design: Kevin Knight; Layout: Francis & Partners

Cover design: Kevin Knight

Set in Goudy and Franklin Gothic

Colour origination by Viscan Graphics (Singapore)

Printed and bound in Kyodo Printing (Singapore)

Dedicated to Steve Davies,
without whose enthusiasm this
work would not have been
completed

CONTENTS

Part 1: Dreams, Designs and Practicalities

Part 2: The Plants

PART ONE

Dreams, Designs and Practicalities

1

Why have an exotic jungle garden?

Gardens are increasingly becoming places of retreat from the hectic pace of life, its stresses and pressures. We view our gardens as havens, our space in which to relax and escape. However, some gardens provide a greater sense of detachment from the outside world by reminding us of places separated by distance or time – of holidays abroad, of childhood memories, perhaps even of imagined places where time exists to savour life rather than just to survive it. These are exotic gardens, and all have an element of unreality, fantasy, fooling the senses into accepting an immediate transition to another place, providing that easy escape.

Gardening must also be a challenge. By its very nature, it involves the taming, controlling and altering of the environment to suit our tastes. In general, we grow plants in our gardens that are not far removed from the natural vegetation of our local area or other parts of the world with a similar climate. The plants are therefore similarly adapted and show the same kinds of characteristics (similar shaped leaves, comparable growth habits and common pollinators), offering little contrast to the plants in the nearby hedge or field boundary. In addition, because they are adapted to our climate they are robust and require relatively little attention. Few of us, however, settle for growing only those plants that will survive all weathers out of doors. We grow houseplants, perhaps a geranium or two for that decorative pot by the door, tomatoes (because we know they taste better grown at home), some alpines in special gritty soil, and a *Camellia* in a tub of ericaceous compost. These provide us with a challenge, to stretch the alteration of our local environment that bit further. We consider these plants worth the extra effort because of the rewards they bring, be it green foliage in winter, flavoursome fruit or exquisite flowers.

An exotic jungle garden is one step further. By introducing leaf shapes different from those of our native and locally adapted plants we can create a contrast that is both dramatic and exciting. The purpose of this book is to show how a garden of exotic interest can be created using plants which are essentially deceptive: many of them are as easy to care for as our natives, but they differ from them in *appearing* to be exotic. Many require only a reasonable soil and position to thrive, while others will require a sheltered site or a little winter protection to do well. A few are worth protecting in an unheated or slightly heated greenhouse, a conservatory or even a garage, as they can contribute those finer touches to the overall scheme. Furthermore, this is not a book written for those lucky few who benefit from a naturally mild climate. Instead, the measures of hardiness provided should be applicable throughout Britain, with the possible exception of eastern Scotland where the climate can be particularly harsh. For this reason, plants such as *Cordyline australis*, which thrive over much of southwest England, are considered here to require some winter protection, principally from excessive moisture.

BELOW **Succulent plants forming an exotic display on the Côte d'Azur, France**

Creating the exotic paradise

If the construction of an exotic garden is what you seek then it is important to remember an important basic in design: the plants come first. These days there is much discussion and demonstration of architectural hard landscaping in gardens, and this is all well and good when dealing with plants that are well behaved, small, delicate or fussy. Exotic or tropical style plants are not small or well behaved (although they may be fussy). The whole concept of a tropical-style garden is that it should appear overgrown and full of vegetation – interesting vegetation. So don't worry too much about an ugly shed (cover it in something rampant such as *Akebia*) or the neighbour's fence (screen it with *Helianthus tuberosus*, the Jerusalem artichoke, or *Miscanthus floridulus*). If the soil is horrible wet clay, use it: dig in plenty of peat substitute and plant *Gunnera*. If you have deep shade, use *Fatsia* and *Aucuba*. If the soil is dry and sandy, plant *Yucca*, and if it's baking hot in summer, try some succulents. Few people have perfect soil so worry not, as there is a wide choice available for whatever you have. This is not a book about how high to build retaining walls or how to construct a pond, nor is it a book about finding the correct shade of lavender to paint the wall or what width of wood slat to use on the decking. Instead, here you will find what to grow over the retaining wall and what will dramatize your pond, what will obscure the awful shade of lavender and what will spill across the decking to break up the hard lines and soften the outline. This is a book about plants.

RIGHT *Cordyline australis* and *Echium* at Trebah, Cornwall, UK

Basic structures

Structure is fundamental in the jungle garden and in most cases will have been predetermined by you or the previous owners of your garden. By structure I mean those features that have a major impact on the immediate surroundings. These include the aspect of your garden, its slope, terracing, existing trees, large shrubs, fences, pergolas, sheds and greenhouses. Most of these structural aspects cannot be changed and some you may not want to change. Aspect and large existing trees are the ones most likely to prevent you achieving your exotic ambitions. A north-facing slope (south-facing in the southern hemisphere) is a problem as such slopes tend to be relatively cold and poorly lit. Don't confuse this with a south-facing slope on the north side of a house, which may be very different. Deep shade cast by existing large (and often protected) trees is also difficult, but both situations can be overcome with correct planting. In the former situation hardier plants and extra winter protection may be the answer, while the dry shade cast by large trees will require plants which can cope with these conditions, such as *Aucuba*, *Bergenia*, some *Euphorbia* and *Heuchera*.

ABOVE **This old archway at Tresco, Isle of Scilly, UK, forms a magnificent feature among the exotic planting**

BELOW **A large pond at Abbotsbury in Dorset, UK, with dense tropical surroundings**

Structures that you can introduce include ponds and other water environments, pergolas and raised beds – these perhaps containing special soil mixes such as a gritty, sunny bed for succulents. Water areas and damp areas are important in the tropical-style garden since many of the larger-leaved perennials are naturally inhabitants of damp areas and will not achieve their full size without abundant soil moisture. Ponds can easily be constructed using preformed plastic moulds, flexible plastic or rubber sheeting or even concrete. All of these (unless they leak) will not affect their surroundings, so remember that the soil around such an unnatural pond could be quite dry. Bog gardens or damp areas can be created by restricting drainage. This is a little like making a pond, but the liner or receptacle is refilled with soil (preferably slightly enriched). Simple plastic sheeting can be used. It is quite important that this does leak a little or it may be too wet, so use a fork to put some holes in the bottom. A good depth is important if you wish to grow *Gunnera*, when excavation to at least 1m (more than 3ft) will be necessary. Raised beds for plants that require extreme drainage or a precise soil type should also be lined, at least around the sides. Ensure that water drains freely from the bottom of such a structure by using a thick layer of stones and coarse grit at the bottom. For acid-loving plants, make sure that any stone material you use is free of lime.

Other very important structural elements for the tropical style garden include supports for climbers. Most gardens have at least one wall (often the house wall) on which to grow plants. Walls are better than other supports where tender plants are concerned since their temperature tends to lag behind changing air temperatures. This means they can remain a little warmer on winter nights but are also a little slower to warm up the following day. South-facing (in the northern hemisphere) and west-facing walls are warmer, as they tend to receive the sun in the day and evening. House walls will radiate a little extra warmth whatever their aspect. Fences and the sides of sheds and gazebos can also be used as supports. With either walls or fences you will need to fix something for the plant to climb through or be tied to, usually wires or trellis. I am a great fan of pergolas as support for climbing plants and lax shrubs. They have the advantage not just of providing vertical support but also of a horizontal 'roof' that enables large climbers to produce a canopy giving an enclosed feeling to the space – a very important aspect of the jungle-style garden. Pergolas need not be free-standing. A 'lean-to' pergola against the house can span a seating area providing shade in summer and giving the effect of an extra room. Obelisks, archways and arbours also provide vertical plant supports.

BELOW *Humulus lupulus* 'Aureus' is an excellent vigorous climber for a shady pergola

Seating areas and patio areas are important structural elements. Although the essential balance between areas of planting and open space is less important in the jungle-style garden than elsewhere, it should still be given full consideration. Sufficiently large areas should be free of plants to allow proper use of the garden for children, entertaining and relaxation. Remember that the jungle should encroach onto such areas: leave a little extra space for it to do so. You may also lose part of your open areas to container displays so, again, if you are planning a patio or open space make it larger than you think you need. Open areas should be constructed of the appropriate materials. Lawns are not a good idea, since they require considerable maintenance and the surrounding jungle will ruin the edges when it nudges into your free space. Nonetheless, if you really want a lawn it can be quite effective as a contrast of texture. Better is paving or brick, but with a weathered look. Perhaps best of all for the exotic style of garden are expanses of wood chips (natural colour, not dyed) or gravel. These should be laid on a weed-proof membrane after which they will be more or less

maintenance-free, although some of the exotics may try to take up residence. In most cases around 5cm (2in) depth of woodchips or gravel will be sufficient. If you need to edge your open area, use split wooden pins or bricks that will blend with the materials used.

Many people consider that a sloping or contoured site is unsatisfactory and makes gardening difficult. Certainly a steep slope can be difficult, but changes in level within a garden can help in the definition of separate areas as well as providing a more interesting aspect. I suspect that the general distaste of slopes stems from the desire to have wonderful, perfectly flat, green lawns. In tropical style gardening, no lawns, no problem. The best way of dealing with a steep slope is to construct a series of terraces. I have adopted this approach in my 1-in-8 west-facing garden in South Wales, where I am 'lucky' enough to have a badly-drained concoction of builder's rubble and heavy clay. The bottom terrace is actually a natural pond. If your slope is more shallow you could consider sloping beds with a little support on the lower side and gently curving paths. It is, however, worth ensuring that some areas are level (for

BELOW *Sedum sedoides* is typical of many succulent plants which grow in dry soils – here in southern France

seating and other activities) and these may entail some excavation or the construction of raised areas. It may be hard work initially, but contoured gardens are much more interesting than flat ones, even flat exotic ones.

Finally, the most important structural aspects are the large plants that will form focal points, screening or shelter within the garden. These include trees and shrubs as well as large perennials such as *Phormium*, bamboo and *Gunnera*. If you are lucky enough to be starting a garden from scratch, as I was two years ago, you can plan exactly which plants you want as structural elements and where best to place them with respect to their particular function. Height is important in the tropical-style garden and what you need to aim for is a series of interconnected small glades between robust upright frames. This means ensuring that there is adequate space between major structural elements so that plenty of light can penetrate between them.

You will need to consider how big some of these plants can become and to provide space accordingly. It is perfectly acceptable to cluster large structural elements together to form bigger 'blocks', especially if you have an extensive garden. This can give the impression of thickets of dense vegetation and will help to produce more sheltered areas of benefit to the large-leaved perennials. Structural planting need not always occupy the middle of beds. A better effect is often achieved if the dominant feature is placed off-centre. What I would urge, though, is that planting should diminish gradually in height away from tall structural plants, or these can appear stark and isolated. This arrangement is merely reflecting the natural circumstance where a large plant will provide peripheral shelter enabling adjacent tall plants to flourish. Furthermore, natural paths will skirt the edges of more dense areas of vegetation, since the larger animals responsible for their formation would be unable to penetrate these thickets. When planning your tropical-style garden, visit a few woodland edges in your local area and look at the shapes and heights of the plants there, particularly in relation to paths, ditches and open areas. This may give you some ideas on where to place structural plants and what to plant next to them.

One or all seasons?

It is very difficult to have an all-year exotic garden. The large leaves and lush foliage that are the essence of the tropical effect rapidly succumb to the vagaries of winter. Even in mild districts, those plants that can contribute the most to richness of the summer garden tend to be deciduous or herbaceous. If you really desire exotic winter effects, concentrate on the evergreen structural plants such as *Yucca*, *Cordyline*, *Aucuba*, *Fatsia* and *Hedera*. These will all provide bold, architectural shapes, even in the darkest days. Exotic flowers at this time of year are hard to come by. Most of the winter-flowering bulbs such as *Crocus* and *Iris* are good, with foliage that rapidly disappears in spring, especially if surrounded by bold herbaceous plants whose growth will conceal any withering leaves.

Spring is still quiet in terms of tropical growth, although there are some exotics that bloom with the early lengthening days. *Acacia dealbata* and *Sophora microphylla* are worth trying in a sheltered spot for their sprays of yellow, and in boggy soils *Lysichiton* will be unfurling its yellow or white cowls. The herbaceous and shrubby *Euphorbia* species are excellent plants for spring colour, providing sprays of lime green, yellow and red. As spring advances, the herbaceous plants seem to explode into growth, and this is especially true of those with large leaves and exotic appearance. *Gunnera* and *Rheum* leaves expand into great sheets of foliage, and many of the large grasses such as *Miscanthus* rocket skyward. If you feel that you lack spring colour, many of the spring bulbs are good because their foliage blends well with the exotic theme. Tulips are fun, particularly the fringed and parrot forms, and *Fritillaria imperialis* is genuinely of exotic appearance with the pineapple-like tuft of leaves above the flowers. All too soon your seedling gourds and marrows will be too big for their pots, the variegated sweet corn will be growing a few centimetres each day and buds will be swelling on the *Brugmansia*. As the first *Kniphofia* extend their vivid pokers, summer is upon us and once again the exotic fun can begin.

Summer should be the time when exotic gardeners can relax and enjoy their surroundings and, indeed, for most of the time this will be the case. However, many of these exotic-appearance plants are fast growers, and established specimens may need cutting back (not too much, mind) to maintain access to paths, through gates and around corners. Lawns are not usually an issue in the jungle garden – I maintain that grasses are only worthwhile if they grow more than 1.5m (5ft) in height in a year – so you can sit back and listen to your neighbours undergoing the weekly mowing chore. Since most of the exotics bloom in summer, there should be no shortage of flowers amongst the dense green foliage.

BELOW *Kniphofia uvaria* is one of many red hot pokers that bloom in summer

Early autumn is a good time for exotics, too. Many of the herbaceous plants need a lengthy spell of growth before they have enough energy to bloom, so flowers are often abundant. Fruits of various kinds will also add interest as the gourds and pumpkins ripen in orange, yellow and red, and the grapes and figs become sweet on the vines and bushes. As the days grow shorter and the nights darker and colder, care should be taken to prevent the tender summer occupants of the garden suffering excessive wetting or damage from early frost. Leaf colour on many plants deepens and reddens, while the leaves of *Hosta* turn a buttery yellow before collapsing to the ground. The cycle of the year is complete as the leaves fall and the exotics rest, sated after the summer feast of sunshine and ready to begin again after the cold of winter.

Up and over

Height is particularly important in the tropical-style garden. One practical reason is that that tall vegetation can provide shelter from the strong winds that can otherwise be a major problem for large-leaved perennials. In real jungles, many plants strive upward to reach what little light penetrates the tree canopy far above, and this means that lengthy vistas in open jungle habitats are rare. In the jungle garden we can use tall plants not only to guide the eye to focal points but to prevent the viewer seeing the entirety of the garden at once, thus creating some mystery and a desire to explore. This is even more important in small gardens where, without tall plants to break up the view, it is all too easy to see everything at once. The introduction of a sense of mystery in a garden is a fundamental aspect of its design and you should certainly give it priority regardless of the size and shape of your garden.

In jungles too, many plants produce much of their growth higher up, away from the forest floor. Climbers and lianas run up almost anything that will support them and expand into leafy canopies well above head height. An exotic garden should reflect this by utilising climbers as much as possible and to ensure that these are able to spread above the head in some way. This can be achieved by supporting them on wires strung from various high points around the garden, on pergolas and obelisks, or by training them into mature trees where they can spread and eventually hang in curtains from the lower branches. Climbers such as *Parthenocissus* (more often seen on walls) and *Humulus* are particularly good for this effect.

BELOW *Parthenocissus* **is an excellent climber, with leaves that take on red tones in autumn**

RIGHT *Platicerium* **is a tropical fern that can be grown outside in summer. However, it needs protection from frost in winter**

In the tropics many plants – particularly ferns, orchids and bromeliads – grow entirely on the branches of trees way up in the canopy. Even at lower levels these epiphytic plants will live supported on tree fern trunks or rocky outcrops. They are not parasites, since they do not damage the plant that supports them. They live on the humus that collects in the forks of branches, and rely on the high humidity and frequent rains to keep them moist. In temperate regions epiphytic plants are far less common, and in Britain, besides numerous mosses and lichens, only the common polypody (*Polypodium vulgare*) properly adopts this mode of existence, and then usually close to ground level. This aspect of a jungle environment is difficult to recreate, but I have found that many ferns, moderately tough orchids such as *Cymbidium* and bromeliads such as *Fascicularia* and *Bilbergia* will do well through the summer in pots strapped to tree trunks or in baskets attached to walls, not to speak of the more traditional hanging baskets. All of these 'fake' epiphytes will need attention to watering as they can quickly dry out, and it is best to use them where possible in a mostly shaded site. Any of these methods helps to get the vegetation off the ground and up to or above eye level, where it will contribute greatly to the tropical feel.

Ground cover

Weeds are less of a problem in the jungle garden than in other styles of garden: the lush foliage and vigorous growth of the plants usually smothers them. In order to reduce weed growth at the outset I would strongly recommend the use of a weed-proof porous membrane. In most cases the beds containing tropical-style plants will require a surface mulch (usually of bark chippings or gravel) and this will cover an otherwise unsightly membrane. Be careful, however, of using a membrane around plants that spread by underground runners, because these may not be able to penetrate it. *Miscanthus floridulus,* for example, can lift whole areas of buried membrane through a surface mulch as its new shoots emerge in spring.

Where you require ground-cover planting, you may have to do without a membrane to enable the plants to spread effectively. *Lamium galeobdolon* and *Ajuga* 'Catlin's Giant' are examples of plants that do better in such a situation. Some spreaders, such as the creeping *Sedum* species, will not mind the presence of a membrane under the gravel in which they grow. Even if you don't use a membrane, it is as well to mulch your beds, as this not only keeps away the weeds but also provides a more constant soil environment that will benefit the plants you do want to thrive. There are various mulches available commercially, and it is really a matter of choice, but

BELOW **Bananas and other plants with lush foliage that cast shade are best mulched with bark chippings or a similar organic material**

remember that succulents and spiky plants look best against a gravel mulch whereas large-leaved perennials are happy with an organic covering such as bark chippings or coco shells. (If you use wood chips or bark, add a nitrogenous fertilizer with this as the decomposition of woody material actually depletes soil nitrogen levels). Grass mowings are also an acceptable organic mulch but should not be piled thickly and are perhaps best mixed with bark chippings or the like before application.

Water

Although water is not an essential feature of the tropical-style garden, there is little doubt that either still or moving water can accentuate the atmosphere we are trying to create. I dislike the term 'water feature', as to me this conjures the idea of formal or quaint trickling affairs that fail utterly to blend with their surroundings. Simple ponds of an irregular shape fit well in the tropical-style garden, however, and they should be as large as you can afford and manage within the space you have: the marginal vegetation and surrounding plants will always diminish the apparent size of your pond once established. Avoid fountains unless you are working within a formal arrangement, perhaps of more Mediterranean plants, where such unnaturalness is acceptable. Moving water is more of a challenge. A slow-moving, deep stream lined with lush vegetation is probably something to aim for as a natural feature but, once established, the planting will obscure your water, probably defeating the object. Masking the edge of an artificial stream with rocks can help but may look fake unless done with care. Try to use flat rocks wherever possible. Lining the edges with inverted turf works well, and it can look quite natural once you have established smaller creeping plants in it. Weeds, however, will be a problem and you may find that a lot of water is drawn out of your circulating system by capillary action. Always consider water in relation to the contours of your garden. Natural ponds always look best in the lowest part of the garden or in a natural hollow. Waterfalls are silly on flat sites, but where you have a slope they are perfect and provide an additional sense of sound into the garden.

ABOVE **Emerging leaves and flowers of *Gunnera* are an imposing sight at the water's edge**

Soils

Soil type dictates to some extent the plants that can be grown in the open ground, but it should not be seen as restricting the diversity of plants that the garden can support. Few of us experience perfect soil and, indeed, the idea of what is perfect depends on what we wish to grow. Those frequently seen as problematic include heavy clay soils, alkaline soils and the combination of rubble and highly compressed soil found around recently built houses. There are plants that will happily survive all of these condtions, and obviously these should be used whenever possible. Some soil improvement will be necessary in order to grow a wider range of plants, and with most problem soils the addition of organic material in the form of well rotted manure or garden compost is the best policy. This should be dug in deeply – if possible down to 0.5m (1½ft) – and thoroughly mixed with the existing soil, preferably in autumn. Where extra drainage is required, grit and sharp sand can be added in the same manner. A newly dug site is best left for a month or so before planting as this gives the mixture time to reach equilibrium and for the soil bacteria to begin work on the material you have added. Try to avoid compressing your soil by walking on it. This will assist drainage and, although plants dislike large cavities around their roots, a certain amount of air in the soil is essential for the well-being of any plant.

Some plants require an acid soil on which to grow. The reason for this is that calcium carbonate (a compound that makes soils alkaline) inhibits the uptake of nutrients by such plants, particularly magnesium and iron, and so the plants gradually starve. Normally these plants grow on soils that are naturally low in calcium and so are neutral or acidic. If you wish to grow acid-loving plants then you must ensure that the compost you intend to use is low in calcium. To make matters more difficult, calcium carbonate is relatively soluble in water and can migrate below soil level. Organic garden compost is usually fairly low in calcium, particularly if you avoid the inclusion of egg shells, and this can be used for acid-loving plants, mixed with sharp sand and grit (make sure that it is not beach sand or limestone grit). For most plants this would need to be mixed with some loam, such as J12 (John Innes potting compost no. 2) potting mixture, but for extreme acid lovers even this can be too alkaline and is therefore best avoided. If in doubt it is possible to buy ready-mixed 'ericaceous' composts suitable for most acid-loving plants. If your natural garden soil is alkaline then you may have to restrict your acid-loving plants to containers with the appropriate soil, although you could also try raised beds – again with the correct soil mix. To avoid seepage of soluble calcium from the surrounding soil, ensure that drainage beneath the bed is good and consider lining the base with polythene (remembering to leave drainage holes). If your acid-lovers begin to look a little yellow and you suspect that they may have become contaminated with calcium, try watering them with a hydrangea blueing compound (aluminium sulphate), following the directions given. This improves the availability of iron salts in the soil by reducing calcium solubility.

BELOW *Crinodendron* is a plant which requires a soil with minimal calcium. Such plants are often termed 'acid loving'

Aesthetic aspects

Open ground

The intention of this book is to provide an introduction to the range of exotic-looking plants that are hardy enough to spend most, if not all, of the year outside. There is no reason therefore that these

BELOW **A spectacular display of subtropical bedding in Badenweiler, Germany**

should not be permanently planted in a suitable site. When positioning plants it is clearly important to consider the conditions under which they would thrive in their natural habitat since this has an immediate bearing on their survival and vigour. In general, the aspects to consider are the amount of sunshine a site receives, drainage and soil moisture, and exposure. Many plants naturally grow in open places and these almost always require full sun (minimal shading from other plants or buildings). Such plants are often also able to cope with an exposed site where winds can be strong. Open sites often occur because the soil is too shallow or too dry to support large tree growth, and so good drainage is also related to a requirement for abundant light. Typical plants that require these conditions are succulents, most grasses and many of the lily-like herbaceous and shrubby perennials.

Other plants are tolerant of shade in varying amounts. These naturally grow in the company of trees (although not necessarily directly beneath them) and share their requirements of a moist deep soil. Because trees reduce wind speed in their immediate surroundings, plants around them can develop large leaves which elsewhere might suffer wind damage and drying. Large leaves also help in compensating for the reduced light levels in shade. Typical plants in this category are *Hosta*, *Rheum* and *Gunnera*. The shapes of plant leaves are therefore often a guide to particular requirements but these are only general guidelines and there are many exceptions (among them *Luzula*, a grassy plant that likes shade, and *Zantedeschia* that likes full sun).

Plants that naturally live in or close to water, such as *Ligularia*, often have large leaves and prefer full sun. They can survive this because their abundant supply of water can prevent dehydration of the leaves. Trees and shrubs follow a similar pattern, with small-leaved types usually requiring sunshine and good drainage while large leaved trees and shrubs such as *Magnolia* and *Fatsia* are happy in more shaded sites with moist soils.

Containers

Plants grown in containers have a number of advantages over those in the open ground. Primarily these plants are moveable and so can be brought under cover in winter. This means that plants grown in containers need not be fully hardy. However, the converse of this is that container-grown plants, if left outside for the winter, will suffer more from very cold night temperatures since their roots will freeze as well as their stems. Containerised plants can also be given specific attention in terms of a precise soil mixture and watering regime. This, for example, enables us to grow acid-loving plants in the appropriate medium, even where the local soil is of an alkaline nature. The mobility of containerised plants also means that they can be placed in full view when the plants are attractive, but moved to another site when they have outlived their welcome. An example of this might be a pot of *Fritillaria imperialis* which is wonderful in bloom, but which looks very sad shortly afterwards as the leaves yellow and wither.

The choice of soil type for container-grown plants is particularly important but should be considered alongside the container to be used. Succulents, for example, require a compost that is free-draining. If an unglazed terracotta pot is used (as I would recommend for these plants) then water loss will be rapid and even drought-adapted plants will need frequent watering when in growth. In glazed terracotta or plastic, water loss through the pot is reduced and waterings may therefore be less frequent. Relatively waterproof containers are therefore better for plants such as *Hosta* that can dry rapidly because of their large leaf area. Soils that are rich in humus tend to retain moisture for longer than soils with a high proportion of sand and grit: again, moisture retention can be improved by incorporating organic material, although if this does dry out it can be difficult to re-wet without considerable and frequent soakings.

Whether you mulch the soil in containers is a matter of choice. A decorative gravel covering can add contrast to a display but can also be used on a number of different pots in a display to link them together. Wood chips could also be used on larger containers. Consider also using other plants as a foil for the surface of large containers. Small annual plants are excellent for this purpose such as *Dorotheanthus* and *Begonia* 'Semperflorens'. Hardy pot sharers include the creeping *Sedum* species, *Ajuga*, and *Saxifraga* x *urbicum*. For pots that are not exposed to frost, try *Soleirolia soleirolii* (mind your own business) or tender creeping *Sedum* and *Crassula* species. In very large containers you could plant ivy-leaved *Pelargonium* and or *Chlorophytum* but take care that these do not compete with the main occupant.

Containers for water plants must clearly be entirely waterproof and without drainage holes. Usefully a number of suppliers provide pots and containers without basal perforations, the larger of which are ideal for growing both hardy and tender aquatics. When planting containerised water plants, choose a container that will hold the appropriate depth of water and soil for the plants you

BELOW **A selection of potted plants around a seat provides cool but exotic surroundings**

intend to grow. Generally a deep tub is needed for water lilies but a shallower bowl may be adequate for normally marginal plants. Allow space for 10–15 cm of soil depth at the base. It helps to use specially prepared, low fertility aquatic soils for this but it is not essential unless you require clear water. Most plants can be planted directly into this soil base but if you prefer, use aquatic baskets containing the same mixture. Site your water-filled container before filling since water is heavier than an equivalent volume of soil.

Flower colour

There has been much written about colour in the garden, usually with respect to flowers. Much of this advice seems to have been written for designers, rather than people who want to grow plants. My only advice on flowers is to avoid putting colours that are very similar next to each other as this can detract from the impact of both. However, if you are the kind of gardener who is concerned about colour schemes then I doubt that the tropical style is what you seek. To be a tropical gardener means not being afraid of bright, garish flowers and actively avoiding those 'ever so pretty' pastel shades. But why should this be the case? There is actually a sound reason: in jungles and places of dense, luxuriant growth, the predominant colour is green. Flowers are relatively rare in relation to the amount of foliage, so a plant needs to be bright if it is to be noticed by a potential pollinator. The same is also true of desert plants that may be scattered over wide distances and need to attract any passing attention while their short-lived flowers are open.

The colours that show up most against green foliage are those which contrast most strongly, especially reds, oranges and yellows, through to magenta and bright pinks. Blue flowers are uncommon, being largely absent, for example, in orchids and cacti. The tropical style garden should reflect this bias towards bright colours and especially reds, oranges and yellows – colours that have in the past been considered as difficult to accommodate in the garden, but perhaps only with pastel shades. Many of the plants I recommend have appropriate flower colours,

ABOVE **Forms of *Canna* provide exotic flowers in bright colours together with tropical foliage**

but there are many more that could be used. Conversely, there are several plants described here that have pale or pastel flowers, but most of these I have chosen for their foliage rather than their blooms.

Foliage colours

The subject of foliage colour is complex and clearly a matter of taste. For some a jungle garden might include a vast array of garish contrasts chosen to give maximum vibrancy to the scene. Participants in the creation of such a vista might include *Canna* 'Striata', *Houttonia cordata* 'Chameleon', *Agave americana* f. *marginata*, and a diversity of *Phormium* cultivars, perhaps with some *Solenostemon* hybrids interplanted. Another concept may include the creation of a scene of grey and silver with *Phormium tenax*,

Melianthus major, Hosta sieboldiana 'Elegans', *Parahebe perfoliata, Eucalyptus globulus* and *Astelia nervosa*. Both are feasible and exotic in appearance, but they do not strike me as offering relaxing or particularly evocative surroundings. Plants with such bold and outstanding colouration are more effective when used in isolation amongst a mass of calming foliage, instead of vying with each other for attention. In general I would advise against many variegated plants which are almost always too strident. Grey-leaved plants combine well with succulents

ABOVE **These succulents in the Jardin Exotique in Monaco have superbly contrasting leaf shape and colour**

(as one might imagine, since in general they are also drought-adapted) but look out of place among the rich, dark greens of the jungle garden.

Some yellow-leaved forms are acceptable if used with care, although many will scorch if given too much direct sunlight. Notable are *Choisya ternata* 'Sundance', *Lysimachia nummularia* 'Aurea', *Humulus lupulus* 'Aureus', *Jasminum officinale* 'Fiona Sunrise', *Hakonechloa macra* 'Aureola', the yellow and gold-leaved *Hosta*, (particularly *H.* 'Sum and Substance') and *Catalpa bignonioides* 'Aurea'. All provide a warm glow, like shafts of sunlight penetrating the forest canopy.

Bronzes, reds, maroons and browns are much safer territory. Many tropical and exotic plants naturally have red or purple leaves, commonly on the underside. Reds and purples are complimentary to the greens of most exotic foliage. Valuable reds and purples are *Cordyline australis* 'Purpurea', *Phormium tenax* 'Purpureum', *Heuchera micrantha* var. *diversifolia* 'Palace Purple', *Canna* 'Wyoming', *Vitis vinifera* 'Purpurea', *Photinia* 'Red Robin' and *Cotinus coggygaria* 'Purpureus'. As with all non-green leaf plants, these too should be distributed among a backcloth of green, but they seldom jar and they provide a powerful, yet subtle contrast.

Leaf shape and texture

The leaf shape and form of any particular plant is often a reflection of the conditions prevalent in its original habitat. Arid habitats result in succulent or small, hairy leaves to reduce water loss. Cold climates lead to thin, deciduous leaves, often with serrated margins. Tropical climates permit the production of large leaves, often with linear tips to shed water from their extensive surfaces. The preponderance of any particular leaf shape may change from place to place, warmer climes frequently having more spiky vegetation. Exotic gardens must exploit these differences and emphasize an alternative selection of shapes and outlines from those that normally occupy our gardens (once again a reminder that we usually grow plants from areas with a similar climate to our own). More than anything else in the jungle garden, it is leaf shape and size that is important in creating atmosphere – that feeling of having been transported in an instant to somewhere exciting and different. In the jungle garden, foliage is the most important aspect and flowers are a secondary bonus.

Exotic gardens should have plants with large leaves, preferably with a simple outline. Typical examples are *Hosta* and *Catalpa*. In natural vegetation, however, plants with many different leaf types combine together to occupy as many different microenvironments as possible. Large leaves are part of this patchwork but cannot be used alone or they will appear unnatural. Mix large-leaved plants with others that have contrasting shapes. For example, large

simple leaves work well with grasses and ferns. Remember also that leaf colour and texture can produce contrasts. A combination of *Trachystemon* and *Hosta sieboldiana* 'Elegans', for example, provides a rough dark green leaf and a smooth blue-green leaf, although both leaves are large and oval. Some large-leaved plants have irregular outlines, such as *Rheum, Gunnera* and *Fatsia*. These seem to work well in almost any combination, but avoid crowding too many large-leaved plants together or the effect will be diminished.

The grassy and spiky-leaved plants make excellent contrasts with the large-leaved plants but can also produce interesting effects on their own. A mixture of grasses and various forms of *Yucca*, interspersed with *Kniphofia* and *Hemerocallis* can produce a very exotic border. *Yucca*

BELOW **Palm leaves have dramatic architectural shapes**

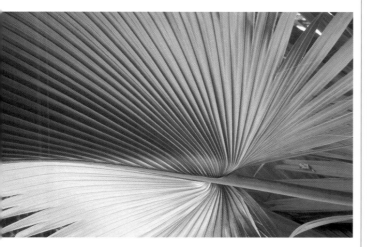

ABOVE **The branches of *Dracaena draco* in silhouette are fascinating, but this and similar plants can also cast equally interesting shadows**

ABOVE **Spiky foliage, such as that of *Cordyline australis*, provides important contrasts in tropical style**

ABOVE *Euphorbia resinifera* is one of many tender succulents that will thrive in pots outside in summer in a sunny position

particularly has a symmetry of structure that is particularly effective, a characteristic shared with the more tender species of *Agave*, *Beschorneria* and *Dasylirion*. All of these plants can be used in containers for striking focal points as well as in combination with other containerised exotics such as *Brugmansia*.

Ferny foliage, consisting of numerous small leaflets, contributes to the exotic feeling in a garden. Ferns apart, plants that produce it in varying proportions include many members of the pea family (*Acacia*, *Sophora*, *Caesalpinia*), *Aralia*, *Dicentra* and *Amorphophallus*. Although I have argued against plants with small leaves in the tropical-style garden, large compound leaves are in keeping with natural tropical systems. Large leaves broken into many small leaflets provide an extensive surface area for photosynthesis but are less easily damaged by wind or

heavy rain/hail, and for this reason they are adopted by many tropical plants.

Finally, succulent plants provide an important textural contrast and, like the spiky leaved plants, often have good symmetrical qualities. Clearly some equatorial areas are periodically dry, and here succulents are widespread and varied. However, even in moist tropical habitats succulent plants are relatively common, often as epiphytes (plants growing supported by other plants) where the small amount of humus in which they root may dry out very quickly.

Use the thick fleshy leaves of various herbaceous *Sedum* species as a dramatic contrast with grasses and *Eryngium*. You can also use other, more tender plants such as *Echeveria* and *Opuntia* as specimens in containers, providing interesting variations of colour and shape.

Features and functionality

Tropical style gardening is interactive. I am a strong believer in using the garden as an outdoor room. Even in Britain, we do occasionally have warm dry evenings when it is possible to relax, perhaps with a glass of wine, and imagine oneself somewhere exotic in the shade of palm trees. How you design and plant your garden should reflect what use you intend to make of it. There are some basic aspects, however, that are common to most gardens. Even the smallest of sites requires seating, and its positioning requires a consideration of function. Seating can, for instance, be used purely to provide a resting point within the garden. This will usually be static and positioned for the individual enjoyment of a particular feature, such as a pond, a vista or a group of strongly scented plants. This form of seating can be of any size and in virtually any position provided that it is comfortable and has adequate access. The second kind of seating is social and more often moveable. Clusters of chairs, usually with a central table, are best sited in open areas with ready all-round access and on a robust surface, such as paving. Ideally the area should be sheltered from wind, screened from neighbours and relatively close to the house, especially if dining outside is an intention.

If entertaining in your garden is a priority, then this should be considered at the outset and the garden designed and built around this function. Remember too, that you may need space adjacent to your social seating area for additional tables, barbecues, portable lighting, prams and dogs. With the prospect of considerable activity in your social area, often involving people and animals unfamiliar with your garden, avoid placing dangerous (spiky, prickly or poisonous) plants or especially valuable or delicate plants in the vicinity.

Sheds and greenhouses commonly occupy gardens, and the tropical style garden must cater for these too. Sheds are less of a problem as these can be painted in colours that blend with the surroundings. Furthermore, they can be concealed by growing climbers over them or by planting tall growing plants as a screen. Greenhouses can be more difficult to incorporate, since they have to receive sufficient light for their occupants. This can restrict the positions in which they can be placed within the garden as well as making them more difficult to conceal. Some expensive greenhouses are quite decorative and can become a feature of interest if well maintained, but the majority are rather ugly with either wooden or aluminium frames. Wood is often painted and this can help, especially if the colour is chosen to blend with other features of the garden. White is not always the best colour although it is commonly used. It is perfectly possible to paint the aluminium frame of a greenhouse with appropriate paints, usually with an undercoat. This can transform an unattractive structure into a much more tolerable feature.

ABOVE **This Japanese-style garden at St Mawgan, Cornwall, UK, shows clever positioning of plants, seating and an ornament**

Garden lighting can extend the period of use of a garden and is particularly effective with tropical-style plants. How you light your garden is largely a matter of choice but it is best, where possible, to use a low voltage system connected to an indoor transformer. Consider lighting seating areas and paths (particularly steps) as a matter of course – but why not illuminate water features, clumps of *Gunnera*, the undersides of tree canopies, groups of containerised plants or outdoor sculptures?

The growing environment

Hardiness: what is it?

Gardeners tend to use the term 'hardy' in a rather loose manner. Clearly hardiness is dependent upon geographical factors: plants hardy in a gentle climate may not be so in a colder one. Hardiness is also dependent upon local factors such as the degree of exposure, soil type and aspect. Probably the most critical factor in the hardiness of a plant is whether it will tolerate being frozen.

As we know, water freezes at 0°C (32°F). When water freezes, it expands slightly – hence ice floats. If the freezing water is constrained, it can rupture the container as it freezes because of the pressure generated in expansion. Plant cells are like little containers of water, and these too can rupture if frozen, destroying the structure of a leaf or stem. However, this freezing point can be changed by the addition of salt, so sea water freezes at a somewhat lower temperature. Most plant cells contain some salts and other dissolved substances, which means that, in practice, ice tends not to form within plant cells until the temperature reaches between 0°C (32°F) and –1°C (30°F). Tender plants will not survive the formation of ice within their cells whereas hardy plants can survive this. 'Fully hardy' plants can go one stage further, in that they can stand extended periods with their cells frozen. These conditions are fatal to many plants, since they cannot photosynthesis or take up water when frozen yet can still lose water through their leaves. Fully hardy plants are therefore generally deciduous, herbaceous or leathery/hairy evergreens.

Frost and ice

In the garden we can take a number of measures to aid the survival of plants that are less than hardy. Covering outdoor plants with straw, bracken or plastic helps reduce the loss of warmth by radiation on cold nights. This may be enough to prevent freezing if the duration of cold is short. Similarly, planting adjacent to a free-standing wall can assist on a temporary basis, but once the wall has radiated any warmth it may have acquired during the day the effect is lost. Neither of these methods is of much use if the temperature is expected to fall much below –4°C (20°F). A plastic covering does, however, confer further advantages in that it is windproof and waterproof. The latter is important. Plants tend to be hardier if dry at the roots because their cells are not completely full of water: when any water they do contain freezes there is space for the expansion to take place without causing so much damage. In addition, the salt content of the cells of a dry plant is effectively higher, which means that the water will actually freeze at a lower temperature. Plants in very well drained soils and at the base of walls (where water supply is limited) will therefore be hardier than plants growing in wet soils. It should be borne in mind however, that sandy and gritty soils lose and gain heat more quickly than humus-rich and clay soils.

ABOVE **The leaves of *Gunnera* can be used to protect the crowns in winter**

Some plants are especially sensitive to freezing near their growing points. In general, all young growth is sensitive to frost, since young cells have less robust walls and are generally full of water. Plants that form resting buds protect their growing points, but others such as palms and bananas do not form buds and their growing points are

ABOVE The banana *Musa basjoo* with winter protection of straw-filled sacking at Paignton Zoological Gardens, Devon, UK

at risk of frost damage even if their older cells can withstand freezing. The growing points may therefore need winter protection. In addition, shoots may be at risk from rain water adjacent to the growing point (i.e. trapped in leaf bases), since this will have a lower salt content and will freeze before the cells of the plant. The growing point may be badly damaged by the expansion of the rain water as it freezes, even if the actual plants cells do not freeze. Keeping the active growing points of such plants dry in winter can considerably improve their chances of survival.

Wind

Exposure to wind is also an important factor. Wind can have both beneficial and detrimental effects. Plants, unlike us, do not suffer wind chill since they do not attempt to keep their body temperatures above the ambient temperature. However, wind increases the rate at which the temperature of the plant equates to that of the surroundings and removes any advantages of a warmer microclimate. For this reason a plastic covering on a still night may protect plants successfully, while on a windy night it will have little effect. In addition, wind will increase the rate of evaporation from leaves. This can help dry plants out, making them a little more frost-resistant, but if they are already frozen it can cause them to burn as

they dry to excess. It is worth bearing in mind that a greenhouse or other protective frame does suffer from wind chill, since the function of such a structure is the artificial raising of the internal temperature. Heating costs will be much greater in windy sites or during windy spells.

ABOVE *Amaryllis belladonna* benefits from the warmth at the base of a wall of the old 'Aroid House', Kew Gardens, UK

Winter protection

We can see how the factors described above provide some general guidelines of how to increase the hardiness of any particular plant. Providing shelter from wind, and perhaps a covering, increases the chances of the immediate surroundings and the plant retaining any warmth from the day for long enough to avert frost damage. Protection from excess wet will assist the plant by decreasing the freezing point of its cells and reducing the risk of external damage by freezing rain water. These factors are found in combination at the base of a stone wall which is why, traditionally, these locations are reserved for more tender subjects. In the northern hemisphere a south- or west-facing wall (or aspect) is the best of all situations, since this is most likely to receive the most warmth during the day and is therefore likely to maintain its warmth for longest on a cold night. In Britain the coldest aspects are north and east with the cold, easterly winds that bring wet snow being the most feared of winter trials for the jungle gardener and the plants.

In this book, I hope to give realistic values of hardiness for the plants described. The various degrees of hardiness are allocated one of five symbols. These are general values only and if you have a warm, sheltered, dry site you can consider plants to be one gradation further on in the sequence, while if you live in a particularly cold locality the values are probably optimistic and the previous symbol is likely to be appropriate.

Values are as follows.

🔵 **8°C** Not really plants for outdoors except from perhaps mid-summer to early autumn. Most of these are best grown as houseplants at a temperature minimum of 8°C (47°F) and stood outdoors in semi-shade for summer effect only.

🔵 **4°C** These plants, although tender, are moderately robust and can usually take what comes outside providing they are taken in before autumn frosts. They need to be kept cool in winter, however, at a minimum of 4°C (39F°), and are less suitable as houseplants. Ideally they should spend the winter in a slightly heated greenhouse, conservatory or poly-tunnel.

🔵 **0°C** This group is relatively tough and will generally tolerate a light frost (that is, a ground frost, but not an air frost where the air temperature falls below freezing). Many are considerably hardier if dry. They

should over-winter in a cold greenhouse, poly-tunnel or under plastic where some heat can be supplied in very cold conditions, just to stop them freezing.

❄️ These are hardy plants that will stand freezing for short intervals. They will do better with some winter protection, especially a plastic sheet to keep the worst of the winter wet from leaves, crowns and buds, but in many cases this is not essential unless on an exposed site. Most will tolerate temperatures a little below −5°C (22°F) but should receive extra protection when temperatures fall below −8°C (18°F).

❄️ No protection is required for these fully hardy plants that will rarely suffer from winter damage. The extra-cautious might cover them with a plastic sheet in very cold conditions, but these plants are generally hardier than their owners.

Rainfall

Rainfall varies considerably from place to place, possibly more than is generally realised. In Britain, most places receive sufficient rainfall to support a tropical-style garden, even through the summer. There are, however, drier areas and drier periods in summer that may mean additional watering of plants in the open ground. Plants in containers do not have the luxury of a deep or widespread root system and will require watering at regular intervals from mid spring to autumn even in wet summers. Although it is possible to use tap water for watering, it is always better to use rainwater if it is available. Do not use 'hard' tap water for acid-loving plants as it contains calcium. In winter, too much water can be a problem, especially combined with cold temperatures. Protect container-grown plants from excessive wet as their roots are more at risk from freezing than plants in the ground. Try also to prevent water collecting in the crowns of plants that form rosettes as, again, this may freeze and cause damage. Cover plants with plastic sheeting if a period of rain is likely to be closely followed by freezing temperatures.

Through the year

So how do you care for your tropical-style garden? Keeping plants alive through the cold, dark, wet months of winter is the biggest problem and some of the methods of doing this have been mentioned already. Once this is achieved, cultivation is moderately simple. Here are some rough guidelines.

Spring

In spring, most plants begin to grow. Hardy plants in the open ground will usually get underway without much assistance from the gardener, but containerised plants may need a little encouragement. Under cover, many plants will show signs of activity by expanding buds or renewed growth in response to increasing warmth and daylight. When this is observed, watering can be increased,

whereupon growth will be even faster. Other plants, however, need to be watered to start them into growth, and it is sometimes more difficult to decide when it is safe to do this. With such plants (e.g. many succulents, summer bulbs and evergreen *Agapanthus*) start in early spring by giving a little water on warm days. Allow the plants to dry before watering again, and do not water if cold nights are expected. Once active growth is seen, a regular watering regime can be resumed.

As spring begins to warm, stand plants outside the greenhouse as often as possible to harden them to external conditions, but make sure that they do not become excessively wet or cold. Frosts may occur into late spring and even early summer, and plants will either need returning to the greenhouse or covering with plastic to ensure that soft new growth is not damaged. On frosty nights in spring be prepared to give extra protection to

BELOW Early growth of plants such as *Agapanthus* is susceptible to frost damage, and may need protection on cold spring nights

hardy plants that have begun to put out soft growth. Plants that will need careful attention include *Decaisnea*, *Akebia*, *Gunnera* and *Hosta*, to name but a few. Other spring jobs include checking that tree ties are not too tight, cutting back dead wood of plants that have been frost damaged and preparing frameworks for annual and herbaceous climbers. Many containerised plants need potting on in spring, and most annuals can be sown either outside or under cover, depending upon their hardiness.

ABOVE Young tender annuals such as these *Cucurbita* should not be subjected to any frost. Plant them out only once all frosts have passed in early summer

Summer

In early summer, pests and diseases can begin to proliferate, and a careful watch should be kept for these. Treat them as soon as possible with the appropriate measures. Containerised plants can be stood outside for increasingly long periods, but a watch must be kept for late frosts. Many plants in the open ground will be growing vigorously, and climbers particularly may need regular training to ensure that they do not smother other plants or collapse away from their supports. Once frosts have passed, tender plants can be stood outside permanetly or planted

ABOVE The luxuriance of tropical planting in late summer

where they are to grow. Half-hardy and tender annuals such as *Phaseolus*, *Cucurbita* and *Zea* can be sown where they are to grow. Watch out for aggressive weeds that can reach sizeable proportions among large exotic plants before they are noticed. Water container plants regularly, even daily, if they are in porous terracotta pots or hanging baskets.

Feed all container-grown plants with a liquid fertilizer on a regular basis, as they can quickly run out of nutrients, especially if frequently watered. Protect bananas and similarly large-leaved plants from hailstorms. Remove faded blooms from plants in order to encourage them to produce more flowers or to prevent them wasting their energy producing seed. Many shrubby plants can be propagated from cuttings at this time of year.

Autumn

As autumn approaches, some leaves and stems of plants may die back. Remove them to keep plants tidy. Many plants are at their best in early autumn when flowers and fruits may be abundant. As the season progresses, however, rainfall may increase considerably. Although this is not generally a problem some plants, such as succulents, summer bulbs, *Canna* and *Fuchsia* plants in containers, should not be allowed to get too wet at this time of year since they may not dry sufficiently before the colder nights arrive and this can encourage rotting. Bring sensitive plants such as these under cover or provide protection well in advance of the first frosts. The top growth of many hardy plants will collapse once frosted and can be removed. Deciduous trees and shrubs will also lose their leaves before or soon after the first frosts and, again, these should be tidied away so that pests and diseases do not spread in the cool damp conditions of autumn.

Many hardy shrubby plants and herbaceous perennials are best planted in autumn so that they can fully establish a root system through the winter. Hardy plants of a delicate disposition will need a mulch of straw or bracken to protect their crowns and some may need the further protection of plastic sheeting. Make sure that this is securely fastened so that protection is not lost in strong winds.

Winter

During winter, most plants will be dormant. Containerised plants under cover will need only enough water to prevent them completely drying, and some will require no water at all. Outside, protect plants from excessive cold and wetness wherever possible. Remove snow from evergreen plants (and greenhouses) before its weight causes damage, but remember that snow can also insulate plants to some extent from very cold air temperatures, so do not remove it, for example, from *Gunnera* crowns. Keep greenhouse glass as clean as possible to admit all the light that is available. Check your greenhouse temperature regularly and ensure that you have a backup heating source. Winter is also a good time to plan any changes for the coming year and also to consult plant and seed catalogues for further additions to your collection.

BELOW **Even in winter some plants produce exotic surprises. Here *Iris foetidissima* reveals its orange seeds**

PART TWO

The Plants

Hardy trees and shrubs

Symbols used in the plant descriptions are:

❀ Evergreen

🚰 Give extra water

🌵 Give less water

☀ Needs full sun

▦ Will tolerate deep shade

ph Requires acidic soil conditions

A reminder of the temperature ratings:

8°C Minimum of 8°C

4°C Minimum of 4°C

0°C Minimum of 0°C

❄ Will survive some frost

❄ Will survive most frosts

It is important to consider trees and shrubs at the very beginning of the creation of a tropical-style garden. Being ultimately of considerable size and permanence, they form its structural basis, along with any hard landscaping such as walls, pergolas and ponds. In addition, unless the expense of a large specimen is to be endured, these must be grown from small plants that will take time to achieve their desired contribution to the overall scheme. Full consideration should be given to size, rate of growth, soil requirements and habit when deciding upon which trees and shrubs to plant.

In the following pages I will list some essential tropical-style plants along with some well-known plants that work successfully in a tropical context. Obviously this list is far from complete, and in the end the choice of what you use is up to you alone. There are, for example, many robust-leaved shrubs that can be used to provide informal hedges and a green background to the summer display of exotics. Among these one would perhaps include *Cotinus coggygria*, *Griselinia littoralis*, *Ligustrum lucidum* and species of *Ilex* (holly), all of which are also available in variegated or coloured forms. You may wish to include trees such as *Davidia* (the handkerchief tree), a *Liquidamber* for its glossy leaves and wonderful autumn colour or *Cercis siliquastrum* (the Judas tree) for its strange rounded leaves and pink flowers borne on the older branches in much the same way as those of many tropical trees. Further, I have not included the acid-loving shrubs *Camellia* and *Rhododendron* in this list, although clearly they have a number of attributes, such as glossy evergreen leaves, which would make them appropriate. Here are suggestions for some of my favourites.

A jungle-like vista at Heligan, Cornwall, UK, relies on the surrounding trees and shrubs to give height and drama.

Aesculus
(buckeye, horse chestnut).
Hippocastanaceae
(horse chestnut family)

The common horse chestnut tree (*Aesculus hippocastanea*) is rather large for most gardens (to 25m; 80ft) and its five-part compound leaves, although large and of tropical shape, lack the glossiness to give them an authentic feel. Of slightly smaller stature and with flowers more in keeping with the exotic theme is A.x *carnea* with similar leaves to the common species but with pink-red flowers. Better for foliage is *Aesculus indica* with dark green, more shiny leaves and larger, less spiny fruits (conkers). It bears pale pink flowers a little later than the other trees. Even better is *Aesculus chinensis*, a smaller

Aesculus x *carnea*

Aesculus indica at Kew

tree (15m; 50ft) with glossy leaves and white flower clusters.

The American buckeyes are more shrubby in stature, and some spread by underground suckers which can become invasive. Leaves are generally similar to those of the trees: that is, palmate compound. Most bloom in summer. A. *parviflora* is vigorous and bears white flower clusters similar in appearance to *Callistemon*, hence the common name of bottlebrush buckeye. A. *pavia* has open clusters of red flowers. All the buckeyes and horse chestnuts are tolerant plants and can be grown in most garden, although mature plants may suffer from canker. Buckeyes can be propagated by removal of suckers, and all may be grown from seed.

Ailanthus
(tree of heaven).
Simaroubaceae
(tree of heaven family)

Ailanthus altissima is a Chinese tree and is the fastest growing of all hardy deciduous trees. The enormous pinnate compound leaves can be well over 1m (3¼ft) in length on young saplings. Fortunately the rate of growth and leaf size decreases as the plants age, ultimately to reach 15m (50ft). Flowers and fruits are similar to those of the ash (*Fraxinus*). These plants are spectacular as young specimens, and to maintain this state they can be cut back to near the base in early spring to encourage the production of vigorous young shoots. Unfortunately this method promotes the production of suckers that may become invasive, although they do provide a means of propagation.

Albizia
(silk tree).
Fabaceae
(pea family)

Albizia julibrissin var. *rosea* is a small tree with an open, branching habit. Its chief attraction is its clusters of pink flowers. These consist mainly of long stamens that extend from the small flowers by up to 2cm (¾in), giving the flower clusters the appearance of a fibre-

Albizia julibrissin var. *rosea*

optic lamp. The large leaves are compound and consist of many tiny leaflets. Despite its tropical appearance, this tree is relatively hardy – especially in the pink-flowered form. *Albizia* can be a shy-flowering plant, especially in Britain, and to encourage bud production it should be planted in a sunny site and given some protection from late spring frosts. Plant in a well-drained neutral soil, but avoid excess fertilizer as this can inhibit flowering. *Albizia* can be propagated from cuttings taken in summer with some heat, but it is

easily raised from seed and, like other pea family plants, is quick to reach maturity.

Aralia
(Hercules' club).
Araliaceae
(ivy family)

Aralia elata (A. chinensis) is vigorous suckering shrub or small tree (to 8m; 25ft) with complex compound leaves formed of numerous leaflets. These can be a metre or so (about 3¼ft) in length. Large clusters of tiny white flowers are produced in late summer on mature stems. There is a variegated form. Better in some respects is *Aralia spinosa*, which is a little faster growing. It forms upright prickly stems from a spreading rootstock and bears similar, slightly larger leaves that have the added interest (or danger) of spines on the upper and lower surface of the leaves

as well as on the stems and petioles. Flower clusters are similar to A. *elata*. Both species colour well in autumn as the large leaves slowly fall apart, leaflet by leaflet.

There are herbaceous forms of *Aralia* which should not be overlooked. A. *racemosa* and A. *cachemirica* are both tall (to 2m; 6½ft or more) with compound leaves and terminal clusters of white flowers. They have a bold, arching habit that looks well with bamboo or other grasses. All *Aralia* species like protection from wind and a moist soil, and all can be propagated by suckers or by division work which should be undertaken in early spring.

Aucuba
(Japanese laurel).
Cornaceae
(dogwood family)

Aucuba japonica is an excellent dense, rounded shrub, commonly planted, but rarely is it given the position and the respect that it deserves. Large (10cm; 4in) waxy evergreen leaves are produced on thick green stems. The leaves may have variously toothed edges depending upon the variety. Female plants bloom in late spring, producing branching clusters of rather inconspicuous purple-brown flowers that have a pleasant scent. Much loved by insects, these are regularly pollinated (providing a male is

Aralia elata

Aucuba japonica

nearby) and give rise to fruits about the size of an olive. These take a year to become brilliant red. By this time, unfortunately, they have often been obscured by subsequent growth. Forms with variously spotted or blotched leaves (e.g. spotted laurel, *A. japonica* 'Crotonifolia') are commonly available while the dark green plain-leaved forms such as *A.* 'Rozannie' are also particularly attractive. The value of these plants lies in their very accommodating nature. They will grow well in almost any soil provided that it does not dry out: indeed, they thrive in quite heavy soils. These are vigorous plants even in quite deep shade, and are spectacular against north-facing walls where the leaves can reach 15cm (6in). Although they will also stand bright sunshine, the variegated forms can scorch. *Aucuba* plants are easily raised from semi-hardwood cuttings taken in autumn. These can be rooted in the open ground. Layering of low branches is also successful. In addition, self-sown seedlings are usually abundant beneath mature plants, and these can exhibit interesting variegations or leaf forms different from the parent.

Buddleja
(butterfly bush).
Loganiaceae
(Buddleja family)

The common butterfly bush (*Buddleja davidii*), originally from the Himalayas, is a familiar sight, particularly to those who frequently travel by train, for it seems to thrive on the neglected track sides and banks of our rail network. *Buddleja* bushes are vigorous and thrive in most conditions, although they prefer well-drained soils. *B. davidii*, through natural variation, has given rise to a wide range of cultivated colour forms in anything from deep rose (*B.* 'Royal Red') to dark purple (*B.* 'Black Knight', my favourite) and white (*B.* 'White Profusion', the butterfly's favourite). There are some variegated forms available, but these seem to lack the vigour of the usual form. *B. davidii* is best cut back hard (almost to ground level) in early spring. This promotes the formation of robust stems (to 2m; 6½ft) that will produce numerous pairs of lance-shaped leaves and an abundance of flowers in late summer. *Buddleja globosa* is evergreen and more tropical in appearance than *B. davidii*. It generally forms a larger bush (3–4m; 10–13ft) and certainly does not respond to the severe pruning recommended for *B. davidii*. *B. globosa* (from Chile) produces interesting pairs of spherical orange-yellow flower clusters in early summer. There is a splendid hybrid between these two species that combines the best qualities of each. *B.* x *weyeriana* 'Sungold' produces clusters of orange-yellow flowers with a dark centre in late summer to autumn.

Other *Buddleja* species worth considering include *B. colvilei* with large, dark red flowers, *Buddleja fallowiana* with silvery leaves and lavender or white strongly-scented flowers in narrow spikes and *B. lindleyana* with loose spikes of lavender-purple flowers and dark green leaves. These three Chinese species, like all *Buddleja* plants are easily propagated from softwood cuttings taken in late summer, a worthwhile exercise as these rapid-growing shrubs tend to be short-lived.

Catalpa bignonioides

Catalpa
(Indian bean).
Bignoniaceae
(Jacaranda family)

atalpa bignonioides is one of the more commonly planted large-leaved trees. It can attain 15m (50ft) but is usually shorter than this and quite broad. Heart-shaped leaves are produced late in spring and rapidly expand to 25cm (10in) or more. White flowers with darker markings are borne in upright clusters rather resembling those of the horse chestnut (*Aesculus*). Subsequent fruits are long and bean-like (although they

contain fluffy seeds), and it is these that give the plant its common name. This is one of the best small trees for the tropical-style garden and works well as a backdrop to grasses such as *Miscanthus* and as a support for vines such as *Actinidia*. The golden-leaved form (C. *bignonioides* 'Aurea') is pretty but can look starved and suffers from leaf scorch. The purple leaved form (C. x *erubescens* 'Purpurea') is interesting but the leaves soon turn to green following their early colour. *Catalpa speciosa* (also North American) is similar but has leaves that are glossy above and hairy below. C. *ovata* (from China) has darker flowers. All species enjoy a fertile soil and lots of sunshine but at the same time require protection from wind. Young plants can be delicate. Propagate from seed or from cuttings of soft wood in early summer.

Choisya
(Mexican orange blossom).
Rutaceae
(Citrus family)

hoisya ternata is a hardy plant related to the oranges and lemons, and it shares with them a wonderful fragrance from its white, 5- or 6-petalled blossoms. It is a medium-sized, dense evergreen shrub that reaches around 2m (6½ft). Stems tend to remain green and bear bright green leaves which are composed of three glossy leaflets (an arrangement known as ternate). Flowering occurs mainly in late spring but clusters of flowers can appear at almost any time, even in mid-winter. There is a strange yellow-leaved form, C. *ternata* 'Sundance', which if given shade from the brightest sunshine will not scorch

Choisya ternata

but will probably not flower either. C. 'Aztec Pearl' is similar but has very narrow leaflets. *Choisya* is not fussy over soil and will tolerate quite dry situations. Propagate from cuttings taken in summer, but protect them from snails and slugs that particularly like the young foliage.

Colletia
(caltrop bush).
Rhamnaceae
(buckthorn family)

There are two species of these amazingly thorny shrubs available, but the names are rather confused. *Colletia paradoxa (C. cruciata)* is perhaps the more unusual of the two. It forms, in time, a large shrub composed of robust stems. At intervals a large thorn is produced, and this extends away from the stem on a triangular wing-like base at least as robust as the stem. Thorns are borne opposite each other up the stem, and each pair is set at a right angle to those above and below, giving the appearance of a series of caltrops – those spiked devices used by the military to lame cavalry horses or puncture tyres. The stems and thorns are a grey-green at maturity. Young growth is produced in early summer, is bright green and includes numerous small leaves that are shed as the stem system expands. Clusters of small, white, scented flowers are borne among the thorns in autumn

Colletia armata

and early winter. *C. armata (C. histrix)* is similar in habit, but the thorns are more linear and the stem systems as a whole are more narrow, giving the bush the appearance of a prickly broom (*Cytisus*). It has similar leaves and flowers to *C. paradoxa*. Both bushes are slow-growing. They are relatively tough and relish dry sunny positions in almost any well-drained soil type. Wall protection is an advantage in preventing wind damage. These plants are generally increased from cuttings of young shoots taken in late summer although they often prove reluctant to strike. Like *Ceanothus* (Californian lilac, to which they are related) *Colletia* has a bacterial soil symbiont which may be important in encouraging root

Colletia paradoxa

development. The addition of small amounts of soil from around the roots of the parent plant to the rooting mixture may be beneficial.

Crinodendron
(Chile lantern tree).
Elaeocarpaceae
(karanda nut family)

This evergreen shrub or small tree is sometimes mistaken for a *Fuchsia. Crinodendron hookerianum* forms a dense mass of upright shoots clothed in rather small dark green leaves. If protected from severe frosts, the plants produce an abundance of 2–3cm (¾–1⅛in) long bright red

Crinodendron hookerianum

Cytisus
(broom).
Fabaceae
(pea family)

The brooms are generally switch plants (drought-adapted plants with whip-like green stems and minimal leaves) but one species has broad leaves and deserves a place in the exotic garden. *Cytisus battandieri*, the pineapple broom from Morocco, has compound leaves with three rounded leaflets of a grey-green colour, largely as a result of the abundant silvery hairs on the surface. It forms an upright, sparse shrub that is well suited to training on a wall or trellis. The bright yellow flowers are produced in cylindrical clusters, not

lantern-like flowers. Although this is not the most exotic of foliage plants, the flowers certainly justify its inclusion in this list. *Crinodendron* is fussy about position and only blooms well if happy. Plant them in acidic compost consisting largely of peat substitute. They don't mind shade but certainly like a sheltered site, preferably west-facing. Propagate by cuttings of soft wood in early summer or mature wood in late summer.

Cytisus battandieri

Spartium junceum

unlike a short lupin, in late summer. Their main attraction is the strong scent of pineapple that they emit. Propagate by seed or by cuttings taken in summer. A related plant is *Spartium junceum* which is more typically broom-like with relatively leafless rush-like stems reaching a height of 2.5m (8ft). In summer numerous bright yellow pea flowers are produced that have a strong honey scent. Grow both in warm sunny positions or against a wall where the slightly less hardy pineapple broom will appreciate the extra protection.

Decaisnea
(blue bean).
Lardizabalaceae
(Akebia family)

Decaisnea fargesii, from China, is a tall, lax, deciduous shrub with compound leaves around 30cm (12in) in length, the leaflets of which have a slightly velvet surface. Leaves are produced from waxy brown buds in early spring and are easily damaged by late frosts. For this reason *Decaisnea* requires a sheltered site. Young shoots and emerging leaves are a strange blue-green colour. The greenish flowers are produced in terminal tassels in early summer and are of no great interest. The resulting fruits, however, are very unusual being not unlike a small broad bean in shape, but of a striking, almost luminescent, blue-green. Grow *Decaisnea* in semi-

Embothrium coccineum

shade in a position protected from wind and late frost. The soil should be moist, but well drained and preferably slightly acid. Sow seed in autumn and allow it to stratify over the winter.

Embothrium
(Chilean firebush).
Proteaceae
(Protea family)

Embothrium coccineum is a spectacular shrub or small tree (to 8m; 25ft) that bears truly vibrant red tubular flowers in clusters in early summer. The smallish leaves are lance-shaped and of a mid-green colour. The more narrow the leaf, the hardier the plant. Indeed, a relatively tough form, *E. coccineum* var. *lanceolatum* 'Norquinco', is supposed

to be fully hardy. *Embothrium* enjoys a sunny but sheltered site and is best in acid soil, although it will tolerate neutral conditions if well drained. The plants tend to sucker, the removal of these providing the best means of propagation.

Eriobotrya
(loquat).
Rosaceae
(rose family)

The edible fruit of the loquat is a little like an apricot but is, sadly, rarely produced in Britain. However, loquats are well worth growing for their bold evergreen foliage. *Eriobotrya japonica* is a large shrub or small tree that will benefit from wall protection or a sheltered site, as the

Eriobotrya japonica

large leaves tend to burn if exposed to excessive cold or wind. The wrinkled leaves are around 25cm (10in) long and are a pointed oval shape. In late summer to early winter, small scented white flowers are produced in clusters. All parts of the plant, including the small stems bearing the flowers, are distinctly hairy. The large, dark green leaves of the loquat make an excellent backdrop to lighter grasses and grey or purple-leaved perennials. Take cuttings of softer growth in summer or raise from seed in spring.

Eucalyptus
(gum tree).
Myrtaceae
(myrtle family)

There is an increasing number of *Eucalyptus* species that are becoming available and have been found to be moderately hardy. Most form large trees in time and are very hungry, often causing soil depletion. They are really only suitable for large gardens but are often grown for their blue-green foliage and scented leaves. They add interest to the exotic garden as their foliage is evergreen and usually partly weeping. The hardiest of these Australasian plants is probably *Eucalyptus pauciflora* subsp. *niphophila* which has a spreading habit to 6m (20ft) in height and interesting white-flaking bark. The leaves are around 15cm (6in) long and lance shaped (oval in juveniles). White

flowers are produced on mature specimens in late spring. *E. dalrympleana* is similar but more columnar in shape with white bark and bright green mature leaves. It is said to be lime-tolerant. *Eucalyptus gunnii* is similar.

Less hardy is *Eucalyptus perriniana* with waxy blue linear leaves and white flowers. It forms a large shrub or small tree to around 6m (20ft). *Eucalyptus globulus* is commonly encountered as a juvenile grown for its striking blue green ovate leaves that have a white waxy bloom on the surface. The plants mature to tall spreading trees with sickle-shaped leaves and white flowers.

Of the tender eucalypts worth growing in large tubs are *E. cinerea* which has silver-blue circular leaves

Young growth of *Eucalpytus dalrympleana*

Eucalyptus erythrocorys

on juveniles and *E. ficifolia* which is the best, and probably hardiest, of the red flowered species. *E. erythrocorys* forms a small shrub with greyish leaves and yellow flowers offset by bright red flower caps.

Although trees, many eucalypts may be kept for their early years in tubs and pruned hard back in early spring to encourage the production of abundant juvenile growth with its associated bright foliage. Seed of a wide range of *Eucalyptus* is available, and this is the best method of propagation. It is well worth growing a few extra plants in pots to be planted out where they might survive the winter months. All eucalypts are sun lovers, and although they like plenty of water when in growth, they resent a waterlogged soil.

Euphorbia characias, wulfenii form

Euphorbia
(spurge).
Euphorbiaceae
(spurge family)

  some

The spurges form a large group of diverse plants, ranging from sizeable shrubs to hummock-forming succulents and annuals. All have characteristic flowers consisting of stamens and stigmas borne in a small cup-shaped structure surrounded by a pair of bracts known as a cyathium. In addition, all species when injured exude a milky sap that can cause skin burns in the allergic. The toxic sap, however, is no good reason for ignoring these wonderfully structural plants. There are three principal groups of euphorbs: the woody shrubs and subshrubs; the herbaceous perennials; and the succulent species.

Euphorbia characias is probably the best known of the shrubby spurges. This Mediterranean shrub bears clusters of spirally-arranged blue-green willow-like leaves on green stems. The leaves are slightly hairy. Flowers are borne from early spring and last to early summer in a terminal cylinder. This may be green to almost yellow, and some forms have a dark 'eye' to the cyathium. These can be short-lived shrubs, but removal of the flowering branches from close to soil level before they set seed helps to prolong life and encourage the production of future flowering stems. Many forms are in cultivation, some listed as *E. wulfenii*. *E. x martinii* is apparently a dwarf form of *E. characias* but is in fact a hybrid of this with *E. amygdaloides*. It has slightly broader, more glossy leaves than *E. characias*. *E. stygiana* from the Azores is particularly exotic. It has broad leaves to 15cm (6in) in length borne on lax spreading stems. It is unfortunately rather tender. *Euphorbia mellifera* from Madeira is also well worth trying in a sheltered position. Ultimately it forms a large woody shrub with sparse branches bearing bright green, slightly spoon-shaped leaves. Sweet-smelling brown-pink flowers are borne in loose clusters in late spring. Propagate all of these from seed or from long cuttings of non-flowering shoots in summer. Allow the white latex to dry thoroughly before inserting the cuttings in a sandy potting mixture.

Euphorbia rigida and *E. myrsinites*, from the Mediterranean, are two dwarf shrubs with triangular blue-grey leaves borne in a tight spiral around fleshy stems. *E. rigida* is the larger, producing arching mounds of 0.5m (1½ft) stems terminating in sulphur-yellow flower clusters. *E. myrsinites* is much smaller but of very similar habit. Its stems seldom exceed 15cm (6in) in length. It is commonly listed as an 'alpine', but if planted in quantity it forms a spectacular carpet in combination with species of *Eryngium* and *Sedum*. Both can be raised from seed and will flower in their second or third year.

Euphorbia amygdaloides is a small short-lived (often biennial) subshrub which bears almost flat clusters of broad green leaves. In spring, these elongate into spikes of brilliant green flowers. There is a form flushed with purple known as 'Rubra' and a spreading, more

Euphorbia myrsinites

37

Euphorbia stygiana

persistent form with glossy leaves (known as *E. robbiae*). All are very attractive with ferns and sedges. A true herbaceous perennial is *E. griffithii* which is available in a number of named varieties. The reddish stems emerge early in spring and elongate rapidly to flower in late spring. The flowers are varying shades of orange. Other shoots that emerge later do not flower, but branch repeatedly and bear numerous bright green oval leaves. Both of these species will tolerate shade.

The succulent species of *Euphorbia* are mostly tender and require winter protection. Most species are from southern Africa and require dry winters. Much more tolerant of some winter moisture are those from the Canary Isles and North Africa. As specimen plants to be taken into the house or greenhouse for the winter, try *E. canariensis* and *E. resinifera*. *E. canariensis* ultimately forms a large clump of erect, cactus-like stems with tiny brown-purple or yellow flower clusters born toward the top of mature stems. The stems are a strange silvery-green-brown. *Euphorbia resinifera* forms low mounds of spiny succulent stems that ultimately produce small yellow flowers. Both enjoy a summer outside in full sun where they need only the rain that falls (see general comments on succulents, p. 154). *Euphorbia* species may be propagated from cuttings, but this is a complex process. Most are easily raised from seed, as is the large biennial spurge *Euphorbia lathyris* (caper spurge) which, with its symmetrical appearance and bright green flowers, will reach all of 1.2m (4ft) in its second season.

Fatsia
(false caster oil plant).
Araliaceae
(ivy family)

Fatsia japonica (also known as *Aralia seiboldii*) is an excellent shrub of both remarkable hardiness and exotic appearance. Its main requirements are a moist soil that does not dry out in summer (heavy clay is fine) and protection from strong winds. Principally grown as a foliage plant, it rewards with large leathery leaves similar in form to those of *Ricinus communis*, the caster oil plant, and this accounts for the popular name. Up to 30cm (12in) in diameter, the leaves consist of a number of wavy-edged lobes, the whole being a fresh, dark green at maturity, paler when young. There is an attractive variegated form with cream edges to the leaves.

Fatsia is a lax shrub as it seldom branches. Shoots arise from the base, grow for few years, flower, and may then die, usually to be replaced by further shoots. The flowers are like those of ivy, but in much larger clusters. They are generally produced

Fatsia japonica

in late autumn/winter. Indeed, ivies (*Hedera*) and *Fatsia* are closely related, and there is a hybrid between the two genera, x *Fatshedera lizei*, which is between the two in characteristics.

Fatsia, like ivy, is shade tolerant, and this is also true of the variegated forms. *Fatsia* will often thrive in dark corners where little else will grow, and looks well if accompanied by *Aucuba japonica*.

Pseudopanax laetus is similar in appearance to *Fatsia* but has more distinctly separate rounded leaflets. They are a bright glossy green. The plant is less hardy than *Fatsia* and requires a sheltered shady position in humus-rich soil.

Feijoa
(pineapple guava).
Myrtaceae
(myrtle family)

Feijoa sellowiana (*Acca sellowiana*) is a bushy shrub with small (6cm; 2½in) oval leaves of a greyish green, paler beneath and slightly woolly. Unusual red and white flowers with long protruding red stamens are produced in mid-summer on plants in sheltered positions. Occasionally, in hot summers, large green berries follow the flowers. These are edible and said to taste of guava. *Feijoa* is a tough plant and withstands considerable neglect readily tolerating a dry soil. It will flourish particularly

against a south- or west-facing wall where it is more likely to fruit. Try it with *Passiflora*, a grape vine (*Vitis vinifera* 'Müller Thurgau') and *Ficus carica* in a warm location and you may be able to pick a tropical fruit salad. Cuttings can be rooted in summer with a little warmth.

Ficus
(fig).
Moraceae
(mulberry family)

The common fig is the only fully hardy representative of a large genus of trees, shrubs and climbers which includes a number of popular houseplants. *Ficus carica* is widely cultivated for its fruits, which may ripen outside in favourable summers. Cultivated figs are commonly grown as wall shrubs where fruiting is better and where the roots can be confined to improve cropping. For the jungle garden, figs are principally grown for their foliage, which is light green in colour, each leaf being variously lobed and rather bristly. Leaves are borne on robust but rather sprawling branches along which fruits may form. Figs tend to leaf late in spring and shed their leaves quite early, and so should occupy a sunny, but sheltered position within the garden. Although not particularly fast growing, they will become sizeable in time. They will stand pruning provided this is not into very old wood. Grow figs in any well-drained soil. They will tolerate

Ficus carica

poor soils and indeed may thrive on these. They dislike cold, wet clay. Figs do not generally require feeding as the roots spread widely and deep, although a feed may increase foliage size. In general, figs require little maintenance. F. 'Brown Turkey' is commonly available and fruits well, while 'White Marseilles' is less hardy but has a better flavour.

Other species of *Ficus* are generally not suitable other than as evergreen pot plants to stand out in the garden during the summer. The common rubber plant (*Ficus elastica*) in its various forms can be useful as a summer foliage plant. *Ficus pumila* is a small-leaved climbing plant on the borderline of hardiness and may be successfully encouraged up a warm wall in sheltered parts.

Fraxinus
(ash).
Oleaceae
(olive family)

Ash trees are a useful group for the tropical-style garden, bearing large compound leaves. Two species are generally available, although others are becoming more common. *Fraxinus excelsior* (common ash) is a vigorous tree, ultimately attaining very large proportions (30m; 100ft). Ash produces leaves late in spring from distinctive black buds. The leaflets are bright green in colour and born on a yellowish petiole. The flowers are relatively insignificant but develop into hanging clusters of

Fraxinus ornus

elongate flat fruits (ash keys). Although deciduous, the branches of ash are decorative in winter and especially in the form F. 'Jaspidea' in which much of the young bark is suffused with butter yellow.

Fraxinus ornus (manna ash) from the Mediterranean has large, dark green leaves and pretty branching spikes of feathery white flowers borne in early summer. *F. velutina* from North America has leathery leaves of a grey-green colour. Both these species will reach around 12m (40ft). *F. sieboldiana* (from China) is smaller with dark green leaves and white flower clusters borne rather like those of *Buddleja*. The flowers are strongly fragrant. Ash trees are not fussy about soils providing they are not too acid. They prefer a sunny location. Seeds are sometimes available of the less common species. Particular forms are usually grafted.

Fuchsia

see under Slightly tender trees and shrubs (p. 112)

Ginkgo
(maidenhair tree).
Ginkgoaceae
(maidenhair tree family)

Ginkgo biloba is a truly astounding tree. It is the last of its kind, there having been many more species in the time of the dinosaurs. *Ginkgo* is unique and is distantly related to the

Ginkgo biloba

flowering plants and cycads. A rather slow-growing tree, it bears strange, wedge-shaped grey-green leaves with a central cleft and other subsidiary clefts in the ends of the resulting lobes. The leaves turn a lovely yellow in autumn. Mature specimens bear either short male catkins or female, paired berry-like structures which if fertilized by a nearby male, will produce plum-like green-orange foul-smelling fruit. These plants are not especially tropical-looking but are so unusual in appearance that they certainly warrant consideration. *Ginkgo* likes a sunny position with a moist fertile soil but is none the less tolerant of a less than perfect site. *Ginkgo* is easily raised from seed sown in a little warmth in spring.

Gleditsia
(honey locust).
Fabaceae
(pea family)

Gleditsia triacanthos is a spiny North American tree ultimately reaching 25m (80ft). The leaves are compound and are composed of numerous small glossy leaflets. The insignificant flowers give rise to pendant seed pods which may reach 30cm (12in) in length. Commonly cultivated are the smaller-growing G. 'Sunburst' which has butter-yellow leaves in spring and again in autumn, lacks thorns and fruit, and G. 'Rubylace' with purple spring leaves. To my mind 'Sunburst' is a much superior plant to *Robinia pseudoacacia* 'Frisia', the rather insipid yellow form of the false acacia, with which it may be compared. Grow *Gleditsia* in a sunny site in any reasonable soil. Plants are easily raised from seed but specific forms will have to be grafted.

Hibiscus
(China rose).
Malvaceae
(hollyhock family)

  or

Most of the bright, flamboyant species of these flowering shrubs are tropical and require warm conditions in the greenhouse in winter. *Hibiscus rosa-sinensis* can be cultivated in large tubs that

Gleditsia 'Sunburst'

may be stood outside in the summer. Much better, although a little less exotic, is the fully hardy Chinese *Hibiscus syriacus*. This is an upright shrub that produces its lobed, mid-green leaves in late spring. Flower buds occur in the leaf axils and open in late summer. Flowers occur in a range of reds and pinks. Best for the tropical-style are those with strong colours such as 'Diana' white, 'Woodbridge' red, and 'Blue Bird' which is a lavender-blue with darker throat markings. I suggest that you try any or all of these surrounded by *Kniphofia* and *Agapanthus*, which flower at the same time.

To flower well, *Hibiscus* needs a sunny location and a protected site will encourage slightly earlier flowering. They are not fussy over soil so long as it is not too wet. Propagate by semi-ripe cuttings in late summer, or layer in late spring or summer.

Hydrangea
(hydrangea).
Hydrangeaceae
(Hydrangea family)

Everyone is familiar with *Hydrangea macrophylla* which has a variable flower colour depending upon the pH of the soil, ranging from pink-red in alkaline to deep blue in acid soils. Some named cultivars retain their colour independent of soil type but none of these has the exuberant tropical feel for which we are looking. Try instead the Chinese *Hydrangea paniculata* 'Grandiflora' which forms a large, upright shrub (to 3m; 10ft) with oval, pointed leaves of a bright green colour and large flowerheads of many white (sterile) flowers that are green-white at first and fade to pink-white. Also good, although smaller, is *H. quercifolia* from

Hibiscus syriacus 'Blue Bird'

41

Hydrangea paniculata 'Grandiflora'

North America, which has (as the name suggests) large oak-like leaves that have an unusual velvet surface texture. The leaves turn red in autumn. Spikes of white flowers are borne in late summer. *Hydrangea villosa* is a large Chinese shrub (to 3m; 10ft) with lance-shaped to oval velvety leaves and flower clusters with few pale sterile outer blooms, but a pleasing mass of lavender-pink fertile flowers much loved by insects. All hydrangeas are fully hardy and enjoy a semi-shaded position in a moist, rich soil. They can be increased easily from cuttings of soft wood taken in spring.

Juglans
(walnut).
Juglandaceae
(walnut family)

The walnuts are excellent trees for the tropical-style garden, having particularly good foliage. The common edible walnut (*Juglans regia*) is ultimately a large tree to 15m (50ft) or so. The leaves, which have a pleasing odour, are pinnate compound with 3 to 9 leaflets that are purplish when young. The best forms have glossy leaflets with an entire margin. The flowers, borne in catkins, are insignificant. *Juglans nigra* from North America has very large leaves with up to 25 leaflets and also has edible fruit. *Juglans ailantifolia* from Japan is similar. These three species are hardy and enjoy a sunny position (which helps to ripen their stems). They like a deep, fertile soil that is well-drained. All are best propagated from seed (which requires stratification), while named varieties are usually grafted.

Koelreuteria
(golden rain tree).
Sapindaceae
(akee family)

Koelreuteria paniculata is a lovely Chinese shrubby tree not grown as much as it should be since, although deciduous, it has a long season of interest. First pinkish,

unfurling leaves in spring, then *Mahonia*-like spikes of tiny yellow flowers, after which appear peculiar inflated fruits and, finally, yellow autumn tints. The large leaves are pinnate compound, consisting of small ovate leaflets rather like those of the ash. Although fully hardy, it resents cool summers and mild winters and so grows best away from coasts and in a sunny position where it can get a good roasting.

Koelreuteria looks good as a specimen tree, but you could grow it against a south-facing wall which it would particularly enjoy. Grow *Koelreuteria* in fertile, well-drained soil. It resents pruning and so is best propagated from root cuttings, a strategy borne out by its readiness to sucker in its native habitat.

Koelreuteria paniculata

Laurus nobilis

Laurus
(bay).
Lauraceae
(bay family)

Most species of *Laurus* are tropical or warm temperate trees or shrubs. The Mediterranean *L. nobilis* is, however, moderately hardy and has the added bonus of strongly scented leaves that are of great culinary value (bay leaves). The slightly grey-green leathery leaves are elliptic with a point, and can reach 10cm (4in) in length. Relatively insignificant yellowish flowers clusters are borne in spring. There is a moderately attractive golden-leaved form (*Laurus nobilis* 'Aurea') that has greenish-yellow leaves, but these can scorch in a very sunny or windy position. A popular use for bay is as a topiary subject, commonly trained as a spiral cone or a ball-topped standard. If you like topiary, try it, but it is not really appropriate to a tropical-style garden. *Laurus* likes a sheltered site and will take some shade. The soil should be light and well-drained. Take semi-ripe cuttings in late summer.

Leycesteria
(Himalayan honeysuckle).
Caprifoliaceae
(honeysuckle family)

Leycesteria formosa is an unusual shrub, more like a shrubby herbaceous perennial, with ovate, dark green leaves borne on long, arching blue-green stems. The plant grows rapidly from basal shoots in early spring, at which point old, flowered stems should be removed. The stems are rather bamboo-like and can reach as much as 2m (6½ft) before breaking into numerous pendulous flower clusters. The individual flowers are white but are borne in amongst numerous green-red-purple bracts. The flowers are followed by purple fruits that have a strange musty smell. Although rather subdued in flower, the plants are particularly architectural and combine well with bamboo or *Fatsia*. *Leycesteria* will tolerate deep shade, but flowers best in a reasonably light situation out of intense sun. Plant them in a loamy, moist soil. It is possible to take cuttings in summer, but a ready supply of self-sown seedlings around mature plants is the best method of propagation.

Lomatia
(rust tree).
Proteaceae
(Protea family)

Lomatia ferruginea is large bush or small tree from Chile that bears complex compound pinnate dark green leaves on brown furry shoots. The individual oval leaflets have a furry underside. Hanging clusters of numerous yellow and red flowers are produced in summer, however, in order to achieve this display, the plant needs a warm sheltered site and for this reason is best grown against a south- or west-facing wall. *Lomatia* looks spectacular under-planted with *Eryngium* and *Fascicularia*, perhaps with some *Hedychium* if the soil is moist enough. Grow in a moderately fertile, slightly acid soil and provide some protection in winter when young. Take softwood cuttings in late spring.

Magnolia
(magnolia).
Magnoliaceae
(Magnolia family)

 - some

Magnolia delavayi

One of the oldest of flowering plants, *Magnolia* species were consumed by dinosaurs and have easily outlived them. The various species bear solitary, often waxy flowers with large leaf-like petals and stamens all spirally arranged. However, despite the beauty of their flowers, it is the leaves that make them valuable in the tropical-style garden. The largest leaved of all is the North American *Magnolia macrophylla* with, as its name suggests, leaves of banana-like proportions. This is not an especially delicate species

but the massive oval leaves of up to 1m (3¼ft) in length require a sheltered site if they are to survive wind damage. The white flowers are the size of dinner plates but are only borne toward the top of mature trees (10m; 33ft or more) in late summer. M. *hypoleuca* (from Japan) is a large (40cm; 16in) ovate-leaved fully hardy species with large white flowers sporting reddish stamens, borne in early summer. Many other species and varieties of deciduous *Magnolia* can be considered for the exotic garden as they often have large oval, simple-edged leaves, often rather glossy and tropical-looking.

Magnolia grandiflora from North America is rather different to the preceding species. It is an evergreen with large glossy mid-green oval leaves with a brownish underside which bear a passing resemblance to *Ficus elastica*. This is a slow-growing

Magnolia that enjoys a warm location. It is perfectly happy as a specimen tree or large bush but is most often seen as a wall shrub where it flowers more prolifically. The flowers of this species are particularly lovely, being

Magnolia macrophylla

Magnolia grandiflora

Liliodendron tulipifera

large (to 15cm; 6in diameter) white and strongly scented of honey and lemon. There are a number of named varieties but all are valuable garden plants. *Magnolia delavayi* is similar but has larger, greyer leaves and short-lived flowers.

Liriodendron tulipifera is a close relative of *Magnolia*. For those expecting tulips there is a long wait and probable disappointment as the flowers are mostly green and borne only on older trees. The deciduous leaves, however, are most unusual. They are leathery, bright green and similar in shape to a plane tree leaf but without the central pointed lobe.

All *Magnolia* species like semi-shaded woodland-like conditions with a moist, humus-rich acid to neutral soil. They do not like to dry out, so

ensure plenty of moisture and a good soil depth. Make sure you plant them in the right place because moving *Magnolia* saplings, with their rather fleshy roots, is not easy and can be very damaging to the plant. Similarly, take care with the roots when planting. Propagate either from stratified seed or from semi-ripe cuttings in late summer.

Mahonia
(holly grape).
Berberidaceae
(barberry family)

There are an number of these prickly shrubs, but the most tropical-looking are those with upright growth and large, dark blue-green pinnate compound leaves made up of leaflets that individually resemble those of holly. *Mahonia* x *media* and one of its parents, the Chinese M. *japonica*, are both tough, rugged shrubs (to 3m; 10ft) which will stand almost any conditions except full sun. There are a number of forms of which M. 'Charity' is one of the best. Although rather coarse, they warrant a place in the exotic garden as architectural foliage plants and because they are winter-flowering, producing sprays of spikes, each covered with tiny scented bell-like yellow flowers. They are best propagated from cuttings in late summer – and do not be surprised by the brilliant yellow wood.

Morus
(mulberry).
Moraceae
(mulberry family)

Mulberries are now little planted, although in the past they were more popular. There are a few hardy species, but the best for the tropical-style garden is *Morus alba*, from China. This has the largest leaves, reaching up to 20cm (8in) in length, more or less heart-shaped and slightly glossy. They are the staple diet of silkworm caterpillars. Flower clusters are insignificant but give rise to pale pink-purple fruits. They are borne in late summer, but in this species are not really edible (although birds will readily consume them). *Morus alba* will eventually form a tree of 8m (25ft) or more. M. *nigra* is usually smaller and lacks the glossy leaves of M. *alba*. You should root hardwood cuttings in the open ground in autumn.

Morus nigra

Paulownia
(foxglove tree).
Scrophulariaceae
(foxglove family)

Easily raised from seed is this fast-growing tree that bears large, shallow-lobed hairy leaves. Eventually reaching 10m (33ft), *Paulownia tomentosa* is particularly amenable to pollarding, the practice of cutting stems back to the base to encourage vigorous spring and summer growth. If this is done, the resulting leaves can reach 50cm (20in) although the plants will never flower. If left uncut, older specimens will produce spikes of lavender-pink foxglove-like flowers borne in late spring. Although fully hardy, this Chinese plant may suffer from late spring frosts that will destroy the flowers. Plant *Paulownia* in a moist, humus-rich soil.

Paulownia tomentosa

Photinia x *fraseri* 'Red Robin'

Photinia
(scarlet leaf).
Rosaceae
(rose family)

The small number of *Photinia* species are laurel-like shrubs that are notable for producing red young foliage much as do many tropical shrubs and trees such as the mango. All produce small cherry blossom flowers that are insignificant compared with the foliage. *Photinia* x *fraseri* 'Red Robin' is commonly available and is an excellent bushy shrub to 3m (10ft) with lance-shaped leaves up to 16cm (6½in) in length. These are produced in at least two flushes each year, the leaves remaining a purple-red until the emergence of the next flush. *P.* 'Redstart' is similar. Grow *Photinia* in

a fertile, moist, but well-drained soils in full sun and with some protection from wind to prevent scorch of the foliage. They can suffer from a number of diseases and pests that result in leaf curl, although this is rarely serious. Spray aphids and remove seriously damaged shoots. Propagate the plants by semi-ripe cuttings in summer.

Pittosporum
(lemonwood, Japanese mock orange).
Pittosporaceae
(lemonwood family)

 -

Most species of *Pittosporum* are slightly tender and require a protected site, especially from cold winds. The toughest species is *P. tenuifolium* from New Zealand, of which there are a number of ornamental varieties. *P.* 'Irene Paterson' is a small to large slow-growing shrub with wiry black stems and small (4cm; 1⅝) ovate leaves which are pale green and white with strongly undulating edges.

'Silver Queen' is similar but with a distinct white margin to the leaves as is *P.* 'Garnettii' which is larger with purple flowers. 'Tom Thumb' is a small variety with very dark purple-red leaves. Although the flowers of these *Pittosporum* are relatively insignificant, you will find that the strange valved fruits are quite decorative when produced.

Pittosporum 'Tom Thumb'

Pittosporum dallii is a larger shrub with dark green elliptic leaves with a toothed margin and small fragrant flowers. It has decorative purple young stems. *Pittosporum tobira* is a superb shrub from China. It bears glossy dark green leaves around 8cm (3in) in length somewhat like those of a small *Rhododendron*. In late spring it bears clusters of strongly scented white flowers that are followed by green spherical fruits 2cm (¾in) in diameter. These turn yellowish before releasing their red seeds.

Grow *Pittosporum* species in a sheltered location or in large pots or tubs that can be over wintered in a cold greenhouse or under the protection of a plastic sheet. Plant them in a well-drained, fertile soil in a sunny or slightly shaded position. Plants in containers should be potted in JI3 with a little peat substitute to lighten the mixture. Propagate plants from cuttings in summer or layer them in spring. The species can be raised from seed.

Poncirus
(Japanese bitter orange).
Rutaceae
(Citrus family

Poncirus trifoliata is a rather untidy, semi-deciduous shrub, but for those looking for a hardy, fruiting *Citrus*, this is probably the best option. Like other *Citrus*, the branches grow rather unevenly, often terminating and redeveloping in an irregular direction. The stems are persistently green and produce robust thorns at intervals. The sparse leaves are compound, consisting of one terminal leaflet and two subsidiary leaflets all borne at the end of a broad petiole. The white, few-petalled flowers are produced in late spring

Poncirus trifoliata

Prunus laurocerasus

and are scented. In ideal growing conditions, these will give rise to fruit rather like a small tangerine in autumn. The fruit are strongly scented and can be used for preserves. To fruit well, *Poncirus* requires a warm site with ample sunshine and protection from wind. The soil should be neutral to acid and well-drained. *Poncirus* can be propagated from cuttings taken in summer in the same way as other *Citrus*.

Prunus
(cherry laurel).
Rosaceae
(rose family)

This enormous genus, which includes the cherries, plums and almonds, has little to contribute to the exotic garden but for one species: *Prunus laurocerasus*, the cherry laurel. This is an excellent, very robust shrub or small tree that bears large, oval, bright green leaves with a glossy upper surface. The leathery leaves have a slightly toothed margin and strong veins. Spikes of white flowers are produced on mature specimens in late spring. These have a pleasant fragrance. There is a number of varieties available, some with variegated leaves, but for the exotic garden, the species is probably the best. *P. laurocerasus* is a coarse plant but very useful for providing bold evergreen structure or a shelter hedge. It is very vigorous and fortunately stands pruning well, although then it will rarely flower. It is not fussy over soil or position but may suffer on chalk. Easily propagated from semi-ripe cuttings rooted in the open ground in autumn.

Punicia
(pomegranate).
Puniciaceae
(pomegranate family)

The Asian pomegranates flower freely in cooler climates, but rarely produce fruit. In contrast, however, the dwarf form *Punicia granatum* var. *nana* fruits quite freely, although these are smaller than in the species. All pomegranates have small, olive-green or bright green narrow leaves with a coppery tint when young. In summer, small (3cm; 1in), tubular, bright orange-red flowers are produced in abundance and are

followed by small gourd-like fruits in the dwarf. Pomegranates love sunshine and should be planted in an open but sheltered position in a well-drained soil. The dwarf form should be propagated from cuttings of semi-ripe wood taken in summer.

Rhus
(vinegar tree).
Anacardiaceae
(mango family)

The various species of North American *Rhus* suitable for the tropical-style garden are valuable for both their pinnate compound leaved and brilliant autumn colours. Most commonly encountered is the fast-growing small tree *Rhus typhina* with large pinnate leaves borne of furry stems. In summer, erect conical flower clusters are produced which develop

Punicia granatum

Rhus typhina 'Dissecta'

into purple hairy fruits. There is a form *R. typhina* 'Dissecta' or 'Lacinata' which has leaflets with a ragged margin. *Rhus glabra*, which is similar to *R. typhina*, lacks any hairs and so the leaves and stems are rather glossy in appearance. Both sucker enthusiastically, causing problems in lawns and paths (often under the garden fence) but providing a ready means of propagation. Many species of *Rhus* are poisonous and should be treated with caution.

Ruscus
(butcher's broom).
Ruscaceae
(butcher's broom family)

The butcher's brooms are strange plants consisting of stems bearing flattened subsidiary branches instead of leaves. *Ruscus aculeatus* produces tiny white flowers in the centre of the

Ruscus aculeatus

flattened branches. These are followed by small red berries. The flattened branches are a glossy dark green colour, rhombic in shape with a distinct spine tip. The individual branch systems are short-lived, but new ones are produced readily from the base. *Ruscus* species come from Europe and the Mediterranean region (*R. aculeatus* is a British native). They like relatively dry soils and semi-shade, although they will tolerate deep shade. They dislike very acid soils. Propagate by division of the underground stems in spring.

Sciadopitys
(umbrella pine).
Taxodiaceae
(swamp cypress family)

Few conifers are worthy of a place in the exotic garden because by their very nature they tend to be plants of colder environments. Some, such as the numerous species of

Podocarpus, are tropical but are of relatively little interest. *Sciadopitys verticillata* differs in being strongly architectural with its tiers (umbrellas) of strange leaf-like grooved branches which are linear and a pleasing mid-green in colour, often turning more olive green in winter. *Sciadopitys* is reasonably fast-growing and will attain a conical height of 3m (10ft) in ten years. Small cones are produced on mature trees.

One of the best uses of this small tree is as a tub plant, where it does surprisingly well and makes a superb patio specimen along with *Citrus* and *Brugmansia*. In a container or the open ground, *Sciadopitys* likes a moderately fertile soil that is well-drained. Propagate from semi-ripened wood in late summer.

Sciadopitys verticillata

Sophora microphylla

Sophora
(kowhai).
Fabaceae
(pea family)

The more or less evergreen species of *Sophora* are splendid shrubs or small trees for a moderately sheltered site. *Sophora microphylla* has pinnate leaflets (to 12cm; 4½in) that are formed from numerous small, oval, dark green, glossy leaflets. In spring, clusters of quite large bright yellow pea-flowers are produced. S. 'Sun King' is a smaller bushy form that is very early to flower. *S. tetraptera* is a similar species, but tends to form a small tree. Grow both species in well-drained soil in a sunny position (without which they will not flower). The more sheltered their position, the more likely they are to remain fully evergreen. *Sophora* makes an excellent specimen for near the front of a tropical border where its foliage combines well with bold leaves and grassy leaves alike.

Climbers

Climbing and scrambling plants form a fundamental part of tropical-style garden structure. They play a role in softening hard landscaping such as walls and fences but, more importantly, they provide a vertical accent while at the same time occupying relatively little ground area. Climbers are also valuable when trained over pergolas or arches, as they give dappled shade and may have the added advantage of displaying hanging flowers best seen from beneath. Climbers can also be encouraged to ramble through mature trees and shrubs where they can provide contrasts of leaf and flower. In addition, many of the more vigorous climbers – among them *Parthenocissus* will festoon small trees, hanging like tropical lianas to create a genuine jungle effect.

Included in the following list of climbing plants are woody plants, herbaceous and annual climbers and a few lax shrubs more usually grown against a wall. Some of the annual climbers are actually perennial in their native habitats: where frosts are light or rare these may survive a winter, after which producing abundant growth and flowers. The protective nature of walls mean that climbers and wall shrubs are often the most tender of the plants that we can grow, and so they are often some of the most exotic-looking plants. By the same token, training a tender shrub against a wall is the most suitable means of providing a warm microclimate in which it has the best chance of surviving short periods of cold temperatures.

The list of climbers which follows is by no means exhaustive. There are no roses, for example, no pale-flowered *Wisteria,* and very few *Clematis*. Instead I have included a range of familiar and unfamiliar plants which are appropriate to an exotic theme, many of which have interesting (or edible) fruits, since these are generally a more persistent feature than flowers.

Tropical climbers are fast-growing and often have the most extraordinary flowers. This gigantic *Aristolochia* bloom is 40cm (16in) from top to bottom

In its native China, near Nanjing, *Akebia quinata* can be found clambering over *Koelreuteria paniculata*

Actinidia deliciosa

Actinidia
(Chinese gooseberry,
kiwi fruit).
Actinidiaceae
(Chinese gooseberry family)

Actinidia deliciosa (*A. chinensis*) is well known for its brown, furry fruit with juicy green flesh and black seeds. The plant is a very vigorous scrambling climber with robust stems covered in reddish-brown fur. The leaves are large, to 20cm (¾in), and are roughly heart-shaped. The small flowers are white, shading yellow and are borne in early summer. These plants tend to be either male or female and although they both look similar, only the females bear fruit. If you want fruiting plants (and who doesn't?) make sure that you plant a

male and a female or one of the varieties such as A. 'Blake' that are self-fertile. To support the extremely vigorous growth, and feed the fruit, plant *Actinidia* in a fertile soil enriched with plenty of garden compost. They need a moist soil and plenty of sunshine to crop well, and are best sheltered from strong winds. Ideal as a shade plant over a pergola, perhaps with *Vitis vinifera* 'Purpurea'.

Akebia
(chocolate vine).
Lardizabalaceae
(Akebia family)

 some

The three forms of *Akebia* commonly available are superb vigorous twining woody climbers, ideal for clothing pergolas where the hanging flower clusters can be seen

Akebia x 'Pentaphylla'

from beneath. The Chinese *Akebia trifoliata* is the smaller of the three with slightly glossy leaves consisting of three oval leaflets of a mid-green colour borne at intervals on the rapidly extending stems. Flower clusters are produced in spring as the new leaves emerge, and consist of catkin-like spikes. Individual flowers are dark purple-brown, the larger female flowers at the base of the spike having three petals while the smaller male flowers have six. *Akebia quinata*, also from China, is similar but has 5-parted light green leaves, the leaflets with an undulating margin. The flowers are larger than those of *A. trifoliata*, paler in colour, and produce a strong scent of chocolate. Both may produce gherkin-like fruits. A. x 'Pentaphylla' is a very vigorous, but sterile, hybrid between the preceding two species and is midway in most characteristics including a semi-deciduous habit. Cuttings of all forms should be rooted in summer or the plants may be layered through the winter months.

Aristolochia
(Dutchman's pipe).
Aristolochiaceae
(birthwort family)

The tropical climbing species of *Aristolochia* bear some of the largest of all flowers, some up to 40cm (16in) long and almost as wide. Unfortunately those that can be

Aristolochia clematitis

cultivated in colder climes have much smaller flowers, although they can bear tropical-sized heart-shaped leaves. Most species of *Aristolochia* are climbing plants but some are herbaceous perennials. Principal among these is the European *Aristolochia clematitis* (birthwort) which forms upright, stiff stems with regularly arranged heart-shaped leathery leaves. Small, curved tubular yellow flowers emerge from among the leaves in summer. It likes a moist, fertile soil and can run vigorously although it resents disturbance.

Aristolochia macrophylla, as its name suggests, bears large (15cm; 6in) heart-shaped leaves on mature plants. It is moderately fast-growing once established. The stems are naturally twining but may need some training in their first few years. The flowers are insignificant. *A. macrophylla* is

ideal for a semi-shaded trellis or pergola, perhaps in combination with the golden hop, as the leaves will scorch in full sun. It requires a moist, well-drained soil. Although *A. macrophylla* produces its leaves quite late and loses them (in a show of butter yellow) relatively early, it is none the less a most deserving plant. *Aristolochia littoralis* (*A. elegans*) is a tender climber that may be grown on a support in a large tub for summer decoration. The flowers are strange, flared trumpets in mottled brownish-pink and white and have a resemblance to the traps of certain insectivorous plants. *A. clematitis* can be increased by division of the roots in spring. Other species are propagated from cuttings of softer growth in late spring or early summer with some bottom heat.

Aristolochia macrophylla

Billardiera longiflora

Billardiera
(blueberry).
Pittosporaceae
(lemonwood family)

Billardiera longiflora is a twining wiry shrub with narrow dark green leaves around 3cm (1in) in length. It will eventually scramble to 1.5m (4½ft) in height with support. The yellow-green *Fuchsia*-like tubular flowers are produced in early summer and, although small, stand out due to a strange luminous quality. The flowers are followed by pea-sized fruits which ripen to purple-blue and are most attractive. *Billardiera* likes a warm wall and moist soil. It can be propagated from cuttings of semi-ripe stems taken in summer. Protect the young growth from slugs and snails.

Campsis
(trumpet vine).
Bignoniaceae
(Jacaranda family)

These are vigorous woody climbers that cling by means of aerial roots. The two commonly available species (the North American *Campsis radicans* and Chinese *C. grandiflora*) bear large foxglove-like trumpet-shaped flowers in clusters in orange-red. The leaves are large and pinnate compound, the individual leaflets having rather jagged edges. There is a yellow flowered form *C. radicans* f. *flava*, and a hybrid *C.* x *tagliabuana*. Only matured stems will survive the winter so expect some dieback that will need to be removed if extensive. Once established, growth is rapid and

Clematis armandii

plants will reach 10m (33ft) if support is available. They like warm walls on which they flower well but the aerial roots can be a problem with mortar. They will also scale trees if encouraged. Best grown in well-drained, fertile soil in full sun. Layer stems with roots in autumn and remove from the parent the following autumn.

Clematis
(traveller's joy).
Ranunculaceae
(buttercup family)

 some

Although there are many *Clematis* varieties available, few have (in my view) the necessary qualities for consideration in the tropical-style garden. None the less, if you like them, grow them. The best exotic-looking species is *Clematis armandii*. This is an evergreen from China with long, wedge-shaped glossy leaves that appreciates the shelter of a wall rather than an open position (although it enjoys plenty of sunshine) where it will produce its flowers. These are borne in spring and are quite small (5 cm), white and fragrant. Rather different are the deciduous *C. tangutica* and *C. orientalis*. These have ferny foliage and wiry stems. The flowers are yellow with four thick petals resembling lemon peel. The stamens are purple. *C.* 'Bill MacKenzie' is probably a hybrid between the two and is a rampant climber, as indeed are its parents. All

will reach 8m (25ft) or so if support is available and may swamp weaker shrubs if allowed to spread at will. *C. rehderiana*, from China, is also a pretty, pale yellow-flowered clematis, the flowers of which are bell-shaped and pleasantly scented. *Clematis* 'Niobe' and *C. texensis* 'Gravetye Beauty' are both good purple/red-flowered forms suitable for inclusion in the tropical-style garden on the basis of their unusual colour.

All *Clematis* like a deep moist soil that does not dry out in summer. Grow them in sun or semi-shade. They enjoy a cool root run and the base of the plant should be shaded by stones or a thick mulch.

It is always a good idea to plant clematis a little deeper than they grew in the pot in which they were purchased. This guards against the

Clematis 'Bill MacKenzie' scrambling over *Aucuba japonica* 'Crotonofilia'

possibility of *Clematis* wilt, a nasty disease that rapidly affects the aerial parts. Deep-planted specimens may recover by sending up shoots from below ground level.

Cobaea
(cup-and-saucer vine).
Polemoniaceae
(Jacob's ladder family)

Cobaea scandens is a vigorous South American perennial climber grown as an annual in temperate climes. In a good season it may attain 6m (20ft) or more. The flat seeds should be sown on edge in moist peaty compost in early spring. Plants should be potted on as soon as the first true leaf has developed (the compound mature leaves are very different from the simple, rounded seed leaves). Plant out individuals as soon as frost has passed in a rich soil or in large pots of JI3 with a little added peat substitute to lighten the mixture. As they grow, the plants will cling to any support with their exploratory tendrils. In late summer, daffodil-like flowers are produced. These consist of a trumpet of petals surrounded by a rather fleshy ring of 5 sepals. At first these are green, but over a few days, the trumpet turns a deep purple and develops a less musty scent. In its native habitat the young green flowers of *Cobaea* are pollinated by bats while the purple flowers are pollinated by humming birds. Since,

Cobaea scandens

occasionally, fruits develop where neither of these pollinators are present, one may presume that bees are also adequate pollinators. The arrangement of trumpet and sepals resembles a cup and saucer, hence the vernacular name.

Cucumis
(melon).
Cucurbitaceae
(squash family)

Usually grown under glass, the many cultivated varieties of melon (*Cucumis melo*) make unusual annual climbers. These tender plants are fast-growing in a warm sunny situation in the richest available compost. Outside, fruits are less readily produced but the foliage is worth the effort, the leaves being roughly heart-shaped, slightly hairy and up to 30cm (12in) in length. C. *metuliferus* (the horny cucumber) is a tougher but smaller melon that can be grown in a large pot with overhead support such as a cane and wires. It has lobed leaves and decorative spiny orange fruits. More alarming still is the non-climbing *Ecballium elaterium*, the squirting cucumber, that has small white flowers followed by 4cm (1⅝in) hairy green fruits that readily expel water, seeds and pulp when disturbed. These latter plants are smaller than typical melon plants and have lobed, hairy leaves. They like full sun and abundant water and feed in summer. All melons are easily raised from seed sown in late spring and planted or placed outside when all danger of frost has passed. Mildew can be a problem and some forms of the plant are susceptible to virus.

Cucurbita
(squash, marrow).
Cucurbitaceae
(squash family)

The marrows, pumpkins, squashes and gourds are excellent fast-growing annuals with both decorative flowers and fruits. All are easily grown from seed sown on edge in a peat substitute potting mixture in late April under glass (preferably in a warm environment). Seedlings develop rapidly but should only be

Cucurbita pepo

planted out once all danger of frost is passed. None the less, it is important to keep the plants moving and they should therefore be potted on at regular intervals in a rich medium at regular intervals. Some forms develop tendrils and are self-clinging while others will require some training. All can be grown as spreading ground cover or over a support such as trellis work, wires or even over robust shrubs. The large-fruited marrows look well on a pergola where the mature hanging fruits resemble tropical loofahs (*Luffa*). Large-fruited pumpkins are best grown as trailing ground cover as the fruits may be too heavy for the vine to support. Smaller squashes and ornamental gourds can be used in either manner. Flowers are either male or female, the latter are recognisable by the slightly swollen immature fruit at the base. It is best to hand pollinate female flowers in order to ensure fruit production. This is easily achieved by removing one of the more numerous male flowers, tearing away the petals from the staminal column, and brushing the stamens directly onto the stigma in the centre of the female flower. Squashes are relatively disease- and pest-free although slugs adore the young seedlings. Mosaic virus can be a problem as can mildew but be careful not to confuse these diseases with the natural silver mottling that some varieties develop. All the cucurbits require a rich soil and abundant moisture. If you want to eat your cucurbits, there are a wide variety of vegetable forms. Recommended are

Marrow 'Long green trailing' and 'Butternut' squash. Seed can be saved from one year's harvest to sow the next year, but the plants will probably not come true to type, especially if you have grown a diversity of cucurbits. Similar, and related to *Cucurbita*, is the genus *Lagenaria*, the bottle gourds. These require the same treatment but produce lacy white flowers and bottle-shaped inedible fruits. They are excellent tendril-bearing climbers and you will find them ideal as an annual cover for a pergola.

Dicentra
(bleeding heart).
Papaveraceae
(poppy family)

Dicentra scandens from the Himalayas is a delicate herbaceous ferny-leaved climber that grows rapidly each year by clinging tendrils. The leaves consist of numerous small well-separated bright green spade-shaped leaflets sometimes with silvery markings. In summer, clusters of tubular bright yellow or purplish flowers are produced, each around 2cm (¾in) in length. The plant enjoys a moist but well-drained fertile compost and a semi-shaded site and is probably at its best scampering through a *Clematis* or *Lonicera*. Even in ideal conditions it can be short-lived but is easily raised from seed sown in early spring. Protect the young shoots from slugs and snails.

Dolichos
(hyacinth bean).
Fabaceae
(pea family)

*D*olichos lablab (or *Lablab purpurescens*) 'Ruby Moon' is an unusual African annual climber to 2m (6½ft) with runner bean-like leaves but of a darker green colour with purple undersides. Pea-like flowers are produced in clusters in summer and autumn and are a pale pink colour. These give rise to short broad pods that are reddish-purple. *Dolichos* is easy to grow in a light compost of equal parts peat substitute and JI3. Grown in pots, the plants can be trained up a small frame or over shrubs and other climbers. Try *Dolichos* with *Eccremocarpus* for an

Eccremocarpus scaber

exotic purple and orange contrast. Sow seed in late spring in warmth, eventually placing outside once all risk of frost has passed.

Eccremocarpus
(Chilean glory vine).
Bignoniaceae
(Jacaranda family)

*E*ccremocarpus scaber is a vigorous climber with pinnate compound fern-like leaves and narrow scrambling stems. Flower clusters are terminal and consist of numerous 2cm (¾in) long tubular orange flowers, each with a slight upward curve. They are borne from mid-summer to autumn. Different colour forms are available of which the yellow is most attractive and is excellent grown together with dark blue morning glory (*Ipomoea*). *Eccremocarpus* is easily

Dolichos lablab 'Ruby Moon'

raised from seed and will flower in its first year if sown early. In mild areas, plants will survive the winter and can eventually reach an impressive 5m (16ft). Plant in a rich, well-drained soil or if grown in pots, in JI3 with a little extra peat substitute.

Fremontodendron
(flannel bush).
Sterculeaceae
(bottle tree family)

*F*remontodendron californicum is a grey-green, rather woolly shrub that is most commonly grown against a sunny wall where it produces large (mallow-like) yellow flowers in abundance from mid-summer. The leaves are lobed and felted below. *F*. 'California Glory' is one of the best varieties with a long flowering period, but all are worthy of growing. They

Fremontodendron californicum

prefer a well-drained soil, but not necessarily a rich one as they are shrubs of the semi-deserts of North America. Propagate these plants from semi-ripe cuttings in late summer.

Hedera
(ivy).
Araliaceae
(ivy family)

Ivies are excellent climbers for shady walls and fences, but can also be used on pergolas or arbours where they may need some assistance to climb. The common ivy, *Hedera helix* has a number of forms with interesting leaves although these are generally rather small compared to those of other species. The largest-leaved of these forms are those

sometimes listed as *Hedera hibernica*. *Hedera helix* 'Glacier' is one of the best variegated types with crisp white edges to the leaves and sometimes patchy inner variegation. 'Goldheart' has pretty creamy-yellow centres to the leaf and 'Buttercup' has leaves which are a pleasing yellow colour in their entirety. 'Cristata' has large ruffled leaves which are a bright green colour.

With much bigger leaves (to 20cm; 8in), although generally less lobed, is *Hedera colchica* 'Dentata'. This is a vigorous plant from western Asia that will scale a support to 5m (16ft) or so. There is a form with an interesting yellow variegation often in the centre of the leaf known as 'Paddy's Pride' or 'Sulphur Heart' and generally more vigorous than the white-edged form *H. colchica*. All

Hedera colchica 'Variegata'

ivies grow well on a shady support where they will cling by aerial roots. These can be damaging to mortar so ivies may not be suitable for certain walls. Ivy is a woodland plant and as such likes a soil rich in leaf mould. Where happy they will produce winter flower clusters of greenish blooms that mature to black berries much loved by birds.

Cuttings of ivy can be taken in summer but beware, because the resulting plants will retain the habit of the cutting. For this reason use trailing shoots for trailing ivies and climbing plants or upright shoots to obtain adults with a bushy habit and less strongly lobed leaves. Ivies can suffer from scale insect and aphids, particularly if in a dry location.

Humulus
(hop).
Cannabidaceae
(hop family)

The common hop is one of the fastest-growing climbers for temperate climates. The green-leaved form is rather coarse and not often grown as a garden plant, but the golden form *Humulus lupulus* 'Aureus' is a superb climber for a semi-shaded pergola or obelisk. The hop is a herbaceous perennial which begins growth in early April with the production of numerous vigorous hairy stems from the shallow rootstock. The leaves produced from

Humulus lupulus 'Aureus'

intense blue flowers with a white centre. 'Crimson Rambler' has red flowers, again with the white centre. The blooms are borne from mid-summer onwards and, as their common name suggests, open in the night, are at their best in the morning, and usually wither by mid afternoon. *I. indica* is more robust with lobed leaves and dark, purple-blue flowers with a pink throat. It is less eager to bloom in its first year from seed than are the other species of *Ipomoea* yet it has perhaps the best blooms. For this reason it is best grown on a small support in a large pot or tub that can be given winter protection. The flowers of *I. lobata* appear very different from those of

the twining stems are lobed and have a wrinkled, bristly surface. They can be up to 15cm (6in) across. The stems will reach around 6m (20ft) whereupon they begin to produce smaller leaves and side branches bearing small, green, flower clusters which sometimes lead to the well-known scented fruits. Cut down the dead stems to the base in winter, being careful not to damage the basal shoots. *H. japonicus* 'Variegata' is a pretty, fast-growing annual hop with large, lobed white variegated leaves and can be used in much the same way as the perennial hop. Plant hops in rich, moist soil. Propagate by separation of rooted parts of the crowns or from seed in early spring.

Ipomoea
(morning glory).
Convovulaceae
(bindweed family)

The South American morning glories now include a number of different vine-like plants, usually with bindweed-like flowers. The species suitable for the tropical-style garden are mostly perennials grown as annuals as they readily flower in their first year if sown in mid-spring. They all have slightly hairy, heart-shaped or lobed leaves borne on vigorously twining stems. *Ipomoea tricolor* 'Heavenly Blue' is one of the best known forms with trumpet-shaped

Ipomoea tricolour 'Heavenly Blue'

the preceding species in that they are small and borne on a one-sided spike. They change from red, through pink-orange, to white as they age.

Grow these and any of the many other forms available in a mix of JI3 and peat substitute or a rich well-drained soil in full sun. It is useful to soak seeds for 24 hours in warm water before sowing because this improves germination. They need warm conditions during the early stages of growth in order to germinate, and will not recover from any shocks incurred at this stage. Similarly, sow only a few seeds in each pot so that they do not need to suffer root disturbance until well established. *I. indica* and other more long-lived species may be increased from cuttings rooted in warmth in summer.

Lonicera
(honeysuckle).
Caprifoliaceae
(honeysuckle family)

  some

The honeysuckles are valuable plants for the exotic garden having colourful flowers and sometimes powerfully fragrant flowers. The climbing species of *Lonicera* all have ovate leaves borne at intervals along twining stems. Flowers are tubular and are produced in clusters on short subsidiary shoots. Some species can be rampant and should be pruned vigorously to keep them within bounds. The common *Lonicera*

periclymenum is available in a number of forms which have slightly differing flower colours and flower at different times. All have wonderfully scented flowers and are ideal for training over a pergola or arbour near a seating area where their fragrance can be appreciated. Although the cultivars are charming, I prefer the wild species that is easily grown from seed. This has pale flowers and a very pervasive scent. *Lonicera* x *brownii* 'Dropmore Scarlet' is a splendid, easily grown climber with grey-green leaves and red tubular flowers with an orange throat. It is sadly weakly scented but is well worth growing, especially since it is semi-evergreen. *Lonicera sempervirens* is similar but with brighter flowers. It is, however, unscented and slightly less hardy than the hybrid. Both really do look as though they could be pollinated by humming birds. Also with spectacular flowers is *Lonicera* x *tellmanniana*. This slightly delicate hybrid has golden yellow flowers and ovate, dark green leaves. It too lacks a scent of any significance.

Most forms of honeysuckle are happy in semi-shaded positions although they tend to flower best where they get bright sunshine for part of the day. They are not fussy over soil but do best in loam that does not dry out excessively in summer. They can be propagated from seed sown in autumn and stratified over winter. Alternatively strike cuttings in summer. Plants can sometimes suffer from aphids.

Parthenocissus quinquefolia in autumn

Parthenocissus
(Virginia creeper).
Vitaceae
(grape family)

These vigorous climbers take time to establish, but once underway they can be almost troublesome. There are two principal species. *P. quinquefolia* has compound leaves of five leaflets each with a jagged margin. The plants climb by means of wiry tendril-like structures that are tipped with little suckers. These initially cling to any support but if later dislodged, may not be able to re-establish. The flowers are insignificant. In autumn, the foliage turns a magnificent red colour. This North American plant is commonly grown on a sunny or semi-shaded wall but is wonderful sent up the trunk of a small tree where it will rapidly run up the branches and then hang down in festoons that may eventually reach the ground forming an encircling curtain. *P. tricuspidata* from Korea has leaves with three lobes. The leaves are a darker green than those of *P. quinquefolia* and are slightly glossy. Grow *Parthenocissus* species in fertile soil in sun or semi-shade and supply plenty of water in summer, especially for young plants. Propagate from hardwood cuttings in winter.

Passiflora
(passion flower).
Passifloraceae
(passion flower family)

Passion flowers are wonderfully exotic and fortunately there are a few that may be grown outside with a little protection. They climb by means of tendrils and twining stems. The South American *Passiflora caerulea* is a well known species which has deeply lobed glossy leaves rather like a large ivy (*Hedera*). The flowers are around 10cm (4in) in diameter and consist of ten white petals and sepals surmounted by a mass of radiating filaments that are purple toward the centre of the flower, becoming white, and finally lavender purple at the tips. Projecting from the centre of the flower are five green stamens and a stigma with three purplish lobes. In warm sites, such as

against a sunny south-facing wall, flowers are followed by tomato-like fruits. These change from green to orange when ripe in late summer. There is a lovely white form *P. 'Constance Elliott'* which is said to be slightly hardier than the blue. *Passiflora incarnata* from North America is a hardy passion vine with flowers that range from pale to to light purple and radiating filaments of similar colour. It has yellow fruits.

Grow passion vines on wires against a wall or over a sheltered trellis or pergola. They enjoy full sun and plenty of water when in growth during the summer months. Plant in a fertile soil with good drainage. In cold areas *P. caerulea* may become almost leafless during the winter. If cut back by frosts the plants commonly regenerate from buds at soil level. Propagate from cuttings in summer or from rooted suckers which have been detached from mature plants.

Phaseolus
(climbing bean).
Fabaceae
(pea family)

It will come as no surprise to discover that the runner bean (*Phaseolus coccineus*) was originally introduced from Mexico as an ornamental climber and has only recently become popular as a vegetable. The striking scarlet pea flowers are familiar to most and certainly combine well with other annual climbers such as *Tropaeolum* and *Ipomoea*. Although the majority of named varieties have red flowers there are some that bear white ('Czar') or bicoloured blooms ('Painted Lady') and these are worth growing in combination with the red forms or on their own. The best to grow in the tropical garden are the tall growing varieties such as 'Scarlet

Passiflora caerulea 'Constance Elliott'

Phaseolus coccineus 'Scarlet Emperor'

Emperor' although dwarf types are now available that form bushy plants. Runner beans can be grown in most fertile soils providing ample water is supplied. They generally prefer a slightly alkaline soil so it may be necessary to incorporate some lime when planting.

Beans should be sown in mid-spring under cover and planted out after risk of frost has passed. Alternatively they may be sown where they are to grow in late spring. Once established, growth is rapid and plants will begin to bloom in early summer. Slugs and blackfly can be a problem in the early stages, but once underway, little interferes with the exuberant growth of a runner bean. If you wish, you can eat the resulting bean pods, but even if you don't like runners to eat, remove the developing pods to encourage further flower

production. You can leave a few pods to mature, but the resulting beans, if sown the following spring, may not produce blossoms that are the same as those of the parents.

Solanum
(potato vine).
Solanaceae
(tomato family)

The South American potato vines are lax shrubs that can be trained over wires or against a wall where they receive the protection they need to flower well. *Solanum crispum* 'Glasnevin' is a robust blue-flowered potato vine with small oval dark green leaves and predominantly green stems. Flowers are produced from late spring to autumn with the main flush occurring in early summer. The

Solanum lacinatum

flowers appear in large clusters and have five purple-blue petals and bright yellow prominent stamens. Sometimes the flowers are followed by small black fruits. This plant will reach 5m (16ft) or more with support but becomes mostly leafless below. *Solanum jasminoides* 'Album' is a more slender, twining, white-flowered

Solanum crispum 'Glasnevin'

potato vine with narrow dark green, often purplish leaves. It is not as hardy as *S. crispum*. *Solanum lacinatum* is a vigorous shrubby relative that is less hardy than the climbing forms but is well worth growing for its large, bindweed-like purple-blue flowers. It can be grown outside with plenty of winter protection but is perhaps better grown in a tub or large pot that can be moved under cover for the winter. All *Solanum* species like a moderately rich soil with plenty of moisture and ample sunshine. Most can be propagated from cuttings rooted in summer in a sandy medium.

Trachelospermum
(star jasmine).
Apocynaceae
(oleander family)

*T*rachelospermum jasminoides is a woody evergreen twining climber from China that will eventually reach 8m (25ft) or so on a suitable support. The 8cm (3⅛in) ovate glossy leaves are dark green in colour and provide an excellent foil to the clusters of white, periwinkle-like flowers.

There is a less vigorous variegated form worth considering. *T. asiaticum* is smaller in every way, but the flowers are wonderfully scented. These plants like a warm, sunny site (preferably a south-facing wall) and a fertile, well-drained acid soil. Best propagated by layering of stems near the ground in autumn.

Tropaeolum
(nasturtium).
Tropaeolaceae
(nasturtium family)

  some

Nasturtiums (*Tropaeolum majus*) are familiar annual plants. There are now many cultivated varieties including dwarf bushy forms (e.g. 'Tom Thumb'), some with variegated foliage ('Alaska') and some double flowered forms that are generally propagated from cuttings. The best, and easiest nasturtiums for the tropical effect are the vigorous long trailing or climbing forms, usually labelled as such. These will happily climb by means of their twisting stems and petioles and can reach 4–5 metres (13–16ft) in length. As vigorous as the common nasturtium, if not more so, is *T. peregrinum*, the canary creeper. It is an active climber and will reach 3–4 metres (10–13ft) in a growing season. It bears lobed leaves as opposed to the round (peltate) leaves of *T. majus*. The flowers are lemon yellow and somewhat smaller than those of the common nasturtium, but are borne profusely until seed is set whereupon the plants generally die. The rapid growth and flowering of this plant often means that a second generation may flower in autumn from seeds shed earlier in the year. Both of the above species will grow in most soils but the better

Tropaeolum speciosum

Tropaeolum majus form

the conditions, the better their performance. Sow both species in early April and plant out as soon as frosts have passed. Train the stems as they grow. *T. majus* will not flower well in rich soils although growth may be very vigorous. In mild areas self-sown seed will over-winter and plants will germinate early. Note that these will need some protection if they are to survive late frosts.

Tropaeolum tuberosum (from South America) is a perennial species over-wintering as small tubers. These have a striking red streaked and marbled surface and are said to be edible (they certainly are by mice). The plant is not as vigorous as the annuals described above. Each tuber produces a number of stems that will actively climb. The leaves are lobed but darker than those of *T. peregrinum*. The flowers are almost tubular with

particularly long spurs and are produced in late summer. The form 'Ken Aslet' is generally more vigorous and most commonly encountered. *Tropaeolum speciosum* is a hardy climbing herbaceous perennial, again with deeply lobed leaves: it bears red flowers in abundance when happy. Achieving this generally requires a sheltered, part shady, position and a peaty, acid soil (also appropriate for *T. tuberosum*). These species will occasionally self-seed. All nasturtiums are susceptible to aphids and caterpillars. The annual species seem to cope with this, probably because of their rate of growth. The perennials may need a dose of insecticide to ensure their survival.

Vitis
(grape).
Vitaceae
(grape family)

There are a number of vines suitable for the exotic garden, not least forms of the grape vine *Vitis vinifera*. As well as the many wine grapes such as *Vitis vinifera* 'Müller Thurgau', there are two forms worth growing for their foliage. *Vitis vinifera* 'Purpurea' has small very sharp black fruit which are much-loved by birds and reddish leaves for much of the year, turning very red in autumn. *V.* 'Brant' has edible fruits and green foliage that becomes a riot of reds, and yellows in autumn. Another

interesting species is the vigorous *Vitis coignetiae* from Korea that can reach 15m (50ft). This has huge, heart-shaped leaves (to 30cm (12in) that are wrinkled, slightly hairy and turn red in autumn. It is superb when encouraged to clamber through a mature tree and allowed to hang in liana-like festoons from the branches.

Grape vines prefer full sun in order to set abundant, well-flavoured fruits. Those forms cultivated for their leaves alone are best grown in semi-shade where leaf size will be larger. Grape vines usually require some training to their support and will, once established, require frequent pruning. The vigorous species can be left to explore any support and need only be cut back when they extend beyond desired limits. Vines generally dislike an acid soil but are otherwise not particularly fussy.

Vitis vinifera 'Purpurea' at Kew.

Hardy herbaceous and biennial plants of diverse affinity

Herbaceous plants (those that die back to the ground in autumn) provide some of the largest leaves available to the exotic gardener, as well as having spiky or grassy leaves. Although essentially herbaceous, many of these plants do retain leaves through the winter, when they may develop stronger colouration. Plants with linear leaves and lily-like flowers belong to a distinct group of plants and are dealt with in other sections. The herbaceous plants described here are from a wide range of other plant groups, mostly with broad or large leaves, and therefore have many different characteristics.

The large-leaved herbaceous plants generally enjoy a moist soil environment and often a semi-shaded site. Conversely, those with linear or spiky leaves usually prefer dry, sunny situations. Whatever your situation, herbaceous plants can provide dramatic, bold structure amongst established architecture formed by hard landscaping, trees and shrubs. Some herbaceous plants are so big during growth (e.g. *Gunnera*) that they too form part of the overall garden design. Other plants, such as *Lamium galeobdolon* and forms of *Ajuga*, form rapidly spreading ground cover which is colourful all the year round.

The plants described here mostly have large, imposing leaves and some have interesting, or bright flowers. All are good plants for contrast with the more 'normal' herbaceous plants, but for a truly tropical feel, try mixing a selection of these bold-leaved specimens with grasses or large ferns, interspersed with *Canna* and perhaps a few bananas.

A young expanding leaf of *Gunnera manicata*.

Ajuga reptans 'Burgundy Glow' is, along with others of its kind, an excellent ground-cover plant with colourful leaves for much of the year

Acanthus
(bear's breeches).
Acanthaceae
(Acanthus family)

There are several of these rather thistle-like plants, of which *Acanthus mollis* is the most suitable for the exotic garden. This architectural plant provided the subject for a great deal of classical stone carving, its lobed, dissected and curled leaves being highly distinctive.

Interesting, too, is the fact that this is one of the few hardy representatives of a large family of tropical plants and yet it has given the family its name. The leaves, which are a lustrous dark green, can reach 1m (3¼ft) in length. They are quite brittle and have spiny tips.

Mature plants produce tall spikes of white tubular flowers largely enclosed by purple spiny bracts in late summer. *Acanthus* is easy to grow in a semi-shaded situation in any soil, although *A. mollis* prefers a deep and fertile soil.

Acanthus can be propagated from seed or by root cuttings. This latter feature also makes them very difficult to eradicate, should you choose to be rid of them. Another hardy acanth is *Strobilanthes atropurpureus* which is rather like a dark purple-flowered sage. It is a more or less herbaceous subshrub with the advantage of flowering in early autumn – a time of year when many other plants have finished blooming.

Amicia zygomeris

Amicia
(cleft leaf pea).
Fabaceae
(pea family)

Amicia zygomeris is a charming plant that in mild areas will be shrubby but regenerates vigorously from the base if cut by frost. From Mexico, it is somewhat delicate, but well worth growing for its unusual appearance. The hollow stems are purple-green and slightly hairy. They support pinnate compound leaves, the leaflets of which are a bright green, rounded, and with a cleft at the tip. One of the striking features of this plant are the large, rounded stipules which are pale green in colour with purple markings. These enclose the developing leaves and are relatively

persistent on mature stems. Pretty, bright yellow pea flowers are produced on contented plants in late summer and occasionally at other times.

Grow *Amicia* in a light but fertile well-drained compost in full sun. In pots or tubs, it flourishes in JI2 with a little extra peat and sand added. Although moderately hardy, this plant appreciates a warm sunny site preferably with some protection from winter wet. Try growing with *Eryngium* and the more robust *Sedum* species for an interesting foliage display. Propagate from stem cuttings taken in summer.

Aristolochia
see under Climbers (p. 51).

Asclepias
(milkweed).
Asclepiadaceae
(milkweed family)

These interesting North American plants have flowers much loved by butterflies. They have paired leathery hairy leaves that are broadly ovate, rather waxy and are commonly a grey-green colour. *Asclepias syriaca* will grow to around 1.5m (5ft), whereupon it produces rounded clusters of five-petalled pink blooms. These occasionally develop into fruits like a pair of inflated horns. They contain fluffy seeds. *A. incarnata* has

Asclepias syriaca

darker flowers in smaller clusters and has whitish woolly leaves. *A. lanceolata* has narrower leaves and red flowers. Rather different is *Asclepias tuberosa* which has orange-yellow flowers on shorter growth with linear bright green leaves. All flower in late summer. Grow in any fertile soil in full sun but watch them as they tend to spread rapidly by underground suckers. These provide an ideal method of propagation.

Astilboides
(dinner plate plant).
Saxifragaceae
(saxifrage family)

The single Chinese species *Astilboides tabularis* (syn. *Rodgersia tabularis*) is a valuable plant for a shady site, its large, flat leaves with a central stalk resembling a small *Gunnera*. Its requirements are similar to the latter monster too in that it requires, a rich, moist soil. *Astilboides* is late to leaf so rarely suffers from frost damage, but it should be planted in a sheltered site in order to reduce wind damage to the large leaves. The position should be shady. Leaves may reach 1.5m (5ft) in height and up to 1m (3¼ft) in diameter, above which, in summer, rise loose spikes of green, *Astilbe*-like flowers which, to my mind, lack any attraction and are therefore perhaps best removed. Propagate by division of the robust rootstock in spring ensuring that each piece has an active bud.

Bergenia
(pig squeak, Siberian saxifrage).
Saxifragaceae
(saxifrage family)

Some consider these to be rather ugly plants, but they are difficult to beat as a robust, more or less evergreen, ground cover of large rounded leaves. Looking rather cabbage-like, *Bergenia* x *schmidtii* produces numerous ovate bright green leaves that are very weatherproof. It is a vigorous spreader and will quickly colonise quite inhospitable situations provided slugs can be controlled. In

Astilboides tabularis

Bergenia x *schmidtii*

dry situations, the sprawling stems may become leafless at the base and if this happens, simply break off and plant the active shoots, where they will rapidly root, and discard the older leafless plants. *Bergenia* 'Ballawley' is the largest-leaved of the varieties, these reaching 30cm (12in) or so in length. This variety also has the advantage of acquiring coppery-red shades during the winter months. Most forms of *Bergenia* produce dark or pale pink flowers on short or long spikes in early spring but *B.* 'Silberlicht' has pretty white flowers that turn pale pink as they age. All varieties enjoy a good rich moist soil but are tolerant of quite a range of conditions. They will survive in shade but flower better and produce more interesting leaf colouration if given ample sunshine.

Cynara
(cardoon).
Asteraceae
(daisy family)

These large thistles from the Mediterranean are sometimes grown as a vegetable but it would be difficult to beat them as an architectural herbaceous perennial. *Cynara cardunculus* produces enormous much dissected grey-green leaves that may become silvery in dry sunny situations. The leaves may reach 60–70cm (24–28in) in length and about half this in width. In summer, tall branched woolly stems support large, 8cm (3⅛in) wide, purple thistle flowers at a height of up to 1.5m (5ft). The related globe artichoke (*Cynara scolymus*) is similar but less silvery, although it can reach a greater size. Almost as architectural is the biennial *Onopordum acanthium* (the Scotch thistle) with large grey woolly and spiny leaves to 40 cm in length. These form a basal rosette in their first year. This subsequently sends up a massive branching silvery stem, unbelievably endowed with vicious spines and terminating in 5cm (2in) wide pale pink thistle flowers.

Grow these giant thistles in fertile, well-drained soil in a warm sunny site and preferably where the winter rosettes can be protected from excess wetness that can cause rot. Sow seed in spring and plant out as soon as possible as they resent root disturbance. Cardoons may also be propagated by division but be prepared for the fact that the small plants can be reluctant to take.

Cynara cardunculus

Darmera
(umbrella plant).
Saxifragaceae
(saxifrage family)

Darmera peltata, formerly known as *Peltiphyllum peltatum* is a delightful plant of exotic appearance and remarkable toughness. In late spring, flower spikes and leaves begin to emerge from *Iris*-like surface rhizomes. The flower spikes rapidly elongate and produce surprisingly tall clusters of pink flowers that are unusual enough to warrant retention. It is, however, the leaves that provide the exotic garden with interest. These are born on 40–80cm (16–32in) stalks and are supported at their centre (peltate) such that a clump resembles an elaborate plate-spinning trick. The upper surface of their wrinkly leaves is slightly glossy and their bright green colour adds to their striking effect. The edges of the leaves are pleasingly scolloped. In late

Darmera peltata

summer and autumn, the leaves take on red tints and finally turn a range of autumnal colours before being shed for the winter.

Darmera is a spreading plant that will clamber slowly over most soils. Plenty of moisture is a bonus, but drainage should be reasonable as well as these are stream-side plants from California. The incorporation of extra grit is advisable. *Darmera* looks splendid next to purple-leaved *Phormium* or some of the taller grasses such as *Glyceria* that will enjoy similar conditions.

Dipsacus
(Teasel).
Dipsacaceae
(Teasel family)

The common teasel *Dipsacus fullonum* is a moderately interesting plant but its relative *D. lacinatus* is an altogether more imposing plant. In its first year this bristly biennial produces a large rosette of mid-green tongue-shaped leaves with strong veining and undulating edges. In spring the following year, the rosette becomes shuttlecock-like and then begins to grow straight up.

The lobed leaves borne on the flowering stem are opposite and joined at the base to form a boat-like surround to the prickly stem. These boats will fill with water making the stem very heavy. At a height of

Dipsacus lacinatus

around 2m (6½ft), the stem branches to produce a number of cone-like flower heads that develop their tiny white flowers in concentric bands.

Sow seed of *D. lacinatus* in early spring in pots and transplant individuals to their final growing positions once they have produced three or four ovate leaves. Teasels are not fussy over soil, although best results are obtained in moist fertile soil. They do, however, like as much sunshine as is available. In view of their tall nature and heavy stems, *Dipsacus* may need some form of support, especially in windy localities.

Euphorbia
see under Hardy trees and shrubs (pp. 36–8).

Galega
(goat's rue).
Fabaceae
(pea family)

These old-fashioned European plants are useful for their lush bright green growth. *Galega officinalis* var. *alba* has pinnate compound leaves composed of around 15 rounded leaflets, bright green in colour borne on stems that reach around 1m (3¼ft) in height, but can be larger, when they will need some support.

The flower spikes are produced over a considerable period from summer into autumn and in this form are white (the pale blue-grey flowered forms are not especially appropriate for the tropical-style). The individual flowers are pea-like and something

Galega officinalis var. *alba*

like 1cm (⅜in) long. G. 'Candida' is an excellent large, white-flowered hybrid also well worth obtaining. *Galega* is vigorous, especially when planted in fertile soils, and may spread. It will tolerate most conditions in sun or part shade. The clumps are easily divided in early spring, just as growth begins.

Gunnera
(giant rhubarb).
Gunneraceae
(Gunnera family)

The two large South American species of *Gunnera* are probably the most imposing of all herbaceous perennials and are certainly of tropical proportions. *Gunnera manicata* is the largest species with robust prickly lobed rhubarb-like leaves up to 2m (6½ft) in diameter. These are borne on spiny stalks that may reach 2.5m (8ft) in height. The flowers are insignificant but are borne in strange 1m (3¼ft) long green cone-like structures. *Gunnera tinctoria* (G. *chilensis*) is similar to G. *manicata* but generally smaller (to only 1.5m; 5ft) and forms dense clumps. It is marginally less hardy. These magnificent plants grow best in a deep, rich, moist (even wet) soil and in full sun or partial shade. When plants die back after the first frost, cover the crowns with the dying leaves to provide winter protection. Young plants can be further protected

Gunnera manicata

by piling straw or bracken over the crowns and subsequently covered with a sheet of polythene, pegged down at the corners. When happy, there is little doubt that these plants are the most exotic hardy perennials available, but do make sure that you have space for a mature specimen before planting.

Amusingly, there are other less well-known tiny *Gunnera* species from New Zealand and South America that make splendid ground cover plants for moist areas in full sun. These include *Gunnera magellanica* and G. *prorepens* both with leaves of only 5–10cm (2–4in) diameter. They are both moderately hardy with a little winter protection. Propagate all species of *Gunnera* by division of the rhizomes in spring.

Heracleum mantegazzianum

Heracleum
(hogweed).
Apiaceae
(parsley family)

Hogweeds are pernicious weeds and this is certainly true of the giant form *Heracleum mantegazzianum* from western Asia. This is an imposing plant that will produce its 50cm (20in) diameter white umbels of hundreds of tiny flowers at a height of around 2m (6½ft) on thick, ribbed, hollow purplish stems. The leaves are no less grand in proportion being dark green, highly dissected with purple markings on the veins and reaching up to 1m (3¼ft) in length. This is a wonderful plant for a moist soil and will seed around if happy, indeed, it has done so with a vengeance in a number of places in Britain and is now a notifiable weed. In addition to this invasive behaviour, the plant contains some dangerous toxins that can cause severe skin blistering in

those who are susceptible or have come into contact with the sap. If you dare grow this monster, plant it in full sun with *Gunnera* and *Miscanthus floridulus* for a giant 'weedy' experience. *Heracleum* resents disturbance so is best grown from seed sown individually in pots and planted where it is to grow as soon as it has a few leaves.

Heuchera
(coral bells).
Saxifragaceae
(saxifrage family)

Few of these lovely plants with decorative foliage are really suitable for the tropical-style garden, simply because in most cases the

Heuchera micrantha var. *diverifolia* 'Palace Purple' (bottom), with *Alchemilla mollis* and *Carex* 'Evergold'

leaves are rather small, but do include them if you like them. *Heuchera micrantha* var. *diversifolia* 'Palace Purple', however, is a larger plant which can hold its own against other robust perennials such as species of *Carex* and *Sedum*, where its large, lobed, dark wine-red leaves make a superb contrast. The flower spikes are around 40cm (16in) in height and consist of numerous small creamy flowers in loose clusters – not tropical, it's true, but pretty.

The shoots of this form of *Heuchera* seems to elongate quite quickly and, since the plants lose vigour when these shoots exceed 10cm (4in) or so, they should be regularly lifted and divided, appropriate parts being replanted with the shoots just above soil level. This is therefore the best method of propagation.

Hosta
see under Lilies and allies, hardy and not so hardy (p. 90).

Houttuynia
(lesser lizard tail).
Saururaceae
(lizard tail family)

This rapidly spreading plant from China can become a nuisance, so plant it where it can invade without annoying. *Houttuynia cordata* 'Chameleon' has wonderful 6cm (2⅜in) long heart-shaped leaves that

Houttuynia cordata 'Chameleon'

Ligularia clivorum 'Othello'

are variegated with cream, yellow and pink, borne alternately upon reddish stems that reach around 25cm (10in). The small summer flowers are insignificant but are surrounded by petal-like white bracts. The plant has pleasantly scented foliage that makes it useful for path edges where invasive stems will be crushed under foot. It is best to plant this lizard tail in moist soil in full sun, where it will develop the brightest leaf colour. Divide plants in spring just as the shoots emerge from the soil.

Ligularia
(golden groundsel).
Asteraceae
(daisy family)

These are splendid plants for the exotic garden, their requirements being ample moisture at the roots and protection from voracious slugs. All have their merits as bold, clump-forming herbaceous perennials, fully hardy and luxuriant.

The best forms are those with large heart-shaped leaves, often with a purple underside, such as *Ligularia clivorum* 'Desdemona' or *L. c.* 'Othello'. Flower stems vary from 1–1.5m (3–4½ft) and are usually purple or black in colour. Flowers are in keeping with the exotic appearance of the plants being orange or yellow. Their only drawback is that the flowers become scruffy once over. *Ligularia* species work well with other moisture-loving plants, especially *Zantedeschia* and *Lysichiton*.

Grow *Ligularia* in sun or partial shade in moist (wet) peaty or even clay soil. Feed amply, preferably with a dressing of manure to encourage large leaves. Water well in summer if

dry (the plants will let you know if they need it, as they wilt readily but recover rapidly). They may suffer from mildew in dry summers. Propagate by division of clumps in autumn or early spring. Species may be raised from seed.

Lobelia
(cardinal flower).
Campanulaceae
(bellflower family)

 some

A few species of this large genus that contains the well-known bedding plant (*Lobelia erinus*) are of interest in the exotic garden. Most imposing is *Lobelia tupa* from Chile. This is a large herbaceous plant that can reach 2m (6½ft) in height at flowering. Each upright stem is clothed in pale, grey-green, slightly furry leaves. In late summer, the stems sport reddish spikes of red tubular flowers, the contrast with the leaves being particularly striking. *L. tupa* is hardy but requires protection from moisture in winter and less than expected in summer. Not surprisingly, excellent drainage is essential and a soil enriched with grit is a great bonus. In exposed positions, the tall stems may require support.

Lobelia cardinalis and *Lobelia splendens* (*L. fulgens*) are altogether different in their requirements, being at home with their feet in wet soil, at the margin of a pond or similar location. These too are herbaceous and tend to be relatively short-lived. The wild forms bear green leaves and these are of limited interest. The red-leaved forms are considerably more valuable and numerous and some

forms have been interbred for large leaf rosettes to emphasize this aspect. A particularly good form is 'Queen Victoria'. They look well with *Carex* 'Evergold' or *Pontederia*. All can be grown in rich, moist soil, or form part of a water feature. In pots, grow in JI2. In mid to late summer, most forms produce spikes of bright red flowers of the typical Lobelia form. Protect from slugs during all stages of growth. A mulch of fern leaves can be beneficial in winter, particularly for forms of *L. splendens* which is the more tender of the two.

Macleaya
(plume poppy).
Papaveraceae
(poppy family)

These tall plants are worthy of a place in the exotic garden for their unusual, leathery lobed leaves. *Macleaya cordata* is the largest species with intricately lobed olive-grey leaves that have a furry white underside. These leaves are borne on the lower part of the tall (2.5m; 8ft) stems, the upper parts of which bear masses of tiny white flowers which seem to consist of little more than stamens. Other species and their forms are generally smaller but have more decorative pinkish flowers. The plants need a sheltered site and even then usually require staking for support. They like abundant sun and moderate amounts of water providing

Macleaya cordata

drainage is good. Propagate by division in spring once the shoots have emerged.

Persicaria
(bistort).
Polygonaceae
(knotweed family)

The bistorts have two useful exotic-looking representatives. *Persicaria amplexicaulis* from China (often listed in the genus *Polygonum*) has dark green pointed, oval dock-like leaves (to 12cm; 4¾in) with strong veins borne on stems that reach more than 1m (3¼ft) when in bloom. The flower spikes are narrow with tiny red flowers and are produced in late summer and autumn. *P. virginiana* 'Painters Palette' is a smaller, almost *Coleus*-like foliage plant with ovate, pointed leaves marked with cream,

Lobelia tupa

Persicaria amplexicaulis

Petasites fragrans

green and red. The late summer flowers are rather insignificant but they do tend to produce seed that can give rise to further variegated plants.

Grow these and other robust-leaved *Persicaria* species in moist soil in full sun or semi-shade. Established clumps can be divided in spring and stray seedlings can be potted up to be planted in appropriate positions once they are large enough.

Petasites
(butterbur, winter heliotrope).
Asteraceae
(daisy family)

These robust, spreading herbs are not for the faint-hearted. Large (70–90cm; 27–35in diameter), almost circular leaves are produced on robust stems by *Petasites japonicus* and *P.*

albus. The leaves are mid-green in colour with a toothed margin. Flowers are borne in early spring before the leaves and are white and borne in a short-stemmed cluster. *P. japonicus* var. *giganteus* is a larger-leaved version with leaves and there is an interesting variegated form.

Rather smaller is *Petasites fragrans* which forms a spreading carpet of kidney-shaped bright green leaves. This bears narrow spikes of grey-purple flowers in late winter that, as a bonus, have a strong fragrance. It makes a splendid groundcover plant but, like other species, can disappear in late summer in a blaze of mildew.

Grow all species in moist (but not wet) soil in semi-shade where the leaves will not scorch. All species are easily propagated by division in late spring once growth is underway.

Petasites alba

73

Physalis
(Cape gooseberry,
Chinese lantern).
Solanaceae
(tomato family)

These plants are grown for their fruits that, in some species, are enclosed in a decorative inflated capsule-like structure. *Physalis alkekengi* is a short herb, growing to around 60cm (2ft). The leaves are quite pretty being heart-shaped and with rather undulating edges. They are quite coarse and often conceal the small, solitary pendulous tomato-like white flowers borne in their axils. From these, the papery capsules develop containing a single berry. As they age, the capsules gradually turn a bright orange, usually at the same time as the leaves are shed, leaving these lovely lanterns arranged on the purplish stems. The lanterns will last for a while outside but are best gathered for indoor use before the autumn rains bleach them. *P. alkekengi* var. *franchetii* is similar but smaller. Both are vigorous spreaders when suited and should be watched. Another interesting *Physalis* is *P. peruviana*. This is usually grown as an annual in much the same way as a tomato plant and bears similar fruits enclosed in papery capsules but the berries are larger, golden orange and edible. Cape gooseberries, as they are known, are sweet and rather like a cherry tomato. Grow the hardy perennials in any well-drained soil

Phytolacca americana with *Euphorbia*

in sun. Cape gooseberries grow well in growbags or in rich soil in the greenhouse border, or a sunny protected site outside.

Phytolacca
(pokeweed).
Phytolaccaceae
(pokeweed family)

Phytolacca americana is an interesting tuberous plant which is grown more for its ornamental fruit than its flowers. In spring, the plant produces branching stems which are reddish in colour from which are borne simple ovate leaves of a bright green colour, each around 20cm (8in) in length. In summer it produces terminal spikes of rather small, dull greenish star-like flowers. These subsequently give rise to fruits that as they ripen pass from green to pink,

then purple and finally black. This contrasts dramatically with the yellowing autumn foliage. *Phytolacca* likes a humus rich soil and plenty of moisture when in growth. Plants are readily increased from seed: indeed, they can become a problem where conditions are ideal. All parts of the plant are highly toxic.

Rheum
(rhubarb).
Polygonaceae
(knotweed family)

The rhubarbs are large, bold perennials with arrow-shaped or much dissected leaves borne on long, thick petioles from a basal crown. The biggest is probably *Rheum palmatum* with dissected leaves that can be almost 1m (3¼ft) in length and nearly this across. The flower spikes are tall (to 2m; 6½ft) and branched and bear numerous tiny greenish-white blooms. The leaves of the type are dark green but various forms have reddish leaves, particularly while they are unfurling and some retain this colour on the underside at maturity. Particularly good in this respect is *R. palmatum* 'Bowles' Crimson' which also has red flowers. *R. palmatum* var. *tanguticum* has large leaves with a jagged edge and can develop a purple hue in full sun. It has particularly tall flower spikes bearing pinkish flowers. Another impressive rhubarb is *Rheum* 'Ace of Hearts' with heart-shaped leaves around 30cm (12in) in length, all with a purple underside. Lacy spikes of cream flowers are borne in summer and reach around 1m (3¼ft) in height.

Because of their large leaves, the rhubarbs are best planted in a sheltered site, especially where strong winds are a problem. The plants will stand full sun providing the soil is always moist, but they generally prefer partial shade. A deep, fertile soil is essential if the largest leaves are to be produced. Large crowns can be divided with a sharp knife in early spring. In very wet areas, it is best to cover the crowns with a plastic sheet in winter to avoid crown rot that can be a problem. Slugs may damage young leaves and small plants.

Rodgersia
(rodgersia).
Saxifragaceae
(saxifrage family)

The various eastern Asian species of *Rodgersia* produce solitary, large palmate compound leaves on stout stalks. Most turn spectacular shades of red and gold in the autumn as they collapse. *Rodgersia aesculifolia* has, as its name suggests, horse chestnut-like leaves about 40cm (16in) in diameter consisting of around seven ovate leaflets with strong veining. These are borne on hairy stalks that reach around 1m (3¼ft) in height. *Rodgersia sambucifolia* is similar. *R. podophylla* is slightly different in having crinkly leaves of five leaflets with a jagged margin. They are less hairy than the other species and as they unfurl in spring are a striking copper colour. They mature to an almost glossy dark green. All species of *Rodgersia* produce shapely plumes of tiny flowers in mid-summer. These range from greenish white to pinkish white and reach

Rodgersia podophylla in spring

a height of around 1.2m (4ft). Grow *Rodgersia* species in moist fertile soil in a sheltered and partly shaded site. They can be divided in early spring as they begin to grow their new leaves.

Rodgersia podophylla

Rheum palmatum

Rumex alpinus

Rumex
(dock).
Polygonaceae
(knotweed family)

Various species of docks can be troublesome weeds but there are two that are good hardy perennials suitable for the exotic garden. *Rumex sanguineus*, the bloody dock, is relatively diminutive with blood-red veins within the 15cm (6in) long ovate leaves. *Rumex alpinus* (monks' rhubarb) is larger with large, oval crinkly leaves of up to 25cm (10in) in length borne on short stems from stout spreading rhizomes. Both species will tolerate some shade but do require a deep, moist, loamy soil. Flowers are insignificant and may be

Sarracenia purpurea

removed. Propagate both species by division of the rhizomes in spring just as growth begins.

Sarracenia
(pitcher plant).
Sarraceniaceae
(pitcher plant family)

Some forms of these North American bog-loving carnivorous plants are relatively hardy and will thrive in a sunny situation in the appropriate soil. This is the crucial aspect of their cultivation, in that they require a moist, peaty but well-drained soil that must be completely lime-free. In containers, a mixture of moss peat, pearlite and sharp sand generally suits. Avoid tap water. In winter, a covering of bracken will help to protect the rhizomes while plants in containers are best kept frost free and moist. *Sarracenia purpurea* is the hardiest form with ground-hugging pitchers with purple veining. The flowers, like long-stemmed umbrellas, are pink to purple-red in colour. *S. flava* has tall pitchers of a lemon yellow and because of their height, the plant succeeds well with a little protection from wind best achieved by co-planting with taller sedges and perhaps ferns such as *Osmunda* or *Blechnum*. The flowers of this species are yellow. In time, the basal rhizomes of these plants spread and branch producing moderate clumps. These can be split up carefully in spring to produce new colonies.

Trachystemon
(giant comfrey).
Boraginaceae
(borage family)

Trachystemon orientalis is a large, vigorous borage-like plant from eastern Europe which bears 25cm (10in) long arrow-shaped hairy leaves from creeping rhizomes. Flowers are borne on short branching stems from the rhizomes, usually before the emergence of the leaves, in early spring. The individual flowers are blue and star-like. Although a rather coarse plant, the size of its leaves make a valuable contribution to the shadier part of the exotic garden. A position sheltered from wind and strong sunlight is essential since either can cause burning of the relatively thin leaves. *Trachystemon* likes a moist soil and will grow under trees if the necessary moisture can be maintained. It can be propagated by division of the rhizomes in autumn or in the early spring.

Trachystemon orientalis

Robust lily-like rosette plants

Large spiky rosette plants evoke the North American deserts and many of them do indeed require relatively dry conditions. Similar plants, however, come from around the world and are often better suited to moist environments. Whatever your situation, these plants are essential architectural components providing a contrasting leaf shape against shrubs and large-leaved perennials. One of the biggest, and most spectacular, of these plants is the Australian *Doryanthes palmeri* that forms clumps metres across and has leaves that reach 3m (10ft) in length. Sadly, this monster is usually too large and not particularly hardy but there are similar (smaller) plants such as *Phormium* that are more adaptable and can even be grown in containers in particularly cold areas.

The following list includes a diversity of plants that will suit a variety of garden conditions ranging from bone dry sunny soil (ideal for *Yucca*) to moist or wet soils (*Astelia* and some *Phormium*). Other rosette plants include the bromeliads and some succulents (such as *Agave*) that are both rather more spiny than the plants described here.

Giant rosettes of *Doryanthes palmeri* in Antibes, France

Astelia
(bush flax).
Asteliaceae
(bush flax family)

Astelia nervosa is an elegant clustering rosette plant with long, silvery-green spineless keeled leaves that may reach over 1m (3¼ft) in length. It comes from boggy parts of New Zealand. The silvery appearance of the leaves results from waxy surface scales which may be lost on older leaves and are always less abundant on the upper surface. The spikes of small flowers are produced in spring but are relatively insignificant although the subsequent orange berries on female plants are decorative. *A. cathamica* is similar. Grow *Astelia* in a partly shaded site in moist humus-rich, preferably acid, soil. In pots or tubs, grow in a soil-less compost. The plants require ample

moisture in summer but the rosettes should be protected from excessive winter wet in cold areas. Divide clumps in spring in order to produce new plants.

Beschorneria
(beschorneria).
Agavaceae
(century plant family)

Rather like a bright green, broad-leaved *Yucca*, *Beschorneria yuccoides* is the hardier of these large rosette plants available to the tropical-style gardener. The mature rosettes consist of around 40 softly spine-tipped leaves that are otherwise inoffensive. Growth of *Beschorneria* is generally faster than that of other lily-like rosette plants but it is correspondingly softer, so protection from excessive wet is particularly important. None the less, to provide for the relatively rapid growth rate, a moderate supply of water should be provided when the plants are in growth. Mature plants produce blooms that consist initially of a pinkish scaly spike (usually curved) that elongates into a tall (1.5m; 5ft) branching structure bearing the individual tubular green flowers. *B. tubiflora* is similar in growth but generally smaller and less hardy but makes a good tub plant. The flowers of this species are reddish and borne on a 1.2m (4ft) spike. Grow *Beschorneria* in a very well-drained

Beschorneria yuccoides: young flower spike

compost (in pots, JI2 with ⅓ grit by volume) in full sun, as these Mexican plants enjoy a good roasting. Propagate from suckers from mature plants separated in late spring.

Cordyline
(Torbay palm, cabbage tree).
Dasypogonaceae
(Cordyline family)

Two species of these woody-stemmed rosette plants are suitable for the tropical-style garden: indeed, the resilience and relatively fast growth rate of *Cordyline australis* probably makes it one of the most widely grown exotics. From New Zealand, *Cordyline australis* has long green narrow leaves that reach nearly 1m (3¼ft) in length on vigorous plants. The leaves are unarmed but the tips are sharply pointed. Each

Astelia nervosa

mature rosette consists of up to 100 tightly spiralled leaves that are gradually shed from the base as new ones form. Eventually, plants will produce large hanging clusters of hundreds of tiny cream-coloured flowers with a pleasing scent. The flowers may be followed by small blue berries. After flowering, the stems usually branch and in time, these plants can develop numerous rosettes at a height of around 3m (10ft) or more. There are now many cultivated forms of *C. australis* with red, pink, purple or yellow leaf markings. Some of these are the result of hybridisation with *C. indivisa*. Hybrids (which include most of the purple-leaved forms) usually have broader leaves than forms of *C. australis* and are less hardy so if you plan to grow *Cordyline* in a cold area, do choose the species or a variety with narrow leaves. Of the coloured forms of *C. australis*, 'Coffee Cream' has coppery purple, rather long leaves and is a tough survivor. 'Torbay Dazzler' is an old form with pinkish midribs and yellow leaf margins. A healthy plant of this

Cordyline australis

Cordyline australis 'Torbay Dazzler'

form is a truly shocking sight and so plants should be sited with care for it will otherwise steal the show. *Cordyline indivisa* (also from New Zealand) is a bolder, slower-growing *Cordyline* with leaves that reach up to 2m (6½ft) and are as much as 10cm (4in) in width on vigorous plants. It is less hardy than *C. australis* but is otherwise similar in form.

Grow species and varieties of *Cordyline* in fertile, well-drained soil in a moderately sunny or partly shaded site. If growing them in tubs, use JI2 with a little extra peat substitute and feed frequently. In winter, protect the crowns of young plants with plastic sheeting in order to prevent water collecting among the bases of the young leaves where, if it freezes, it may kill the growing point. Stems that have lost their growing point usually die, but suckers are commonly produced at the base of

Cordyline indivisa

such stems. These may be left to grow again or can be removed, once they have around 15 leaves and a few centimetres of stem, and encouraged to root to form new plants. Variegated plants may suffer from blotching of the leaves in wet winter weather.

Dasylirion
(Mexican grass plant).
Nolinaceae
(bottle palm family)

These are excellent plants for a dry, frost-free site or as specimen plants grown in a large tub or pot that can be taken under cover for the winter. A number of species are available of which the largest is probably *Dasylirion longissimum*. At first this plant resembles a grassy *Yucca*, but as it ages it gradually

Dasylirious and *Yucca* at Tresco, UK

Dianella
(New Zealand blueberry).
Phormiaceae
(New Zealand flax family)

  mostly

There are two species of this small *Phormium*-like spreading perennial. *Dianella tasmanica* (to around 1m; 3¼ft) and *D. caerulea* (to 70cm; 28in) are similar in form, each bearing fans of dark green keeled leaves arising in clusters from a branching rhizome. In mid-summer, the mature fans produce branched airy clusters of small, pale blue or lavender flowers with large yellow stamens. Pollinated flowers subsequently produce berry-like fruit that gradually turn from dark green to a dramatic dark blue-purple by early autumn. The fruits are undoubtedly the principal attraction of the plants, as the flowers are somewhat inconspicuous. *Dianella* will grow in sun or part shade although the fruit tend to develop more readily

develops a trunk. The rosette contains hundreds of rigid dark green leaves that reach up to 1.5m (4½ft) in length and are edged with small spines. The plants gradually form a robust trunk which may branch when the plants produce their large clusters of small white flowers. *Dasylirion acrotrichum* is smaller with leaves that extend to around 60cm (24in) in length and are borne in such enormous numbers that they can form an almost spherical crown to the robust stems. The flowers of this species are borne on an erect spike that may reach 3m (10ft) in height.

Nolina recurvata (Beaucarnea recurvata) requires similar treatment to *Dasylirion*. It differs in producing a massive bulb-like swollen woody base to the stem that makes an interesting feature in a large pot. The leaf rosette is completely unarmoured making this a safer alternative to *Dasylirion* where children abound. The bulb-like base

is rapidly formed but the subsequent stem elongation is much slower. Mature plants may produce sprays of purplish cream flowers whereupon the main stem may branch. Ultimately *Nolina* can reach 6m (20ft) or more in height, but is unlikely to achieve this in a container.

Grow *Dasylirion* and *Nolina* in very well-drained compost consisting of JI3, peat substitute, coarse sand and grit in approximately equal quantities. Water moderately in summer when the plants are in growth but allow the compost to dry out from autumn to early spring. These plants all require protection from frost but are relatively tolerant of low temperatures if dry at the roots. Avoid excessive water in the growing crowns of the plant as this can cause a fatal stem rot. Provide as much sun as possible at all times of year. Propagate these plants from seed or, alternatively, by the rarely produced basal offsets.

Dianella tasmanica

Phormium tenax 'Variegatum'

and last longer in shady conditions. The plants will grow in most soils but enjoy a moist situation with plenty of organic content and of a slightly acid nature. They object to excess winter wet but are otherwise relatively hardy. *Dianella* is most easily propagated by division of the clumps in spring, but may also be raised from seed.

Phormium
(New Zealand flax).
Phormiaceae
(New Zealand flax family)

The large forms of these robust plants can be absolute monsters reaching 3m (10ft) in height and as much in diameter. *Phormium tenax* is the largest with long upright grey-green keeled leaves around 6cm (2⅜in) at their greatest width. The leaves are produced in iris-like fans. The leaf edges look fierce but are not particularly sharp. In summer, mature fans produce tall dark spikes to 4m (13ft) in height that bear at intervals

clusters of dull orange, upward-curving tubular flowers. There are purple leaved forms that are almost as large as the type and *P. tenax* 'Variegatum' is a giant with yellow-striped margins. 'Yellow Wave' is smaller with internal yellow variegation as well as yellow margins. *Phormium cookianum* is a smaller species reaching 1.5m (5ft). The flowers are yellowish and are

borne on shorter spikes that achieve 2m (6½ft). Most of the *Phormium* hybrids with dramatic foliage colours are derived from this species. *P. cookianum* 'Maori Sunrise' has pinky-orange striped leaves with a darker margin while 'Jester' has pink leaves with a green margin. Particularly good is *Phormium* 'Sundowner' which can make a large specimen. This has dark purplish-green leaves with margins and stripes of pink shading to yellow.

All *Phormium* make excellent plants for the exotic garden, being very tolerant of poor conditions. They look particularly good with *Yucca*, grasses and bamboos. All *Phormium* varieties like plenty of moisture and should not be allowed to dry completely as this can be fatal. Conversely, these plants generally require good drainage, although *P. tenax* will certainly be

Phormium 'Sundowner'

happy in wetter conditions. They all enjoy full sun, especially the brightly coloured forms. Propagate the species from seed and all forms by the removal of small offsets from around the base of mature plants.

Yucca
(Adam's needle).
Agavaceae
(century plant family)

These bushy plants from North America are probably the toughest of all the robust rosette plants and are an essential ingredient for the tropical-style. Not all species are hardy but there is quite a range of habit amongst those that are. *Yucca recurvifolia* is the hardiest of the large species of *Yucca* forming rosettes of up to 1m (3¼ft) diameter and consisting of around 50 lance-shaped leaves that readily bend down to form a surrounding skirt of foliage. The leaves of this species are quite broad reaching 4cm (1⅝in) at their widest point and are greyish green in colour. The leaves have tiny margin teeth and a sharp terminal spine. Eventually this species will form a woody trunk and will sometimes branch after flowering. The autumn flower spike can reach 1.5m (5ft) and bears numerous pendulous cream flowers around 4cm (1⅝in) in diameter. *Yucca gloriosa* is a similar plant but bears slightly narrower leaves that tend to remain straight and are of a brighter blue-green colour. Tall, branched flower spikes, that have purple tints, give rise to numerous white flowers also with a hint of purple. *Y. gloriosa* 'Nobilis' has

Yucca filamentosa

a more intense blue-green foliage and more purple in the flowers and spike while 'Variegata' has cream-margined leaves, sometimes with a pink hue. Be aware that the autumn blooming *Y. gloriosa* is marginally less hardy than *Y. recurvifolia*.

The smaller *Yucca* species form minimal trunks but may branch from below ground level. *Yucca filamentosa* is probably the hardiest of all *Yucca* species forming blue-green, sometimes waxy rosettes around 1 m in diameter. This relatively fast-growing species produces around 50 narrow leaves before blooming. The leaves produce wispy filaments from their margins. Flower spikes reach 1.5m (5ft) or more and branch slightly. They support numerous pendulous creamy-

Yucca gloriosa 'Variegata'

white blooms. Individual rosettes die after blooming. 'Bright Edge' has yellow-margined leaves but is reluctant to bloom. *Yucca flaccida* also has variegated forms. It is a smaller Yucca, reaching only 75cm (2½ft) in diameter with flower spikes to around 1.3m (4¼ft). In other respects it is similar to *Y. filamentosa*. *Yucca whipplei* is less often available. It is like a large form of *Y. filamentosa* but lacks the marginal threads. The flower spike reaches 2m (6½ft) and bears numerous pendant creamy-white fragrant flowers. Sadly the entire plant dies after blooming.

Yucca elephantipes is a rather different plant from tropical Mexico that is commonly available for indoor

Yucca whipplei

Dracaena draco at Icod, Tenerife

cultivation. It is a fast growing stem-forming *Yucca* that thrives in warm, relatively shady positions **8°C**. It has quite soft bright green leaves that may reach 50cm (20in) in length. These readily bend down around the stem to form a skirt before being shed as they die. This species eventually becomes very large but rarely achieves its full height (up to 5m; 16ft) in a container. It will enjoy being stood outside in summer in a shady, sheltered site. *Dracaena draco*, the dragon tree, **8°C** from the Canary Islands is similar when young. It has shorter, often grey-green leaves and is slower growing. Its sap is red and poisonous. Both of these plants will thrive in a well-drained fertile compost (JI3 with a third extra grit by

volume) with moderate watering. Outdoor species of *Yucca* also require a well-drained site and will always do better where they receive some protection from excessive winter wetness that can badly mark the leaves. Full sun is essential if the plants are to bloom. It also helps to toughen the leaves so that they can better survive the winter. Most species and forms produce basal offsets once the plants have matured. These can be removed and rooted to produce new plants. Although *Yucca* plants are less dangerous than their more robust relatives (e.g. *Agave*) they still have relatively dangerous spines on the tips of their leaves and so should be positioned away from where they may cause injury.

Lilies and allies, hardy and not so hardy

Lilies and lily-like plants provide some of the bright, flamboyant colour in the tropical-style garden, particularly through the summer months. Although a few are evergreen, most are herbaceous, arising from bulbs, corms or rhizomes once the cold weather of winter is past. Most of these plants have grassy, linear leaves that are usually borne from ground level but are occasionally borne on stems as in the true lilies. Among this group of plants I have included a number of tender plants that are ideal for standing out of doors in summer, where they can provide an architectural compliment on hard surfaces such as patios. Whether hardy or tender, all of these plants make a good contrast with the broad leaves of other herbaceous perennials and shrubs. They also combine well with grasses where leaves may be similar but flowers vastly different. In general, lily-like plants require plenty of sunshine and good drainage although there are notable exceptions to this.

I have purposely excluded from this list most of the spring flowering bulbs such as tulips and narcissi. They certainly have their place and are wonderful in pots where they can be appreciated close to the house when in bloom and then taken elsewhere for the foliage to die back out of sight. There are some good exotic looking spring bulbs such as *Fritillaria imperialis* with orange or yellow flowers and

glossy green foliage and the various species of *Trillium* with their large, often marbled, leaflets. Species of *Eranthis* (the winter aconite) are also good providing early colour and green foliage. These are long gone when it comes to replanting with summer blooms. This list does, however, contain some important stalwarts of the exotic garden including *Agapanthus*, *Hemerocallis* and *Kniphofia* that are difficult to beat for exuberance of flower and lush appearance.

Fritillaria imperialis 'Aurora'

Crocosmia and similar lily-like perennials blend with other herbaceous plants and shrubs at Dinmore Manor, Herefordshire, UK

Agapanthus
(Africa lily).
Alliaceae
(onion family)

    some

These herbaceous or semi-evergreen perennials from South Africa are hardier than was once believed. In general, the evergreen forms are tender while those that are fully herbaceous are hardy to minor frosts. There are some smaller evergreen varieties that are also moderately hardy and these can be recognised by their relatively narrow leaves. The herbaceous forms can be planted in a sunny site in well-drained soil and will only require a little protection with straw or bracken mulch. The tender forms are best grown in large pots in JI2 compost with a little extra sharp sand. These can then be removed to a frost-free location for the winter. All *Agapanthus* have strap shaped leaves and clusters (umbels) of blue or white flowers borne on stems from 20cm (8in) to 2m (6½ft). Most commonly grown are the so-called Headbourne Hybrids which are a somewhat confused but unfussy group of hardy deciduous forms in a range of colours. Selected forms commonly have a more intense or better defined colour although some of these are a little less tolerant of extreme conditions.

Good small forms of *Agapanthus* include 'Blue Baby' which has clusters of relatively few pale blue strongly tubular flowers borne on arching stems around 30–40cm (1–1½ft) in height. 'Peter Pan' has more open, bright blue flowers that tend to face upward on stiff stems. It is evergreen and relatively early flowering, commonly with the first blooms opening in early summer. 'Snowball' is a good small white flowered form. Larger *Agapanthus* can be particularly imposing especially once the clumps mature. 'Ben Hope' is an old variety with large clusters of dark blue blooms in mid-summer on stems to 1.3m (4¼ft) or more. Forms of *Agapanthus inapertus* are distinct in that they produce clusters of distinctly pendulous, tubular blooms on stems

Agapanthus 'Purple Cloud'

ranging from 1–1.5m (3–4½ft). The usual range of colours is available but the most desirable forms are those with a very dark inky blue colour, often known as *A. inapertus* f. *hollandicus*. *Agapanthus inapertus* is deciduous and moderately hardy.

The evergreen species of *Agapanthus* include *A. africanus* and *A. praecox* subsp. *orientalis* (syn. *A. orientalis*). These commonly have broad, glossy, bright green leaves and large dense flower heads on robust stems. Flowers are generally in strong shades of blue but a good white form of both species is available. 'Purple Cloud' is an excellent evergreen hybrid with exceptionally tall, purple-blue flowers borne in late summer when it contrasts most effectively with *Kniphofia* and other orange-flowered plants. It is marginally hardier than most evergreen forms.

Grow *Agapanthus* in well-drained conditions in moderately fertile soil (in pots grow in JI2 with extra grit). All will appreciate some winter

Agapanthus 'Headbourne Hybrid'

protection such as a mulch or a sheet of polythene. Evergreen species will require protection from frost. *Agapanthus* are sun-loving plants and will not flower if they do not get enough sunshine. They are relatively drought tolerant and will survive a surprising amount of neglect.

Albuca
(tripartite lily).
Hyacinthaceae
(hyacinth family)

 some

Like many lily-like plants from South Africa, the genus *Albuca* contains numerous species that grow in winter and rest in summer. Many of these are admirable for the conservatory in winter but of no great use in the garden. One exception is *Albuca nelsonii* which is not quite hardy and requires protection from frost. It has linear mid-green leaves that arch from a bulb that prefers to sit on the soil surface rather than be buried. In mid-summer, loose spikes of green and white, scented flowers are produced. The flowers are curious in that of the six petals, the outer three open outwards whilst the inner three remain joined at the tip. Spikes last a long time if the lower dead flowers are removed.

Albuca nelsonii is easy to grow in large containers where it will form sizeable clumps. Plant in a mixture of equal parts JI3 and coarse grit. Feed and water regularly during the growing

Albuca nelsonii

season that lasts from spring until early autumn. The bulbs may be left dry for the remainder of the year. Keep the plants tidy by removing dead leaves which often turn an unusual red-brown in colour before drying up. *A. nelsonii* can be propagated by division of the clumps of bulbs (removal of such offsets is not easy as they tend to remain within the outer fleshy scales of the adult bulb), or by seed which may take many years to bloom.

Arthropodium
(rock lily).
Anthericaceae
(St Bernard's lily family)

Arthropodium cirratum from New Zealand is a tufted clump-forming plant to around 1m (3¼ft) in height, bearing curving, simple but

interesting grey-green leaves that are folded at the middle to create a distinct channel in the leaf. Loose clusters of star-shaped white flowers each around 2cm (¾in) in diameter are produced in early summer. The plants are moderately hardy if grown in a light, well-drained soil in full sun, although in particularly wet localities the plants should be covered in winter. These make good specimen plants in pots grown in JI2 with extra grit. Plants in pots should be protected in winter.

Chlorophytum
(spider plant).
Anthericaceae
(St. Bernard's lily family)

The spider plant is familiar in its variegated form as a virtually indestructible house plant. *Chlorophytum comosum* 'Variegatum' forms rosettes of narrow, soft leaves that are creamy white with a dark green central stripe. The leaves have the annoying habit of drying up at the tips, a characteristic that seems to be normal behaviour. At almost any time of year the plants put forth narrow arching flower stems that produce distantly-spaced, white, star-like flowers around 1.5cm (⅝in) in diameter. As the flowers fade, the flower stems sprout miniature versions of the parent complete with roots. These are readily detached to produce new plants. If you can get it, the plain

Chlorophytum comosum 'Variegatum'

green-leaved form is even tougher and will seemingly survive in the darkest corners. Neither form is frost hardy but they will happily tolerate low temperatures if dry. They are excellent plants for 'ground cover' in large tubs and pots where the prodigious offspring will hang around the edges. Propagation from offsets is no problem, but eradication might be.

Clivia
(bush lily).
Amaryllidaceae
(daffodil family)

Clivia miniata is now more commonly available and, although not hardy, has got to be one of the most robust lily-like plants around. From the forests of South Africa, this species is reliant upon a

cool, dry spell in order to persuade it to bloom. Simply, this means keeping it just frost free and dry from autumn to early spring when watering and a little extra warmth can be applied. Flower spikes bearing numerous peachy-orange trumpet-shaped flowers will result from this treatment. Even when not in bloom, the broad, dark green strap-shaped leaves are spectacular and *Clivia* can make a splendid contribution as a container plant in a shady corner of the tropical-style garden: indeed, shade is important otherwise the leaves will scorch. Plants gradually cluster and can be divided at potting which should be done as infrequently as possible as the plants like best to be left alone. Plant them in JI2 and feed them frequently in summer.

There are other species and rare colour variants that are worth obtaining if you can find them. All *Cliva* are mildly poisonous, however, so do take care when handling.

Clivia miniata

Crinum x *powellii*

Crinum
(Cape lily).
Amaryllidaceae
(daffodil family)

  partly

This large genus of bulbous plants hails mostly from tropical Africa. Many are good for glasshouse cultivation but for outside, the hybrid *Crinum* x *powellii* is by far the most satisfactory. The plant is reasonably hardy, and produces dense clusters of arching channelled leaves which are a bright green in colour and reach as much as 1.2m (4ft) in length. In hard winters these may be cut to the ground but generally recover well providing the bulbs are deep enough. Flower clusters are produced by mature bulbs on tall (1.5m; 5ft) stems and are usually produced in late summer. The flowers are large trumpets and are pink although a white-flowered form exists. Plant *Crinum* in deep, rich soil with reasonable drainage. They require full sun and benefit from some winter protection in their early years. They may be propagated by division of the bulb clumps in spring.

Crocosmia
(montbretia).
Iridaceae
(Iris family)

There are many hybrids and forms of the South African monbretia, some of which are rather coarse and can be invasive. They all have relatively narrow, sometimes slightly pleated, upright linear leaves that arise from crocus-like corms. Sometimes the leaves are a coppery colour in full sun.

Monbretias are mostly hardy, but some forms begin growth early and so may need protection from late frosts. Particularly good forms include 'Lucifer' which is tall (to 1.2m; 4ft). In mid-summer it produces somewhat tubular blooms of a striking orange-red which contrasts well with the bright green foliage. 'Emily McKenzie' and 'Star of the East' are shorter with large (5cm; 2in) orange flowers that open wide, the former with dark markings in the throat. 'Solfatere' has small flowers of a wonderful apricot-tinted yellow held above coppery foliage. These smaller forms tend to flower in late summer and autumn. Not to be overlooked is the robust species *C. masoniorum*, which has lush, bright green foliage and arching flower spikes that bear numerous orange upward-facing flowers in mid-summer. It looks well with *Canna* and *Kniphofia*. Look out also for the somewhat similar semi-hardy species of *Watsonia* and *Chasmanthe* which may survive winters if they are planted in a sheltered site.

Crocosmia species and forms enjoy full sun although some will perform in semi shade. They all require a fertile, humus-rich soil that remains moist but well-drained. Plants become overcrowded after a few years and should be lifted. Old corms should be discarded and the vigorous outer corms replanted at a depth of around 10cm (4in).

Crocosmia masoniorum

Eucomis bicolor

Eucomis
(pineapple lily).
Hyacinthaceae
(hyacinth family)

These somewhat inconspicuous bulbs make good specimens for a sunny border or for use in pots. The two commonly available species are fairly hardy, especially if covered by a thick winter mulch. *Eucomis comosa* (syn. *Eucomis punctata*) is the larger of the two. It bears smooth, slightly glossy tongue-like leaves in a basal rosette. In full sun these may become reddish or bronze in colour. In late summer mature bulbs will produce a cylindrical spike of many small creamy pink star-like flowers often with a darker centre. The spikes can reach around 75cm (30in) and are surmounted by a tuft of small leaves rather resembling the top of a pineapple, hence the vernacular.

E. pole-evansii is a larger form of *E. comosa* and is worth obtaining if you find it. *Eucomis bicolor* is smaller and has thinner leaves that are broad, bright green and have an undulating margin. They may have variable amounts of purple spotting on the undersides and toward the base of the leaves. The pale green flowers are borne on a shorter, more club-shaped spike again surmounted by a leafy tuft. The flowers often have strongly marked purple edges and the flower spike and terminal tuft may also have purple spots. Both species are much loved by wasps and when in bloom *E. bicolor* has an unpleasant smell. This apart, they make unusual pot specimens where they should be grown in JI2 with a little extra sandy grit. Propagate *Eucomis* by separating bulbs when potting or lifting for division in spring. Plant the bulbs at about their own depth for protection but, if growing in pots, let their noses poke through the surface. Pot-grown specimens should be given winter protection from frost.

Galtonia
(summer hyacinth).
Hyacinthaceae
(hyacinth family)

Of the three species of *Galtonia* commonly available, *Galtonia candicans* is probably the most useful. This is a charming bulb that should be planted at a depth of around 10cm (4in) and around 5cm (2in) apart in early spring either in a sunny border or in pots. The light green leaves that quickly develop are fleshy and remarkably upright. Tall 80cm (32in) flower spikes emerge from the centre of the leaves. Each flower bud is partly enclosed by a small leaf, but the developing flowers rapidly extend and droop away from these as the spike ascends. Each pendulous flower is white with pale green markings and has a pleasant scent, somewhat reminiscent of hyacinths, hence the common name. The seed pods, which rapidly follow the flowers, should be removed to retain reserves within the bulbs. *Galtonia candicans* looks well with *Agapanthus*, as it flowers at a similar time (late summer) and has a contrasting shape.

Galtonia viridiflora is smaller and rather insignificant with its green flowers. In addition, the leaves and flower spikes are rather floppy and may need support. *Galtonia princeps* is similar to *G. candicans*, but smaller in stature. The individual flowers in this species are more constricted at the base, but open wider at the mouth. Grow these bulbs in a rich, but well-drained soil or compost (equal parts JI3, peat substitute and coarse sand). Leaves generally die off with the first frosts, or even before. The bulbs are best left in the ground or their pots for the winter, but if grown in pots they should be planted afresh in spring. After flowering, bulbs tend to split into small offsets that may take a year or two to reach flowering size.

Plants may be propagated by separating the small bulbs and growing these on, or by seed that will take up to three years to produce flowering-sized bulbs.

Gladiolus
(afrikander).
Iridaceae
(Iris family)

The many colourful hybrid gladioli can be used in the tropical-style garden and it is really a matter of personal preference whether single colours or mixtures are grown and whether they should be in the open ground or in pots.

I would just like to mention two species that I feel contribute in rather different ways. *Gladiolus papilio* has narrow greyish foliage that is in itself

Gladiolus callianthus

quite interesting. The flower spikes bear only a few flowers but each of these is quite tubular, being rather like a foxglove (*Digitalis*) flower and of a pale yellow marked with lavender and dark throat markings. It is almost hardy and will spread slowly in moist, but well-drained soil in full sun. *Gladiolus callianthus* (*Acidanthera bicolor*) is quite the opposite in being rather tender, probably more so than the common *Gladiolus*. These plants are best grown in pots of rich compost (JI3 with a little extra peat substitute) and kept warm right from planting time. Despite the extra care this entails, pots of this plant make a wonderful addition to the exotic garden as the long-stalked white, purple-centred flowers have a delicious scent. This plant rarely performs well for a second season and bulbs are best discarded.

Hemerocallis
(day lily).
Phormiaceae
(New Zealand flax family)

 some

There are literally hundreds of varieties of day lily that have become increasingly popular in recent years. They are available in a wide range of colours and sizes and are suitable for a sunny or semi-shaded site with moist, reasonably fertile soil. All are excellent plants for the tropical-style garden and are very hardy, requiring no winter protection.

Hemerocallis form

Possibly the only drawback with these plants is their relatively short flowering period, but since the various forms have different flowering times, a full display that lasts all summer and autumn can be obtained. As the common name implies, the flowers last but a single day. They are, however, quite spectacular, being usually of trumpet shape with variously ruffled and flared petals. These plants excel in bright yellows, oranges and reds that are all admirable, while the pinks and whites are perhaps less desirable when looking for the tropical feel. *Hemerocallis* take a few years to become fully established and should be moved or disturbed only when they become overcrowded. The roots have numerous small brittle tubers and should be handled with care. Propagation is easiest by division of clumps when replanting.

Hosta
(plantain lily).
Hostaceae
(plantain lily family)

The decorative forms of *Hosta* have a reputation as providing the staple diet of the garden slug. However, do not let this deter you from growing these wonderful plants. Most *Hosta* varieties are grown for their foliage although a few species have such decorative flowers that these become the main attraction. There are an enormous variety of forms available with leaves ranging from heart-shaped to almost linear and from 3cm (1in) to as much as 50cm (20in) in length. It is the large-leaved varieties that are best for the tropical-style garden. Biggest and best (since it is supposed to be slug resistant) is *Hosta* 'Sum and

Hosta sieboldiana 'Elegans'

A diversity of *Hosta* foliage in the author's garden

deterred by encircling the base of the plants in ashes or grit. Despite this though, a few holes are probably inevitable. All *Hosta* forms can be divided in early spring. You will probably need a sharp knife or spade to split the rhizomes.

Iris
(iris, flag).
Iridaceae
(Iris family)

 some

There are many forms of Iris, most of which are not really suitable for the exotic garden, but there are a few which have such vibrant flowers or exotic foliage that they deserve inclusion here. For sheer size, try *Iris* 'Shelford Giant' which can reach 2m (6½ft) in height when in bloom. It has long, sword-like leaves of a grey-green colour and the tall flowers are yellow and white and borne loosely

Substance' which has huge heart-shaped leaves in a yellow green, most pronounced in semi-shade. The leaves have strong veining giving them a puckered appearance. *Hosta sieboldiana* 'Elegans' is a giant blue-leaved plant with leaves to 40cm (16in). Again they are heart-shaped and puckered. *Hosta sieboldiana* 'Frances Williams' is an excellent large blue-leaved variety with broad yellow-green variegation around the edge of the leaf. *H.* 'Big Daddy' is another large blue-leaved form. *H.* 'Krossa Regal' has narrower, taller leaves of a lovely dusty blue. *Hosta fluctuans* 'Sagae' is also taller with narrower yellow variegation. *H.* 'Christmas Tree' has white variegation as does *H.* 'Patriot'. Both of these have slightly smaller leaves.

All of these plants produce spikes of bell-like flowers in dusky lavender or white in summer, some of which

are scented. *Hosta* plants like the shade and will scorch if they receive too much sun. None the less, the yellow and variegated forms do prefer brighter conditions to compensate for their less efficient photosynthesis. All forms like a moist, fertile soil where the leaves will reach their greatest size. Slugs can be a problem but are

Iris lacustris

Iris japonica 'Variegata'

on spikes. It likes a fertile soil in full sun and resents disturbance. Forms of *I. ensata* bear some of the loveliest flowers that can truly be described as orchid-like. These are water irises and like their roots in water or in very wet soil. If you have an acid humus rich soil, some of the American dwarf crested irises can make excellent ground cover. *I. lacustris* and *I. cristata* are very good.

Iris japonica is rather different from the normal iris in that it forms stems which may reach 1m (3¼ft), terminating in fans of dark green leaves. The whole plant can give the impression of a sparse large-leaved bamboo.

I. japonica 'Ledger's Variety' is said to be the hardier form whilst the variegated form is particularly pretty although smaller-growing. This iris will tolerate semi shade and likes a well-drained humus rich soil. Propagate all irises by division in

spring before growth gets underway. There are numerous other semi-hardy iris-like plants from South Africa and New Zealand. Some of these grow in winter and are dormant in summer and so are not suitable for outdoor experimentation as the growth is usually cut by frost. Summer growing species are a better risk. Look out for the various forms and species of *Moraea* and *Libertia* all of which may thrive in a sunny sheltered site. One could also try *Dietes*, *Ixia* and the inevitable *Gladiolus*.

Kniphofia
(red hot poker, torch lily).
Asphodelaceae
(asphodel family)

 mostly

These are probably some of the best herbaceous perennials for the exotic garden with their grassy leaves and crowded spikes of brightly-coloured flowers so similar in structure to the tender succulent *Aloe*. The South African *Kniphofia* come in all sizes from tiny dwarf forms to giants that when in flower tower to 2.5m (8ft). Biggest and boldest are *Kniphofia uvaria* 'Nobilis' (orange fading to yellow) and *K.* 'Prince Igor' (red fading to orange). These are very large clump-forming perennials with tapering channelled leaves that have a slightly serrated margin. They need considerable space but are an amazing sight when in full bloom. Most *Kniphophia* are smaller reaching

around 1–1.2m (3–4½ft) when in bloom and with foliage clumps of narrow leaves around 50 cm in height. The leaves are generally evergreen in most forms although a few die back fully to the base each winter. More normally evergreen forms will also adopt this strategy in severe winters.

There are many named varieties of *Kniphofia* with flowers ranging from red and orange to yellow, green, white and pink. The flowers of most forms fade as they age and this means that any particular spike of flowers is usually paler beneath. Most forms flower in late summer but some forms will produce the odd spike at other times. Particularly good varieties include 'Bees' Sunset' that has pale orange flowers fading to yellow on dark stems, 'Percy's Pride' that has yellow-green flowers, and 'Royal

Kniphofia uvaria

Kniphofia rooperi

Standard' with red flowers fading to pale yellow. Especially interesting are *K. erecta* that bears upward-facing red flowers that fade only a little to orange and 'Atlanta' that blooms earlier than most varieties in late spring and early summer with terracotta and pale yellow flowers. At the other end of the year is *K. rooperi*, often in bloom in late autumn. Of the smaller forms that have very grassy foliage, 'Light of the World' has sparse orange flowers and *K. triangularis* has red/orange flowers. Lastly, *K. caulescens* is worth growing for its wonderful blue-green foliage that forms very exotic-looking rosettes on sprawling rooting stems. The flower spikes are pinkish red fading to yellow but are not as bright as other forms.

All forms of *Kniphofia* perform best in full sun although some will tolerate and bloom in light shade. These plants like a fertile, well-drained soil with extra drainage material added such as sharp sand. Once established, the plants are relatively tough but it is best to protect young plants with a mulch during their first winter and in cold areas protect plants from excessive wet with sheets of polythene. When clumps become crowded, lift them in spring and divide them into manageable groups before replanting in replenished soil.

Lilium
(lily).
Liliaceae
(lily family)

 -   some

There are numerous lily species and varieties available today, many of which are suitable for pot culture as well as the open ground. I have always found pot-grown lilies very useful in the tropical-style garden where their exotic blooms can bring colour and scent to a paved area. Pot-grown plants can also be stood as they are in borders where they are useful gap fillers, perhaps after spring bulb foliage has died away. Lily bulbs are easy to grow in pots, and they respond well as their individual needs can be satisfied. All lilies must have good drainage and a moist rich soil, usually of a neutral or acid nature. Exceptions are *Lilium candidum* and *L. pyrenaicum* which require some lime. Most of the trumpet-flowered lilies will also tolerate some lime.

Lilies require deep planting as many root from the underground portion of stem formed above the bulb. In general, the base of lily plants should be in shade but their flowers and foliage should receive plenty of sunshine. This is particularly important for plants in pots.

Lilies generally have star-shaped open flowers, trumpet-shaped flowers or downward-facing flowers with recurved petals. The trumpet-flowered lilies are very resilient plants although most tend to be of tall growth. They are derived in part from *Lilium regale* and have inherited the wonderful

Lilium regale underplanted with violas

93

Various forms of lily can be propagated from the bulbils that form at the base of the leaves

scent of this species, particularly strong in the evenings. *L. regale* is white with maroon reverse to the petals. 'African Queen' is an apricot orange while 'Golden Splendor' is yellow, again both with dark reverse to the petals. 'Star Gazer' is of similar tall habit but has star-shaped purple-pink flowers with a white margin. It has broader glossy leaves that are exotic in their own right. The various dwarf lilies mostly have star-shaped upward-facing flowers in a wide range of colours. They are all excellent for pot culture. They require plenty of sunshine to ensure that bulbs flower in subsequent years. Of the lilies with recurved flowers, *L. henryi* is very tolerant. It is tall and usually needs support for the branched tiers of orange and green flowers. Shorter is 'Citronella' which has very narrow foliage and lemon-yellow flowers with dark spots.

Lily bulbs should be planted as soon as available as they dislike drying out. Try to plant them without damaging any attached roots. Loose scales may be gently removed and potted up in well-drained compost where they will eventually form new plants. Lilies can suffer from viral diseases and when these occur, the infected plants should be burnt to avoid further contamination. Lily beetle can also be a problem.

Similar in appearance to lilies and with similar requirements are the species and varieties of *Alstroemeria* (Peruvian lily, Alstroemeriaceae). They generally have smaller, funnel-shaped flowers but with interesting speckled markings in the throat and lower petals. Many of these rhizomatous plants have rather pale flowers but the species *A. psittacina* has dark red flowers with golden green edges to the petals and looks much as if it has indeed been gilded. *Alstroemeria* can be difficult to establish, but once settled, will reward with many tiers of blooms in late summer.

Liriope
(lilyturf).
Convallariaceae
(lily-of-the-valley family)

These evergreen grassy plants from China are valuable as ground cover and for their late summer and autumn flower spikes of purple-blue or white flowers. *Liriope muscari* reaches around 30cm (12ft) in height with arching dark green linear leaves produced from a robust branching rhizome. There are a number of named varieties including some variegated forms, and these can be quite effective as a carpet around dark evergreen shrubs. *Liriope spicata* is similar, but smaller. All forms of *Liriope* enjoy semi-shade or even full shade with a moist, humus rich soil. They do better in slightly acid conditions. Propagate from separated portions of rhizome in spring.

Ophiopogon
(snake grass).
Convallariaceae
(lily-of-the-valley family)

Probably the most striking of these plants, closely related to *Liriope*, is *Ophiopogon planiscapus* 'Nigrescens' which is one of those

Ophiopogon planiscapus 'Nigrescens'

plants that always attracts attention. The narrow, grass-like leaves are borne in opposite ranks on branching rhizomes and reach around 10cm (4in) in length. What is significant about the plant, however, is that the leaves are a very dark purple-green and in most conditions appear effectively black. As a result of this, despite its diminutive size, *Ophiopogon* can provide a stark contrast, particularly amongst similarly small, colourful plants such as *Sedum*. *Ophiopogon* occasionally flowers, producing short, loose spikes of pink-purple blooms.

Grow this delightful treasure in a humus rich soil in light shade. It is tolerant of both dry and wet conditions but prefers an acid compost. Proliferation is relatively slow but clumps gradually form. Plants can be propagated by the removal of some of the more distant rhizomes that will usually be found to have rooted independently.

Orchids.
Orchidaceae
(orchid family)

Few flowers are more tropical in appearance than orchids, and it is sad indeed that so few of these exotic plants are suitable for outdoor cultivation in temperate climes. Hardy orchids are in general rather insignificant, although the small flowers have considerable beauty

Cypripedium reginae

when viewed close at hand. They are terrestrial and mostly deciduous. Of the larger-flowered forms, many are rare or protected in their natural environment and are difficult to obtain from reliable horticultural sources. None the less, some forms are available. Some species of the slipper orchids are now available, such as *Cypripedium reginae* from North America. This is a fully hardy plant for sheltered, partly shaded sites in moist acid soil. The leaves are broad and occur in a lax rosette. The solitary or paired flowers are white with a large pink pouch.

Less bright but tall and leafy are species of *Epipactis*. The principal species for gardens is *Epipactis gigantea* (giant helleborine) from North

America. The plants are herbaceous from a creeping rootstock that in late spring sends up stems clothed in linear, slightly undulating strongly-veined leaves. Stems may be up to 1m (3¼ft) in height but are usually much smaller. Relatively large green-purple flowers are borne amongst the upper leaves from early to mid-summer. Although of relatively diminutive stature, the flowers resemble small *Cymbidium* blooms and warrant close inspection. *E. gigantea* is a tolerant orchid and will grow in a variety of positions. It is happiest in a soil rich in leaf mould in semi-shade. Species of *Calanthe* require similar treatment but are not quite so hardy. *Calanthe discolor* is the best species with small flowers from

Epipactis gigantea

pink, white to yellow. Propagate these terrestrial orchids by division of the rhizomes in autumn.

Bletilla striata has *Crocosmia*-like foliage produced from small corms. In a sunny warm situation it produces spikes of a few pink

(sometimes white) typically orchid flowers each about 2cm (¾in) wide. Species of *Pleione* are much sought after and can be expensive to obtain. They are barely hardy but if given protection from excess cold and winter wet, they will produce quite large orchid flowers in pinks, purples and whites (sometimes yellow) before their large pleated leaves. The plants over-winter as conical corm-like pseudobulbs that will gradually colonise a peaty soil lightened with added bark chippings. The most commonly encountered species is *Pleione formosana* but there are numerous variants with flowers in pinks, purples, white and yellow.

Of the tender orchids, forms of *Cymbidium* make good cool-greenhouse plants that may be stood outside in a semi-shaded site in summer. They are easily cultivated in

Sisyrinchium striatum in the rock garden at Kew

a moisture retentive compost of JI2, peat substitute and bark chippings. Divide mature clumps with a sharp knife when potting on in spring.

Sisyrinchium
(blue-eyed grass).
Iridaceae
(Iris family)

One species of these American grassy perennials is of particular use in the exotic garden. *Sisyrinchium striatum* (*Phaiophleps nigricans*) forms clumps of linear pale green leaves around 40cm (16in) tall. These are produced in fans in much the same way as those of *Iris*. In early summer, 60cm (24in) spikes emerge from the larger fans and bear an abundance of small, rather luminous, pale yellow

Bletilla striata

flowers. These last for only a short time but are rapidly replaced by further blooms. There is a variegated form ('Aunt May') that is a rather weak grower. This species, and the smaller *S. californicum* with bright yellow blooms, frequently seed around although they rarely become a problem. They enjoy full sun or partial shade in a moist but well-drained soil. Clumps can be divided in spring. Also with fans of pale green linear leaves are *Aristea ecklonii* and *A. major*, both of which have blue, star-like flowers borne on slightly branched spikes. They are less hardy than *Sisyrinchium*. Similar too is *Belamcanda chinensis* (the blackberry lily) that has orange star-shaped flowers with darker spots followed by clusters of black seed formed in green pods.

Tradescantia
(wandering jew).
Commelinaceae
(Tradescantia family)

 -

The one drawback of these pretty plants is that the flowers tend to open for only a short period during the day and usually only for one day. However there always seems to be a steady supply of them, and certainly enough to keep the plants bright from early to late summer. The flowers have three petals and fluffy stamens and come in a range of colours from dark blue, through to white and pink. *Tradescantia* Andersoniana Group contains most of the garden forms that are hardy and grow well in most soils in a sunny or partly shaded position. The 40–70cm (16–28in) stems are arching and bear clasping bright green (sometimes purplish) linear leaves. The flower clusters are produced between a terminal pair of these leaves. Propagate good forms by dividing clumps in early spring. *Commelina coelestris* is also moderately hardy and is a similar but taller scrambling perennial with very intense small blue flowers borne in lax clusters. It needs a warm sunny or semi-shaded site in a well-drained soil, and appreciates a winter mulch to protect the dormant crowns.

Veratrum
(false hellebore).
Melanthiaceae
(bunchflower family)

These are bold-leaved herbaceous perennials from Asia and North America. They have a rosette of large dark green pleated leaves from which arise branched spikes of pink or white flowers somewhat resembling those of *Rheum*. The largest leaves belong to *Veratrum nigrum*. These are ovate and around 40cm (16in) in length. The flowers are dark red and unpleasantly scented. *V. album* is a little smaller but produces taller spikes of greenish white flowers reaching 2m (6½ft). *V. viride* is similar but enjoys a wetter position. Grow all species in moist fertile soil in partial shade or full sun. Divide these poisonous plants in autumn or spring before growth starts.

Veratrum album

Bromeliads and look-alikes

The South American pineapple family, as one might expect, is largely tropical in its requirements. Some species, however, have become adapted to the colder mountain ranges of South America and are frost- tolerant if kept reasonably dry during winter. Many of these will form imposing clusters of large, spiny evergreen rosettes, in conditions that suit them.

The spines are often very sharp and may be hooked, so they should be avoided if children use the garden. Individual bromeliad rosettes die after flowering but usually produce offsets at the base at this time. The largest genus, *Tillandsia* contains numerous 'air plants' able to survive perched without roots on any available support, taking up moisture from the air or from rain falling on their leaves. These are occasionally sold as house plants and can do well as summer occupants of the exotic garden, strapped to a piece of bark, suspended in semi shade and sprayed regularly. Other houseplant species of bromeliad, including *Aechmea* and *Ananus* (the true pineapple) will enjoy a summer holiday in a semi-shaded spot.

In addition to the genuine bromeliads, I have included here two genera of parsley relatives which, by the convergent processes of evolution acting on plants in similar habitats, have produced a terrestrial bromeliad-like appearance.

Tillandsia plants attached to a hurdle for summer decoration in the South of France

Pineapples in the Princess of Wales House at Kew

Aciphylla
(bayonet plant).
Apiaceae
(parsley family)

These fierce plants are related to *Eryngium* and, like these, seem to have little in common with the humble carrot to which they are related. *Aciphylla scott-thompsonii* (giant spaniard) is the most imposing of the genus, reaching 2.5m (8ft) when in bloom. The leaves form a tight basal clump and are pinnate compound, with each of the linear leaflets extended into a sharp spine. The leaves are an attractive blue-green colour with pale veins and a spiny margin. The small yellowish flowers are produced in a tall spike and are interspersed with horizontal pointed leaf-like spines, the whole very much resembling the flower spike of a species of *Puya*. *A. colensoi* is similarly large but the blue green leaves have dark margins and veins. *A. aurea* is shorter with greyish leaves with a yellow margin and flowers spikes of a pale brown colour. These plants, although hardy, resent winter wetness and should be planted in a well-drained, sunny site where they can be covered with a sheet of plastic to keep the crowns dry. Some species can be divided in spring whilst others are best raised from seed, sown as soon as it is obtained, in pots protected by a cold frame or cold greenhouse. Provide protection from slugs for young plants.

Bilbergia
(queen's tears).
Bromeliaceae
(pineapple family)

This small genus of bromeliads hosts a relatively hardy species and a hybrid that are suitable for the

Bilbergia nutans in a suspended pot, surrounded by *Humulus lupulus* 'Aureus'

exotic garden. *Bilbergia nutans* is almost frost hardy. As a terrestrial bromeliad it is happy in a pot of small size containing a humus-rich compost. A good use of *Bilbergia*, however, is as a summer epiphyte in pots supported on semi-shady walls, tree trunks or other upright structures. Unlike most bromeliads, the plants proliferate quite rapidly, each flowering rosette producing offsets which may themselves flower the following year. *B. nutans* is particularly resilient and will withstand periods of neglect. The leaves are robust and grey-green in colour and will reach 20cm (8in) in length. Flowers, as in most bromeliads are produced on a central spike in late spring. Clusters of flowers are sheathed in pink bracts that are more decorative and longer lasting than the tubular blue-green flowers with

Aciphylla aurea

99

prominent yellow stamens. *B. nutans* and the slightly more tender *B.* x *windii* will thrive in good light, but with shade from strong sunshine. Keep them cool and relatively dry in winter. Feed during the growing season with a liquid fertilizer. *Bilbergia* can be divided a few months after flowering, but should be left pot-bound if possible as this tends to encourage flowering.

Eryngium
(eryngo, caraguata).
Apiaceae
(parsley family)

❄ - 0°C ☀ some ❀

Eryngium is a genus of plants that, although related to carrots, bears little resemblance to these vegetables. *Eryngium* species naturally occur in Europe, Asia and South America. The European species are perhaps most carrot-like in that their leaves are often finely divided into spiny segments, especially on the flower stem when this appears from the basal rosette. In some species (e.g. *Eryngium bourgattii* and *Eryngium alpinum*) the leaves are blue-green with white veins. Flowers in these and the South American species are borne in clusters of teasel-like heads each with a basal ring of spiny bracts. They may be blue, purple or green in colour but it is the bracts that are usually the most showy aspect of the flower head.

It is, however, the evergreen species from South America that qualify the genus as bromeliad-like in that a number of species strongly resemble some of the larger terrestrial pineapples such as *Puya*. *Eryngium agavifolium* forms a rosette of 20cm (8in) long, linear, bright green leaves with sharp teeth along their edges. From the centre of the rosette, a green-brown flower spike around 1m (3¼ft) in height is produced in mid-summer. *E. agavifolium* is a little unusual in that it likes a moist, almost wet soil while its superficially similar relatives (*Eryngium bromeliifolium*, *E. eburneum* and *E. yuccaifolium*) demand better drainage. The most spectacular, but unfortunately the most problematic, of the bromeliad-like eryngiums is *Eryngium pandanifolium* 0°C . Forming a robust clump of thorn-edged, strap-shaped leaves, its flower spike of many small, purple heads will reach 3m (10ft).

Eryngium eburneum

Eryngium pandanifolium

The long leaves alone may arch to 1.5m (5ft), the whole resembling a fierce pampas grass (*Cortaderia*). Unlike the other species of *Eryngium*, *E. pandanifolium* requires some winter protection, particularly from excessive moisture.

The prickly *Eryngium* species (exceptions noted above) require a well-drained compost and benefit from protection from winter wet. If grown in deep pots or tubs, JI3 with extra grit is appropriate. All like plenty of sunshine so an open site is necessary. Fortunately they tolerate wind well. The European species can be propagated by division of clumps and, to some extent, by root cuttings taken in winter. The South American species are best divided in spring as new growth begins.

Fascicularia
(hardy pineapple).
Bromeliaceae
(pineapple family)

Fascicularia bicolour and F. pitcairniifolia are probably the most hardy bromeliads available in Britain. Species of *Puya* and *Abromeitella* are also reasonably hardy but require dry conditions during cold spells. *Fascicularia* is a little more tolerant of winter wet, but will thrive if protection from excess moisture can be provided at this time. *Fascicularia* forms arching rosettes of viciously spiny, dark blue-green leaves from the centre of which a small hemispherical cluster of pale blue flowers is produced. These are of little value in comparison to the bright red of the surrounding leaves at flowering. The individual flowers last for only one day, but the red leaves remain for a number of months. Plants cluster after flowering, or if the main rosette is damaged by frost, and will eventually form substantial clumps up to 1m (3¼ft) in diameter.

As mentioned, *Fascicularia* requires good drainage and responds well if its roots are confined. Cultivation in containers is advised for this reason and to facilitate covering and protection in winter. Grow *Fascicularia* in a mixture of equal parts JI3, peat substitute and grit.

Water them well during summer and stand the container where they receive at most 2 to 3 hours of direct sunshine as they often bloom more readily in partial shade. Propagate these plants by careful division of the clumps in spring.

Ochagavia carnea

Ochagavia
(ochagavia).
Bromeliaceae
(pineapple family)

Ochagavia carnea is superficially similar to *Fascicularia* in producing spiny rosettes of narrow leaves. The central flower cluster is, however, more protruding and the individual flowers are a pink-purple with yellow stamens and are surrounded by a ring of similarly coloured bracts. The plants like abundant sunshine and a well-drained

Fascicularia pitcairniifolia on St Mary's, Isles of Scilly, UK

Puya plants clustered on a rocky outcrop

soil with moderate fertility. They certainly need protection from winter wet and are less hardy than *Fascicularia*. Probably worth a try in a sheltered spot. Propagate by division of clumps in spring.

Puya
(puya).
Bromeliaceae
(pineapple family)

These are very spiny rosette plants from Chile that are remarkably hardy if they can be protected from excessive winter moisture, especially where it is likely to collect in the centre of the rosettes. The toughest is probably *Puya berteroniana*. This produces upright rosettes around 1m (3¼ft) in diameter consisting of numerous spine-edged narrow leaves with white scales on their undersides. Tall, 1m (3¼ft) spikes of dark blue-green flowers are produced on mature plants in early summer. The flowers are interspersed with small spine-edged bracts.

P. chilensis is similar in appearance but is generally larger. The 1.5m (5ft) flower spike bears numerous small branches toward the top giving it a club-like appearance. The individual flowers are yellow green. *Puya coerulea* has whitish leaves and robust spines along the leaf edges. Its flower spike can reach 2m (6½ft) and bears numerous blue-green flowers.

Grow *Puya* plants in JI3 with extra grit in containers (which must be brought under cover in winter) or try them outside in a warm sheltered sunny site where they can be given some winter protection. Individual rosettes usually die after blooming but basal suckers may emerge to continue the clump. Where these are produced, they may be used as cuttings. Otherwise, plants are very easily raised from seed sown in warm conditions in spring.

Puya berteroniana

Grasses

Grasses have undergone a
rediscovery in recent years and
are now established as important
architectural plants. In general they
like open, sunny situations and some
are tolerant of drought. The following
selection of grasses concentrates on
those forms that are large and provide
lush foliage to contribute to a tropical
feel. It includes the bamboos, which
are perhaps more like shrubs than
grasses. Many of these are happy in
semi-shade. Grasses other than
bamboo can easily be raised from
seed, and this can be a way of starting
a collection of more unusual forms.
A mixture of grasses, especially if
interspersed with plants such as
Hemerocallis and *Kniphofia*, can
provide a distinctly exotic vista.
Try using some bananas and *Canna*
as focal points.

Cortaderia beneath an old *Phoenix* palm, Tresco, Isles of Scilly, UK

Arundo
(Spanish cane, giant reed).
Poaceae
(grass family)

  - some

The largest of all the moderately hardy grasses is the giant *Arundo donax* from Asia and the Mediterranean. In a sheltered sunny site the plant is hardy and will send up stems to 5m (16ft). These are clothed with relatively broad, grey-green leaves. Feathery terminal flower spikes are rarely produced in cool climates. *Arundo* is naturally a swamp plant and likes a moist, even wet, soil where the very robust rhizomes can wander to form extensive clumps. In colder sites, *Arundo* will usually be cut to the ground by frost but will recover with new, vigorous shoots in spring. There are a number of variegated forms of *Arundo*, all of which are less

Arundo donax

hardy than the green form. They can be accommodated in large tubs of JI3 kept moist and over-wintered under cover, but be aware that plants grown like this never reach the large proportions of unrestricted specimens. Propagation is achieved by division of the rhizomes in spring.

Bamboo.
Poaceae
(grass family)

Bamboos are generally robust grasses of variable stature and invasiveness. Care should be taken in the choice of bamboo for any particular site, especially in view of their relatively high cost. Some forms of bamboo can become extremely large in time and are only suitable for large gardens. It is true, however, that a large specimen bamboo in a small garden provides a very dramatic feature of great architectural merit.

In general, tall-growing bamboos form dense clumps and spread out from this clump only slowly while the smaller-growing forms often spread rapidly by extremely robust runners that can be very difficult to eradicate. Most bamboos have insignificant flowers and some forms may die after blooming.

One of the largest hardy bamboos is *Chusquea culeou* from Chile. This can form a 6m (20ft) tall arching clump in time, consisting of numerous canes all clothed in shorted stems

Chusquea culeou

with abundant foliage – resulting in a very leafy bamboo. The silvery leaf sheaths are persistent for the first year. Also large are species and forms of the Chinese *Phyllostachys* that again are dense clump-formers but without an invasive habit. *Phyllostachys nigra* is commonly available and forms tall (3m; 10ft) canes that turn black with age, forming a spectacular contrast to the dark green leaves. *P. aurea* and *P. aureosulcata* are similar but in these species the canes turn yellow with age. The leaves of these two are lighter, almost yellow-green. Most *Phyllostachys* are slow to establish and take time to form tall canes and a large clump. They are, however, some of the most graceful of bamboos. *Fargesia murieliae* and *F. nitida* from China are smaller clump formers that ultimately reach around 3m (10ft) in height. They have slender canes which branch above and bear narrow leaves of a bright green colour. The canes can with age become yellow or purple-black. These are excellent, well-behaved bamboos with a decorative arching habit and are suitable for most gardens.

Sasa and *Pseudosasa* are Japanese genera with a more aggressive habit. They will form spreading thickets of sparsely branched canes with relatively few, but large, leaves. *Sasa palmata* is probably the most vigorous, forming extremely tough long underground runners by which it rapidly spreads. It is superb in a semi-wild area in partial shade where it will form open clumps of stems to 2.5m (8ft) terminating in broad leaves up to 35cm (14in) in length. *Sasa veitchii* is a smaller version to only 1.2m (4ft). It has dark green leaves borne in

Sasa veitchii

clusters. These gradually turn papery from the edges, giving the leaves the appearance of a silver margin. *Sasa ramosa* is similar but has a yellowish mid vein. It is dangerously vigorous.

Pseudosasa japonica has narrow leaves with a yellowish mid vein and a silvery underside. It can reach 5m (16ft) in height and also spreads rapidly.

Japanese species and forms of *Pleioblastus* are some of the best dwarf bamboos. *P. pygmaeus* var. *distichus* forms rounded spreading clumps only 40cm (16in) in height. The leaves are borne sparsely up the stems in two ranks. They form attractive bright green fans at the top of each cane. *P. variegatus* is taller (to 1.2m; 4ft) and has striped leaves in dark green and cream. *P. auricomus* is similar but the leaves have abundant bright yellow variegation.

All of the above bamboos are relatively hardy and are easy to grow

in a moist (but not wet) humus-rich soil in full sun or part shade. Bamboos dislike a windy site where the leaves tend to become dry and papery. They should be placed in a sheltered position amongst evergreen shrubs such as *Aucuba* with which they form

Fargesia nitida

Pleioblastus variegatus

an interesting contrast. The invasive forms of bamboo can be constrained to some extent by surrounding them with paving stones buried on edge or with a metal lawn edging. Avoid planting bamboos next to artificial pools or ponds as the rhizomes will easily puncture plastic liners and may even damage a concrete structure.

Most forms of bamboo can be propagated by separation of the outer shoots from the main clump in spring. Ensure that separated canes have a good root system but, even with this, such divisions are often slow to establish.

Briza
(quaking grass).
Poaceae
(grass family)

Three species of this grass are commonly available of which the best is *Briza maxima*, an annual from the Mediterranean. Sown in early spring in a sunny site where it is to

Briza maxima

flower, this grass will form dense patches of bright green leaves from which arise in mid-summer, clusters of pendulous spikelets which are scale-like and around 1cm (⅜in) in length. These are pale green but can turn purple in full sun. Although an excellent and pretty plant, it can self-seed prolifically and may become a nuisance.

Carex
(sedge).
Cyperaceae
(sedge family)

 - mostly

This large genus contains numerous small sedges as well as some larger, more robust plants. The largest and coarsest of the sedges is probably the European *Carex pendula*. It is a very tough plant with green, channelled leaves that are slightly

Carex 'Evergold'

paler beneath. The leaves are produced in tight rosettes that gradually cluster to form a dense hummock to around 70cm (2¼ft) in height. From this in spring arise numerous 1.5m (5ft) fishing rod-like flower spikes, each bearing a number of green catkin flower clusters at the tips. *Carex pendula* likes wet conditions and will grow happily as a pond marginal. It has a habit of seeding around and can become a problem in clay soils. *Carex elata* 'Aurea' is also a lover of wet ground. It is more delicate in appearance than *C. pendula* and its golden variegation makes an excellent contrast with dark-leaved plants such as *Ligularia*. The flower spikes reach around 80cm (more than 30in). *Carex* 'Evergold' is a smaller tufted plant to 20cm (8in) with yellow/white-edged leaves which have a dark green central stripe. It is happy in most situations provided that it is neither too wet nor too dry.

The flowers are brownish and usually hidden by the leaves.

Somewhat less hardy than the above are the *Carex* species with narrow brownish red leaves. These include *C. buchananii* (to 75cm; 30in) and *C. comans* (35cm; 14in). The wiry leaves of these species are particularly architectural and blend well with succulents and other grassy plants. They prefer a little shade and protection from the coldest weather. They gradually form clumps that may be lifted and divided to form additional plants. Some sedges, such as the pretty *C. siderosticha* 'Variegata' with green and white striped leaves are fully hardy and deciduous. These plants can spread rapidly by underground stems when growing in moist, fertile soils.

Cortaderia
(pampas grass).
Poaceae
(grass family)

These robust grasses are notorious for their difficult-to-eradicate habit. Pampas grasses can be coarse and somewhat less than interesting, especially if planted as lawn specimen plants. However, as part of the tropical scene they combine well with other grassy plants such as bamboos, palms and *Fatsia*. *Cortaderia selloana* is the principal species, of which *C. selloana* 'Pumila' and 'Sunningdale Silver' are the best forms. They

Cortaderia selloana two weeks after burning

produce dense creamy-white feathery plumes in autumn on culms 1.5m (5ft) and 2.5m (8ft) respectively. The leaves of both of these are a grey-green but those of *C. selloana* 'Aureolineata' ('Gold Band') are edged in yellow.

C. selloana 'Rendatleri' is a giant, up to 3m (10ft), with broader leaves. The flowers can be a delicate pink but are more often a rather soggy grey. Much better is *C. richardii* from New Zealand. This is a smaller plant (to about 2m; 6½ft) with feathery white flowers in summer. The leaves are an olive green and may turn golden in

cold winter weather. All pampas grasses are hungry subjects and require a rich compost and subsequent feeding to keep them flowering well. Setting fire to established clumps is an excellent method of rejuvenation, but warn your neighbours first. Propagate these grasses from divisions from the parent clump. They can be raised from seed, but the plants may be poor in relation to the named forms. Beware of 'paper cuts' from the sharp leaf edges.

Cyperus
(umbrella grass).
Cyperaceae
(sedge family)

This genus contains the papyrus reed of the Nile but sadly *Cyperus papyrus* is tender. *Cyperus longus* from Europe and Asia is a

Cortaderia selloana

Cyperus alternifolius

smaller version that is fully hardy. It is a tufted plant with glossy grassy leaves produced in markedly three-angled rosettes. In late summer these produce tall clusters of tiny flowers reaching 1.2m (4ft). The terminal flower clusters are surrounded by a ring of leaf-like bracts. *C. eragrostis* from North America is similar but a little less hardy. *Cyperus alternifolius* is commonly grown as a house plant. Like most other species of *Cyperus*, it enjoys wet growing conditions and should therefore be grown in a pot which stands in a tray of water. This species will enjoy a 'summer holiday' in the garden in a semi-shaded humid position. Most species of *Cyperus* can be divided in spring while the hardy species can be raised from seed.

Glyceria
(manna grass).
Poaceae
(grass family)

 -    partly

Glyceria maxima 'Variegata' is a vigorous spreading upright deciduous grass that, when suited, can reach 1.2m (4ft). The leaves are long and strap like, around 1cm (⅜in) in width, and in this form are prettily striped with cream and green. Young leaves, and often mature leaves in full sun, are marked with pink and purple. Flower spikes of numerous small spikelets are produced in late summer. The plant enjoys sunshine and is very happy in sticky clay or in 10cm (4in) of water at the edge of a pond. It spreads by underground rhizomes that can travel a considerable distance before surfacing. They can be troublesome but certainly provide an effective means of propagation.

Hakonechloa
(Japanese mountain grass).
Poaceae
(grass family)

Hakonechloa macra 'Aureola' is a splendid small clump-forming grass which looks at its best amongst large-leaved perennials such as *Hosta*. This is a deciduous grass that produces slowly spreading tufts of arching (25cm; 10in long) leaves with a bright green and yellow striped variegation. They are produced quite late in spring and are followed by tiny lax clusters of insignificant flowers which emerge in late summer.

This grass can also be grown in pots of JI2 with extra humus in semi-shade where the arching leaves can be seen at their best. Propagate by removing rooted sections of mature clumps in early spring.

Hakonecholoa macra 'Aureola' (left) with *Athryrium nipponicum* 'Pictum' and *Uncinia rubra*

Juncus
(rush).
Juncaceae
(rush family)

The two forms of spiralled rush are interesting curiosities for the wet ground at the edge of a pond or grown at the edge of a damp border. *Juncus effusus* 'Spiralis' and *J. inflexus* 'Afro' are similar producing evergreen corkscrew twisted wiry leaves in untidy clumps. More imposing by far is *Juncus pallidus* from New Zealand which produces dense clumps of sharply-pointed arching blue-green leaves that can reach 1.4m (4½ft) or more in length and up to 5cm (3in) in diameter at the base. Small flower clusters are produced in summer toward the end of some of the arching leaves.

This plant will also thrive in moist or wet ground in full sun where it can become a giant (but very architectural). Propagate rushes by dividing the clumps in spring.

Luzula
(woodrush).
Juncaceae
(rush family)

One form of woodrush that is well worth including in the tropical-style garden is *Luzula sylvatica*. It is a pretty, clump-forming plant that makes robust spreading clumps of soft

Luzula sylvatica 'Aurea'

green leaves. In late spring it produces 60–80cm (24–30in) clusters of brownish flowers. Prettier still is the golden-leaved form *L. sylvatica* 'Aurea' which in summer is a bright apple green but through the autumn and winter attains glowing yellow hues. I have clusters of this delight beneath *Acacia dealbata*, where its bright yellow spring flowers blend well with the golden leafy carpet. There are also some variegated forms of *Luzula* which are well worth acquiring. Grow all *Luzula* forms in humus-rich soil with ample moisture in semi-shade where the leaves will not scorch. Propagate by division of the clumps in late spring.

Miscanthus
(eulalia, feather grass).
Poaceae
(grass family)

There are now many forms and varieties of these popular grasses. All are excellent tropical-style plants forming dense clumps. *Miscanthus floridulus* is the largest with tall stems

up to 2.5m (8ft) in a sheltered site. The leaves are quite broad and are borne at intervals up the bamboo-like stems. Each leaf has a lighter, silvery mid vein. This and the similar but smaller *M. sacchariflorus* resemble sugar cane in their overall structure and must be some of the most imposing hardy grasses available. These species rarely flower in cooler climates. *Miscanthus sinensis* is a smaller grass usually reaching around 1.2m (4ft) when in bloom. All forms have lovely feathery plumes that vary from silvery white to almost purple. 'Silberfeder' is an excellent form. Stems bear linear leaves at intervals and terminate in fluffy plumes that last well into the winter as decorative features in their own right. They may be cut and dried for indoor use. *M. sinensis* var. *purpurescens* is a good

Miscanthus floridulus at How Caple Manor, Herefordshire, UK

Miscanthus sinensis 'Variegatus'

dark-leaved form with pinkish midribs, while 'Zebrinus' has leaves which are interrupted at intervals by cream horizontal markings. M. *sinensis* 'Variegatus' has white stripes running the length of the leaf.

Grow the various forms of *Miscanthus* in a sunny site in moist, but well-drained, fertile soil. They dislike excessive winter wet and may need some protection in very cold areas. Divide clumps as the new growth begins to emerge in spring.

Some forms are rather slow to establish in a new site but they will eventually settle down. M. *floridulus* has particularly robust rhizomes which can spread quite quickly, so do not plant this monster where it can overwhelm more delicate companions.

Pennisetum
(squirrel tail grass).
Poaceae
(grass family)

These are wonderful tropical grasses that are consequently slightly tender. They form dense clumps of narrow foliage from which arise in summer dense elongated heads of bristly flowers rather like the tail of a squirrel. Although those described here are perennial, they all tend to be short-lived. *Pennisetum setaceum* is probably the hardiest. The form 'Purpureum' has purple leaves and flowers and is a spectacular sight. It is probably worth growing in a container where it can be brought

Phalaris arundinacea var. *picta*

under cover and given winter protection from excess wetness. *P. alopecuroides* is similar but has shorter flower heads. These are purplish and borne above dark green foliage. These grasses need a well-drained soil in full sun to thrive and, if outside, will require a protective winter mulch. Propagate from seed sown in early spring or divide established clumps at the same time.

Phalaris
(canary grass).
Poaceae
(grass family)

Phalaris arundinacea var. *picta* has a long history as a garden plant. This pretty variegated grass can be invasive, so needs to be planted where it can spread without harm. The variegation is variable but usually consists of white and dark green stripes running the length of the leaf. Some forms have a pinkish tint to the stems and young leaves. When in flower this grass can reach 1m (3¼ft) or more in height with leaves borne up much of the stem. The relatively small flower clusters are silvery or pinkish and are borne in mid-summer.

Phalaris likes a moist soil with full sun or part shade. Old clumps can become thin in the centre. Dig them up and replace only with actively growing portions in spring as the new shoots emerge. Discard parts that have lost their variegation.

Uncinia
(hook sedge).
Cyperaceae
(sedge family)

Uncinia rubra is a small tufted sedge from New Zealand that thrives in a moist but well-drained soil in sun or semi-shade. It is valuable for the edge of the border or planted in drifts where its red, brown and steely blue leaves are a useful contrast to other small grassy plants such as *Carex* or *Ophiopogon*. Tufts reach around 20cm (8in) in height and gradually increase in diameter. The leaves are narrow and channelled. Flower spikes are dark brown and relatively insignificant. Propagate by division in late spring.

Zea
(corn).
Poaceae
(grass family)

This annual grass is well known as the vegetable 'corn on the cob' and is worth growing for its bold structure and architectural appearance, but there are a number of varieties that are grown specifically for their interesting foliage or fruits. Look out for seed of forms such as *Zea mays* 'Harlequin' with red, cream and green leaf variegation and small orange red cobs. 'Variegata' has leaves marked with cream. 'Amero' has cobs

Uncinia rubra

with yellow, orange, white, black and blue seeds which can be cut and dried for winter decoration. These decorative forms of corn are often smaller in stature than those grown for their fruits (usually around 1.2m; 4ft) but retain the bold structure. Sow all forms in late spring individually in small pots, and plant out when all danger of frost has passed. They like a warm, sheltered site with plenty of sun and moisture and a fertile, well-drained soil. Remember to plant them in a close group if you want cobs, because isolated plants can escape pollination.

There are some other annual grasses that require similar cultivation. Try species of *Sorgum* or perhaps even sow some of your budgie millet.

Zea mays form

Slightly tender trees and shrubs

Although there is a wide range of fully hardy, tropical-looking plants available to the gardener, there is little doubt that the introduction of a few genuine exotics to the summer garden scene can contribute much to an overall tropical appearance. For this reason I include below some commonly available tender plants which can be cultivated in large pots or tubs and so can be moved to a protected site or under glass for the winter months.

Amongst these plants there are inevitably some forms that are hardier than others, and these I have given a little more coverage as they may be risked outside in mild localities. Should you not wish to be adventurous with your valued plants, these forms, being hardier, will at least be a little easier (and cheaper) to care for in winter. Most of them are quite vigorous and will require a rich compost. A combination of two parts JI3 and one part peat substitute is generally appropriate, and the addition of some slow release fertilizer such as bone meal can be useful for particularly rapid growers.

Senna in southern Portugal

A shrubby species of *Echium* growing wild in Tenerife

Abutilon
(Indian mallow).
Malvaceae
(hollyhock family)

Abutilon forms a large group of rather coarse lax shrubby plants with maple-like bristly leaves and cup-shaped hibiscus-like flowers. *Abutilon vitifolium* from Chile and its various hybrids (*A.* x *suntense*) are relatively hardy and will survive winters outside in mild areas especially with some protection although it may lose many leaves. The flowers are quite large and resemble those of the common tree mallow (*Lavatera*). They appear in shades of pink, lavender and blue, often with darker veining. These plants are generally short-lived, but can reach some size (3m; 10ft) particularly when grown against a south- or west-facing wall.

Abutilon vitifolium

Abutilon megapotamicum is a small, very lax shrub from Brazil. Its habit makes it amenable to training on supports and wires. I have seen it as a splendid mixed low hedge with *Solanum jasminoides* 'Album' along the side of a greenhouse where there was sufficient winter warmth to keep them happy. The leaves of *A. megapotamicum* are small (3–4cm; 1–1⅝in) and arrow-shaped. A. 'Kentish Belle' is similar but larger. The flowers of both are relatively small and a peach-yellow colour offset by the striking red calyx and dark staminal mass. There is a form with mottled leaves that, to me, always looks rather diseased. This is perhaps not surprising since the mottling is the result of a virus. *Abutilon pictum* (*A. striatum*) 'Thompsonii', a maple-leaved form, also has this virus and is similarly mottled. *Abutilon pictum* is a parent of many of the named forms of *Abutilon* commonly available. These are all shrubby plants that grow quickly and produce an abundance of cup-shaped mallow flowers in a wide range of colours, mainly reds, pinks and yellows. They all have bristly, maple-like leaves in mid to dark green.

A. *pictum* 'Souvenir de Bonn' has a white variegation to the leaf edges but tends to revert to green. It has rather alarming flowers of a dull orange with red veining, leading to my calling it the 'blood-shot eyeball bush'.

All Indian mallows are vigorously growing plants that like a rich compost and abundant water when in growth. Small plants can be grown in pots of JI2 with a little addition of peat substitute while large plants will be in tubs of JI3. All will stand quite severe pruning if they begin to get out of hand. Propagation is by cuttings of semi-soft growth in summer although some varieties are now available from seed. If sown early, plants will flower in their first year.

Acacia
(wattle).
Fabaceae
(pea family)

 -

This is a large genus of African and Australasian shrubs and trees, most of which are tender. There are, however, a few species that are worth trying in a sheltered site

Acacia pravissima

outside. Toughest is probably *Acacia dealbata* - that ultimately forms a small tree of 6m (20ft) height or more. The leaves and young stems are grey-green. The evergreen leaves are fern-like consisting of numerous tiny leaflets. Clusters of small fluffy ball flowers are borne in early spring. They are bright yellow and have a honey scent. Similar, but with smaller leaves, is A. *baileyana* of which the form 'Purpurea' is probably the best. This has blue-green ferny leaves that, as they emerge on the young shoots, are a wonderful grey purple colour. The contrast of the fluffy yellow-ball flowers in late winter and early spring with the foliage is particularly effective. The relatively hardy *Acacia pravissima* - has pendent branches that bear small triangular 'leaves' (actually expanded petioles known as phyllodes) of grey-green or dark green colour. The clusters of yellow flowers are scented. Dangerous, but especially exotic, are the very thorny African species such as *Acacia karroo* . These have long thorns borne at the base of each leaf. Many Acacia species are naturally short-lived and most resent pruning being reluctant to break from old wood. If you want to experiment with some of the more exotic *Acacia* species try raising them from seed. It is quite easy to germinate and provides the best method of propagation. *Acacia* species usually dislike lime in the soil, so use an ericaceous compost as a mix with some neutral, fertile loam-based compost. They all adore sunshine and will not flower without properly sun-ripened shoots.

Brachychiton
(bottle tree).
Sterculeaceae
(bottle tree family)

Brachychiton acerifolium is an excellent evergreen or semi-evergreen tree for container cultivation, with wonderful glossy leaves that are rather like those of a maple but with the points rounded off. They are leathery and bright green. Although ultimately reaching a great size, this Australian plant seems reasonably happy as a 'bonsai' specimen and although you might be very lucky to get any of the red flowers, the foliage is worth the effort. Plants naturally form a rather stout trunk for their height and look well proportioned as container specimen.

Grow them in JI2 or 3 with extra grit to help with drainage. *Brachychiton* likes plenty of sunshine and water in the summer, but will enjoy a drier winter spell when some, occasionally all, of its leaves will fall. Probably best grown from seed sown in a little warmth in spring.

Brugmansia
(angel's trumpet).
Solanaceae
(tomato family)

These poisonous plants from South America are now commonly available in a variety of flower colour, from white to yellow and pink. They are very striking bushes with large ovate, softly hairy leaves borne on persistently green stems. Like tomatoes, to which they are related, these plants enjoy a humus-rich, fertile compost and abundant moisture when in growth. To ensure

Brugmanisa arborea in southern Portugal

Brugmansia aurea

that they remain in a fertile soil they should be fed frequently with a liquid plant food through the summer months. Young plants will require protection from slugs, but once tall enough they usually fend for themselves. They are not quite hardy, and require protection from frosts.

The common white angel's trumpet is *Brugmansia arborea*. This bears 20–30cm (8–12in) long, hanging, trumpet-like, strongly scented blooms that extend from green sheaths at intervals through the summer. *B. aurea* is similar but a pale buttery yellow. It, too, has a pleasant scent most noticeable in the afternoon and at night. Very exotic but a little more tender is *B. sanguinea*, which has smaller flowers but of red and yellow – contrasting well with the green flower sheaths. Grow all *Brugmansia* species and hybrids in JI3 and ensure good

drainage with extra grit at the base of the pot. They like full sun or a little shade.

Bring under cover and decrease watering in winter, when they may shed quite a lot of leaves: clear these away to avoid mildew. Cuttings of most forms can be rooted with bottom heat in summer.

Caesalpinia
(Paradise Flower).
Fabaceae
(Pea family)

There are two commonly encountered species of shrubby South American *Caesalpinia* of which *C. gilliesii* is probably the hardier. Both really require protection from frost in order to survive winters and bloom. *Caesalpinia gilliesii* has ferny

foliage consisting of numerous small leaflets. On mature plants conical clusters of yellow flowers with long red stamens are produced in summer. *C. pulcherrima* is a more robust shrub with larger, bright green leaflets. The flowers are produced in loose clusters and are bright orange-red or occasionally yellow. Grow these very decorative shrubs in JI3 with a little extra sharp sand. They enjoy abundant sunshine and will flower only if they get this. They can be pruned if necessary, but they may be reluctant to break from old wood. Although it is possible to take cuttings in late spring, seed sown at the same time is easy to germinate and young plants grow rapidly.

Similar in requirements are the various species of *Cassia* and *Senna*

Caesalpinia gilliesii

115

Callistemon pallidus

clusters, the principal part of which are the numerous long coloured stamens, in many cases red in colour. The hardiest are generally those species and forms with narrow, lance-shaped leaves borne close to the stems. Unfortunately these are also commonly those with pale green-yellow flowers such as *Callistemon pityoides*, *C. pinifolius* and *C. pallidus* . The red-flowered species and hybrids are more tender, but some, such as *Callistemon linearis* and *C. viminalis*, will survive light frosts and even the broader-leaved *C. citrinus* 'Splendens' will survive short periods of frost. The leaves of all bottlebrushes appear tough and leathery and one would presume from

this that they are somewhat drought-tolerant. In fact these plants can dry out quite easily and a moderate water supply, even in winter, is essential for their well-being. Most forms of *Callistemon* have an open lax habit and they can become quite untidy. To compound the problem, they often resent pruning and can be reluctant to break from even the previous year's wood. For this reason, grow *Callistemon* in a bright sunny position to encourage compact growth. They should be grown in a neutral to acid soil outside or in containers of JI3 mixed with ericaceous peat substitute compost in proportions of around 2-to-1. Cuttings can be rooted in summer with a little bottom heat.

that are now commonly available. These have an abundance of yellow or pink flowers with relatively prominent stamens and pinnate leaves with rounded leaflets.

Callistemon
(bottlebrush).
Myrtaceae
(myrtle family)

 -

These are tough shrubs from Australia, most of which will require some winter protection. A few, however, are hardy enough to risk outside in mild areas. They are renowned for their bright flower

Callistemon citrinus

Iochroma cyanea

Cestrum
(bastard jasmine).
Solanaceae
(tomato family)

These are surprisingly resilient moderately tender arching shrubs from South America. Although the tubular flowers are usually colourful and attractive, the foliage commonly has a rather less than pleasant odour. None the less, these make good container plants and one species, *Cestrum parqui* is moderately hardy as is C. *fasciculatum* 'Newellii' and both will survive outside in mild localities but the late summer flowers in yellow or red are not as spectacular as those of the more tender forms. C. *roseum* with pinkish flowers is also said to be quite hardy. The leaves of most species are rounded and bright to dark green in colour. Those of C. *parqui* are more linear. Flowers are usually around 2.5cm (10in) in length and may be constricted or flared at the ends. *Cestrum aurantiacum* has orange flowers in spring and summer while C. *elegans* is red. Most *Cestrum* species will reach around 2m (6½ft) in height if unpruned, but they can be kept shorter by cutting out old stems to the base in spring. They will then send out vigorous new shoots that in most cases will bloom that year. Similar in appearance to *Cestrum* are species of *Iochroma*. I. *cyanea* has very dark, almost blue-black tubular flowers which are particularly unusual and contrast well with the grey-green slightly downy leaves. The flowers are most often produced in summer. Grow *Cestrum* and *Iochroma* in JI2 or 3 in a sunny position. C. *parqui* is happy in a well-drained, fertile soil in sun or part shade. Propagate from seed or from softwood cuttings taken in summer. I have seen *Cestrum* infested with mealy bug, so beware.

Chorisia
(yachan).
Bombacaceae
(baobab family)

This is an interesting small tree that responds to container cultivation in much the same way as *Brachychiton* and requires similar treatment. The leaves of *Chorisia speciosa* are compound palmate with around 7 leaflets. The leaves are shed at the onset of the dry season that comfortably corresponds with winter, but they may be lost at other times if the plant becomes very dry. Container-grown specimens rarely

Chorisia speciosa

produce the large pink, red or yellow flowers and subsequent kapok-like fruits. However they do rapidly develop the considerably swollen trunk, covered in thorns that increase a little in size each year. Older plants in containers will reach a certain height before branching to produce a small crown. Growth then slows considerably, such that plants can be maintained from year to year with little more than a good feed of liquid fertilizer. New plants are easily raised from seed sown in warmth in spring.

Citrus
(citrus, lemon, orange).
Rutaceae
(Citrus family)

Probably some of the most widely grown containerized shrubs, the Chinese *Citrus* fruits are both decorative and productive if given adequate care. All require the same treatment, this being abundant sunshine and moisture in summer and a cooler 4°C, drier period in winter during which they will rest. In general they should have an acid soil. Most will thrive in JI2 or 3 mixed 2-to-1 with ericaceous peat substitute. Toughest is 'Meyer's lemon' (*Citrus limon* 'Meyer'), which may survive short periods of frost 0°C and can be grown against a warm wall in very sheltered sites. Most forms of *Citrus* have ovate, glossy, bright to dark green leaves that are borne on

strangely broad petioles. Many forms have robust spines among the foliage. The flowers are mostly white and are usually strongly scented. Fertilised flowers will give rise to the familiar fruits but the ripening process can take up to a year, which unfortunately means that you'll have to wait a while to eat them.

Lemons (*Citrus limon*), oranges (*Citrus aurantium*, *Citrus reticulata* and *C. sinensis*) are the most commonly available forms, but there are many other varieties and hybrids available from specialists. They are all tolerant of pruning at virtually any time and can be propagated from cuttings of softwood in summer (although all but *C. aurantium* are normally grafted onto a rootstock which is more tolerant of cold and wet soil). Seed

germinates readily at high temperatures, but will not necessarily give rise to plants similar to the parent. It is also a rather slow process to produce a fruiting bush from seed.

Other *Citrus*-like plants that respond to similar cultivation are the kumquat (*Fortunella japonica*), which bears small orange-like fruits, and the hybrid between this and *Citrus*, the calamondin orange (x *Citrofortunella microcarpa*, sometimes listed as *Citrus mitis*) with small round fruits. These and other *Citrus* can suffer from a variety of pests, including mealy bug and scale insect. These are often first noticed as a result of their sticky secretions that can harbour black moulds. Red spider can also be a problem on plants that are mostly grown in the greenhouse.

Citrus aurantium

Echium candicans

Echium
(bugloss).
Boraginaceae
(borage family)

This genus of annuals, biennials and shrubby plants is wide ranging in origin but those of interest to the exotic gardener are from the Canary Isles and Madeira. *Echium candicans* is typical of the shrubby forms, with lance-shaped bristly leaves of a grey-green colour clothing branching stems white woolly stems. Spikes of small densely-packed white, blue or purple flowers are born terminally on these branches in early summer. Of the biennials, *Echium pininana* is the largest. This forms a large rosette of tongue-shaped bristly leaves up to 25cm (10in) in length. The rosette gradually forms a dark bristly stem and in its second or third year rapidly elongates into a flower spike that can reach around 3m (10ft) or more in height and that produces thousands of small grey-blue flowers over a long summer period. This species is almost hardy and will survive outside in mild sites. When suited, it will self-seed enthusiastically.

All *Echium* species enjoy a sunny situation in a well-drained, fertile soil. In containers, grow them in JI2 with extra grit. Seed is the best means of propagation for the biennial species as well as the shrubby forms, although the latter can also be increased from semi-ripe cuttings taken in summer.

Erythrina
(Christ's thorn, coral tree).
Fabaceae
(pea family)

There are a number of species of *Erythrina,* most of which are shrubs or trees. *Erythrina crista-galli* from South America and *E. herbacea* from North America are more often seen as woody herbaceous perennials and because of this habit, they are moderately hardy especially if they are protected from excessive wet in winter. These plants can also be grown in containers and given winter protection in which case *E. crista-galli* will become more shrubby. Species of *Erythrina* have compound leaves with usually three slightly glossy ovate leaflets, sometimes with spines at the base. The vibrant bright red flowers are produced in spikes, are typically pea-like and about 5cm (2in) in length. The blooms open in late summer. Grow these plants in a fertile soil in a sunny position. In containers, use JI3. Water the plants well when in growth in summer and feed frequently. In winter, keep the plants just moist. These species are easy to propagate from seed sown in spring in a little warmth.

Erythrina crista-galli

Fuchsia
(fuchsia).
Onagraceae
(evening primrose family)

 - some

There are probably thousands of varieties of these popular shrubs almost all of which are graceful and colourful. The familiar *Fuchsia* is a tender shrub, but there are now many forms available that are quite hardy. While the toughest of these will survive frosts to form quite large shrubs, others that are less resilient will be cut to the ground in winter but will sprout again from just below soil level in late spring. As these forms are relatively fast growing they can still form small shrubs again in a single season. The hardiest *Fuchsia* is probably *F. magellanica* (*F.* 'Riccartonii') which commonly forms a large shrub. The flowers are red (flared outer petals) and purple (tubular inner petals) but rather narrow in structure. This form has given rise to other moderately hardy hybrids such as 'Tom Thumb' and 'Genii' (that has golden foliage), both of which are quite tough and have slightly more robust flowers, although of similar flower colour. There are many other varieties of the so-called 'hardy fuchsias', some now with more interesting flower colours. When purchasing *Fuchsia* plants check with the grower about the hardiness of your choices if you intend to try them outside where they will require fertile soil and a sunny or semi-shaded position. *Fuchsia* plants

Grevillea rosmarinifolia

make excellent container specimens or partners for other tender shrubs, perennials and bulbs. They should be planted in JI3 with a little extra peat substitute to lighten the compost. In summer water freely, but in winter allow the compost to become almost dry, at which time the plants will lose most or all of their leaves. *Fuchsia* plants over-wintered in this manner can be pruned more or less as desired once watering and growth resumes in spring. Propagation is by cuttings of softwood taken in spring or summer.

Grevillea
(grevillea).
Proteaceae
(Protea family)

This is a variable genus that contains trees and shrubs from Australia. The lax shrubs have numerous needle-like leaves giving them some resemblance to dwarf pine trees. However, the flowers instantly mark them out as very different. Most

Grevillea juniperina 'Sulphurea'

Leonotis leonurus

species and forms of *Grevillea* are tender but make excellent container specimens. Two that are of interest in being somewhat hardier are *Grevillea juniperina* and *G. rosmarinifolia*. The leaves of these species are grey-green, and when young the growth is relatively soft. With age the leaves become more rigid and spiky. The flowers of these plants are borne in small clusters. Individual flowers are quite small, but the long, colourful stamens are prominent. In *G. rosmarinifolia* the flowers and stamens are red, while those of *G. juniperina* tend toward yellow and are particularly bright in the form 'Sulphurea'. Grow *Grevillea* in a sunny position in a rich acid soil. In

containers use an ericaceous compost mix and feed frequently with a liquid fertilizer suitable for acid-loving plants. Propagation is not easy but is best by cuttings taken in summer and given some bottom heat.

Leonotis
(lion's ears).
Lamiaceae
(mint family)

Leonotis leonurus is a small shrubby plant from South Africa. It has the typical features of the mint family with lance-shaped aromatic leaves and four-angled stems. Grown in JI2 in full sun, and given plenty of water when in growth it will reach around

Melianthus major

1.5m (5ft) in height. The orange-red tubular flowers are produced in encircling clusters at intervals on the upper parts of stems in late summer and autumn. It is moderately fast growing but can be short-lived. Propagation is simple from seed sown in spring. A similar but larger plant (to 2m; 6½ft) is *Colquhounia coccinea* from China. This has broader furry leaves and terminal clusters of tubular red-orange flowers. It is rather hardier than *Leonotis* but not as pretty.

Melianthus
(honey flower).
Melianthaceae
(honey flower family)

  some

This architectural shrubby plant from South Africa has large (40cm; 16in) pinnate leaves composed of slightly folded leaflets with a serrated edge. The leaves are rather waxy and are an elegant grey-green in colour. Large stipules occur at the junction of leaf and stem. Plants can reach around 2m (6½ft) in height. In late summer, 50cm (20in) spikes of red-brown flowers are produced. Grow *Melianthus major* in JI2 in a sunny position.

If frosted, the plant will usually produce new shoots from the base and these, if they already possess roots, are the easiest means of propagation. Otherwise, take softwood cuttings in early summer.

Nerium oleander

Metrosideros
(rata).
Myrtaceae
(myrtle family)

These small trees and shrubs from New Zealand have dark grey-green felted ovate leaves around 5cm (2in) long. Those commonly grown have white fur beneath and also coating the young stems. *Meterosideros excelsus* produces almost bottlebrush-like clusters of flowers consisting mostly of long red stamens borne in late spring and summer. These, to my mind, make better container plants than the true bottlebrushes (*Callistemon*), as they tend to remain more compact and respond to pruning in a better manner. Grow them in JI2 with a little ericaceous humus-rich compost added. Take cuttings of soft wood in summer. Provide some bottom heat to aid rooting.

Nerium
(oleander).
Apocynaceae
(oleander family)

Oleanders are willowy shrubs (to 4m; 13ft in height) which when not in bloom can appear rather coarse. Flowers are, however, produced over quite a long period on happy plants, and these are ample compensation for the greyish-green narrow foliage. Flowers are produced in reddish, branched clusters, each bud opening into a propeller-like five-petal bloom. These come in a range of colours from white, pink, apricot and pale yellow. 'Variegatum' has creamy yellow margins to the leaves. The variety 'Little Red' is said to be hardy . Grow *Nerium oleander* in JI3 with a little sharp sand to assist the drainage, and provide plenty of sunshine. The plants resent excessively dry conditions, so keep them well watered in summer. Mealy bugs and scale insects can be a problem, which is surprising considering the extreme toxicity of all parts of the plant. Propagate from cuttings taken in summer and rooted with bottom heat.

Protea
(protea).
Proteaceae
(protea family)

Protea species are now becoming more readily available as their cultivation requirements are understood. Essentially this means providing a well-drained lime-free compost of relatively low fertility with plenty of sunshine. The addition of some charcoal to the soil mixture also helps recreate their natural environment where scrub fires are common, and if yellowing occurs rectify with a dilute magnesium sulphate application. Water moderately in summer but reduce watering in winter when they require a cool resting period. Most species are quite tough given these conditions, but they will not tolerate the winter wet outside. For a long time only *Protea cynaroides* was available. This is certainly quite an amenable plant, producing 20cm (8in) bowl-shaped scaly flower heads with pink bracts in early summer. Perhaps more striking are the slightly smaller-flowered plants such as *P. neriifolia*. The leaves of most *Protea* species are grey-green and leathery. They vary in shape from linear to almost spade-shaped. Propagation of *Protea* plants is best achieved from seed sown in warmth as soon as available, or from cuttings taken of semi-ripe wood in summer.

Protea neriifolia

Tetrapanax papyrifer

Tetrapanax
(ricepaper plant).
Araliaceae
(ivy family)

 -

Somewhat like a giant version of *Fatsia japonica* in appearance, this too is an oversized ivy. *Tetrapanax papyrifer* produces large, 50cm (20in) diameter, rounded, lobed leaves with strong veins. They are mid-green in colour with a dull surface and felted beneath. The leaves are held on long robust straight petioles. Inevitably this plant requires a semi-shaded position with ample shelter from strong winds that would otherwise shred the large leaves. Grow in JI2 or 3 with abundant water in summer and a little less in winter. Ultimately plants form tall stems and will also branch from the base. In autumn, large clusters of white flowers may be produced from the taller stems. *Tetrapanax* is quite easy from seed sown in spring or can be propagated by the removal of suckers which may already have abundant roots.

Tibouchina
(glory flower).
Melastomataceae
(glory flower family)

Tibouchina organensis (*T. semidecandra*) is a lax Brazilian shrub with large (12cm; 5in) oval hairy leaves with distinctive mid veins that run from base to tip. The leaves sometimes take on reddish tints. Purple-blue flowers are produced in clusters in late summer. These reach around 8cm (3in) in diameter and have prominent stamens that give rise to its other name of 'spider flower'.

Grow these plants in a rich compost (JI3) with extra sharp sand for drainage and place them in a sunny site. Reaching up to 5m (16ft) or more, this shrub will need regular pruning to keep it in order. Semi-ripe wood can be used as cutting material rooted with some bottom heat.

Palms and palm-like plants

Palms and palm-like plants are essential in the exotic garden. However, realistically, only a few species are hardy in any reliable manner and only one true palm is common in colder regions. A number of palms are of borderline hardiness and may spend much of the year in the garden, but they should be brought under cover before frosts occur. Sadly, most palms are not suitable for outdoor exposure, even during the summer, since the atmosphere is rather dry and the nights rather cool, resulting in very slow growth. Only a few palms will flower in cool climates or in pots so these are not really an issue, nor are the resulting fruits. Propagation of palms is almost exclusively by seed sown in warm conditions in spring. Seedlings should be acclimatised to cooler conditions gradually in their first-year and, however hardy, give first year seedlings winter protection 4°C. Here, only those palms that are hardy or nearly so are described.

Chamaerops humilis in its native habitat in southern Portugal

Phoenix canariensis in a sheltered valley bottom in Tenerife

Brahea
(blue fan palm).
Arecaceae
(palm family)

Although one of the most beautiful of blue-grey leaved palms, this is also one of the most slow-growing. *Brahea armata* (*Erythea armata*) is a palmate-leaved palm with leaves that arch on long spiny petioles. Their colour is remarkable and makes a strong accent in the tropical display. However, a specimen of any size will take years to mature, and to purchase a large specimen will be especially expensive. As one might expect from the colour of the leaves, these are relatively drought-tolerant palms, but it is probably best not to put this to the test on pot-grown specimens. Water well in summer and

Brahea armata

Chamaerops humilis

less in winter. They like JI2 potting compost and plenty of sunshine to bring out their best colour.

Chamaerops
(European dwarf fan palm).
Arecaceae
(palm family)

These are small tough palms that will stand considerable neglect. *Chamaerops humilis* is the only palm native to Europe, where it inhabits dry, sunny, usually coastal sites. It is, as the name suggests, a small palm, and it is unusual in a number of respects. This is one of the few of the hardier palms, for instance, that will bloom in a large pot or tub, although the small creamy-yellow flower clusters borne close to the trunk are not especially significant (orange fruits may develop subsequently). In addition, *Chamaerops* is naturally a suckering palm, and mature

specimens will readily produce basal offsets that will ultimately form a sizeable clump. These suckers can, after a few years, be removed with a sharp knife if further plants are desired. The leaves of *Chamaerops* vary depending upon how it is grown but always have strongly spine-edged petioles. In shade, the leaves are broad and mid-green, but if grown 'hard' in full sun, the leaves become more blue-green with white waxy scales and the leaf segments become more narrow. Hard-grown plants are generally hardier and will stand mild frosts, especially if the crown of the plant is dry. The suckering nature of *Chamaerops* means that even if the main crown is lost, basal suckers will emerge to replace it. These palms enjoy a rich compost (JI3) with abundant moisture in summer and much less in winter, when they will rest. Feed mature plants regularly. A blue/grey-leaved form is also available, although this seems to be a very dwarf- and slow-growing variant.

Cordyline,

see Robust lily-like rosette plants
(p. 77).

Cycas
(sago palm).
Cycadaceae
(cycad family).

Cycas revoluta is probably the most commonly available of the cycads, ancient plants which resemble palms at maturity, but which are more closely related to the non-flowering plants such as *Ginkgo* and conifers. All cycads are slow-growing and C. *revoluta* is no exception. Young plants bear palm-like leaves with narrow, dark green, stiff leaflets that generally arise in a cluster in early summer from the pineapple-like stem. For the remainder of the growing season the stem produces brown, slightly furry scales in place of leaves. The leaflets of *Cycas* are inrolled like those of a fern, and gradually unfurl over a number of weeks. Mature plants of *Cycas revoluta* have the beginnings of

Encephalartos frederici-guilielmi in the South of France

a scaly trunk and produce new leaves simultaneously in a ring. Cycads are either male or female. Female plants of *Cycas revoluta* produce rings of reduced, furry leaves on which large seeds are produced. Male plants produce structures resembling elongate spruce cones. However, reproduction is rare in plants confined to pots.

Grow *Cycas revoluta* in a well-drained compost (JI3 with extra peat substitute and sharp sand) and allow it to more or less dry out between waterings. It is important not to let the soil become stagnant, as this will cause rotting of the rather large, fleshy roots. Healthy plants of *Cycas* will develop strange, foreshortened clusters of roots at the soil surface. These should not be buried or removed as they contain a bacterium which takes in atmospheric nitrogen and supplements the plant's supply of nutrients. *Cycas* will grow in sun or

Cycas revoluta (female)

shade, but leaves develop differently according to their environment, and plants that have been grown in shade may scorch if placed in direct sun. Cycads are generally trouble-free, but may suffer from scale insect and mealy bug if kept mainly under cover.

The Indian *Cycas circinalis* is sometimes available, but this is a more tender species and will not tolerate periods of cold that the Japanese *C. revoluta* can survive. Other species of cycad are rarely available but are worth acquiring. Species of the genus *Encephalartos* are fiercely protected in their native South Africa, but are gradually becoming available. *Encephalartos frederici-guilielmi* (white-haired cycad) is relatively hardy 4°C and other species from harsh environments may also prove equally robust.

A number of cycads are also available as seed, particularly members of the Australian genus *Macrozamia*, (e.g. *Macrozamia spiralis*). These are quite easy to germinate and within as little as five years can make a reasonable pot plant!

Jubaea
(Chilean wine palm).
Arecaceae
(palm family)

Jubaea chilensis is another slow growing palm which in its native habitat will achieve enormous proportions and which, even in cooler

Jubaea chilensis at Antibes, France

climates, can reach 10–15m (30–50ft). This is a pinnate-leaved palm with pale to mid-green, long, arching fronds to a few metres in length on mature plants. Grow *Jubaea* in JI2 with a little extra peat substitute and feed regularly through the summer when water should be plentiful. Provide plenty of sunshine for larger specimens. Keep these palms cool and drier in winter, when they will rest. Mature specimens are probably much hardier than youngsters so look after them carefully for the first few years.

Phoenix
(date palm).
Arecaceae
(palm family)

Phoenix canariensis is probably the most widely available and inexpensive palm available at present.

It is a robust pinnate-leaved form with dark green fronds (to 1m; 3¼ft or more on young plants) of stiff leaflets borne on spiny yellowish petioles. In addition it is relatively fast-growing and will produce three or more new leaves each year as a young plant. Although very decorative as a summer patio palm, this is a hungry creature and will require ample feeding through the summer when plenty of water and sunshine should be provided. Pot on regularly in JI3. In winter, provide frost protection, especially for young plants. Keep them on the dry side and especially avoid getting water into the crown of the plant, since this can cause a fatal rot. Although commonly sold as though they are hardy, these palms are really not suitable for outdoor use except in more or less frost-free places. *Phoenix dactylifera*, the true date palm is less hardy but is

Phoenix at Tresco, Isles of Scilly, UK

easily raised from date stones left over from Christmas. They require a high temperature to germinate and are fast-growing as young plants.

Rhapidophyllum
(porcupine palm).
Arecaceae
(palm family)

Rather like *Chamaerops* in both habit and appearance is *Rhapidophyllum hystrix* from the southern USA. It is a palmate-leaved palm that suckers from the base to form clumps. The leaves are bright green with a greyish underside and emerge from particularly spiny sheathes. Said to be hardy, it is rarely available and, since it is rather slow-growing, is probably not worth risking outside if you have one.

Grow in full sun or part shade in JI3 with some additional peat substitute. Water plentifully in summer with less in winter.

Sabal
(palmetto).
Arecaceae
(palm family)

Sabal minor, as its name suggests, is a small palm in terms of height but can produce enormous (1.5m; 5ft) blue-green palmate leaves. It forms an underground trunk from

127

Sabal minor

which the leaves arise in a thicket. In its native habitat of the southern USA it grows happily in places that are seasonally flooded, a feature which may be useful in cooler, wetter climates such as the UK. Somewhat larger, with a trunk above ground, is S. palmetto. This has large green fans that are deeply divided. Both species require plenty of sunshine but will

Trachycarpus fortunei at Heligan, Cornwall, UK

tolerate a little shade. They require abundant water and feeding in summer, less so in winter when they will rest. Pot them in JI3 with a little extra sharp sand and peat substitute.

Trachycarpus
(Chusan palm).
Arecaceae
(palm family)

As in most widely distributed plant groups, there are always representatives that stretch the range to its maximum by becoming tolerant of adverse conditions. In this case, it is Central China that hosts the most cold-tolerant of the palms, *Trachycarpus fortunei*, the Chusan palm. *Trachycarpus* is, for instance, reliably hardy throughout much of Britain, with the exception of central and eastern Scotland and northeast England. Soil should be well-drained, but not dry and, as with most 'exotic' plants, some shelter should be given to youngsters (potted specimens will require JI3). *Trachycarpus* is relatively quick-growing, all things considered, but sadly, to my mind, is not a particularly exciting palm. Leaves are large on mature specimens, palmate with individual leaflets separating for around one-third of their length. The leaves are dark green and slightly glossy but can yellow in exposed conditions. As plants mature, the leaf bases decay into a tough enclosing mass of fibres that probably assists in

Trachycarpus fortunei

insulating the developing trunk. However, it is not the trunk which may require protection in extreme weather, but the soft-growing shoot in the centre of the crown of leaves (the palm heart). Damage to this growing point is usually fatal since, like most palms, *Trachycarpus* is unable to branch or sucker. *Trachycarpus* can reach a considerable size, particularly in sheltered sites. On mature plants, large sprays of flowers may develop from yellow sheaths. In warm years small black fruits may be produced.

Only *Trachycarpus fortunii* is grown extensively and is widely available as young plants. Other forms with a similar natural distribution may prove hardy, such as T. wagnerianus with smaller, pleated leaves and T. nanus, a dwarf palm. Grow all *Trachycarpus* in sun or partial shade, and provide ample water in summer when they are at maximum growth rate.

Ginger, bananas and relatives

Bananas and gingers form a group of closely related herbaceous perennials that, by virtue of their sheathing leaf bases, may form false 'trunks' or stems. Most spread by underground rhizomes, and multiply quickly under good cultivation. Leaves are commonly large, oval and strongly veined, commanding instant attention and providing an air of tropical luxuriance. For the jungle garden they are indispensable as foliage plants, and many also produce spectacular flowers. Surprisingly, some are hardy, although the range can be considerably extended by the use of over-wintered containerised specimens. In general, these plants require a rich garden soil with abundant organic matter such as leaf mould, peat substitute or incorporated kitchen waste. In containers, a mixture of equal parts soil-less compost and JI3 is effective. All gingers respond well to high nitrogen feeds of pelleted or well-rotted manure. When in growth they appreciate abundant moisture. Most will tolerate partial shade but succeed best with at least three hours of full sun per day. The larger leaves of the bananas and species of *Canna* make them particularly susceptible to wind damage. Always site these with shelter from prevailing winds.

Canna leaves have a bold structure and in large groups can form an interesting foliage texture

129

Canna
(Indian shot).
Cannaceae
(Indian shot family)

  0°C - 4°C

Canna has long been cultivated as an ornamental, and as a result is the best known of the gingers. The common name is derived from the seeds that are round and hard, resembling lead shot. Many hybrids are obtainable and are known as *Canna* x *generalis* or *Canna* x *hybrida*. These have a diversity of flower and leaf colour and vary in height from 1–1.5m (3–4½ft) or more. *Canna* plants are adaptable and of easy cultivation. In the open ground, plant the rhizomes 15–20cm (6–8in) deep in late spring after starting into growth in moist peat substitute in late winter. In containers, plant the rhizomes, two to a 20cm (8in) diameter pot at a similar depth. Keep the compost just moist until the shoots emerge and then water well. Keep containerised plants indoors at a

Canna varieties in the Nanjing Botanical Gardens, China

cool temperature (around 10°C; 50°F) until all likelihood of frost has passed. Protect the shoots of outdoor plants from frost, using upturned buckets, plastic sheeting or horticultural fleece. The young shoots may be damaged by slugs.

Once underway, *Canna* plants grow quickly, producing their large, oval leaves in abundance. The largest shoots will flower in late summer. Flowers are borne on a terminal spike. A subsidiary spike may form at the point of the lowest flower and flower spikes should therefore not be removed. Individual flowers last for only a day or two, but many are borne sequentially up the spike.

The flowers are curiously irregular in shape and are commonly in shades of red, yellow, orange and pink, sometimes spotted or striped. Some forms of *Canna* can change their flower colour depending on where and how they are grown. *Canna*

plants may be left in the open ground until blackened by the first frost. Lift them gently, and trim off the dead stems and leaves to about 2cm (¾in) below the original ground level. Store them over winter in dry or barely damp peat substitute. Container-grown plants can also be left outdoors until frosted or brought inside to complete their growth cycle. Remove the foliage when black or brown, severing the stems at soil level. Store the rhizomes dry in their existing containers or treat as above.

Container-grown plants generally require replanting in fresh compost each spring.

Canna forms may be propagated by seed, although this is relatively difficult owing to the hard outer coating. Chipping off this coat with a knife can aid germination, but may also introduce disease. Soaking of the seed for 24 hours before sowing is advantageous. Propagation by division

A display of *Canna* varieties at
Heligan, Cornwall, UK

of the rhizomes with a knife is easier and can be undertaken when starting the rhizomes into growth in early spring. Ensure that each section of rhizome has a bud and dust the cut ends with a fungicide. Allow them to dry for a day or two before placing in moist compost.

Of the many forms of *Canna,* one of the best for the exotic garden is 'Wyoming'. It is tall, to 1.5m (5ft), with striking purple-green foliage and large flowers, apricot-orange in colour. 'Red King Humbert' is also large with bright red flowers and grey-green leaves; 'President' is similar, but shorter with very large leaves. 'Rosamund Coles' is a shocker with red and yellow striped flowers and dark leaves. 'Lucifer' is similar, but shorter. 'Picasso' is yellow with bright crimson spots.

To be used with care is C. 'Striata' which has leaves of yellow and green variegation and is truly shocking and difficult to place. If you can, obtain some of the species. These have a grace that is lacking in the hybrids although in general their flowers are smaller. *C. iridiflora* likes a moist soil and rewards with wands of pink-red bloom. *C. indica* (*C. edulis*) is a spectacular red. The flowers are small but abundant and spikes often branch. This species has very robust rhizomes that like to be just below soil level. Beware as, more than other forms, it will burst through the side of a container as the new rhizomes expand in late summer. *C. glauca* has blue-green foliage and yellow flowers.

Cautleya
(cautleya).
Zingiberaceae
(ginger family)

The principal species grown is the Himalayan *Cautleya spicata,* and that usually in the form C. *spicata* f. *robusta. Cautleya* is almost hardy: if planted with the rhizomes 10–15cm (4–6in) down and covered with some form of protection it should survive most winters. Ideally, it suits the base of a west-facing wall as it objects to too much sun, which can scorch the large oval leaves. *Cautleya* is excellent in a container, where it can remain from year to year provided that a good dressing of manure is supplied once or twice in the growing season. Water abundantly during growth (which starts in late spring) but withhold water during dormancy in winter, when it should be kept just frost-free. Start into growth with a good watering in early spring. *Cautleya* is best propagated by division of the rhizomes in early spring before growth starts. Take care to minimise damage to the brittle roots and ensure that each division bears a few 'crowns' in order to establish a reasonable clump.

As mentioned C. *spicata* f. *robusta* (sometimes seen as C. *robusta*) is the usual form encountered. This bears maroon spikes from which emerge, in sequence, short-lived primrose yellow, sage-like flowers that are orange in bud. This combination is more striking than in the normal form of C. *spicata* that has green spikes and a more diminutive habit.

Cautleya robusta

131

Ensete
(Abyssinian banana).
Musaceae
(banana family)

These banana-like plants form gigantic leaves on a false stem of leaf bases. They are monocarpic (dying once they have flowered) and do not sucker, so they can only be raised from seed sown in warm conditions in spring. *Ensete ventricosum* is the most commonly available species and is relatively tough, being suitable for outdoor use in summer. This species produces lance-shaped leaves up to 3m (10ft) in length on mature specimens, and these will inevitably require a sheltered site in order to avoid shredding by wind. The leaves are bright green and are supported on red leaf stalks. Like true bananas these are hungry feeders and require a rich compost (JI3 with a little extra peat substitute) and frequent feeding. Rapidly growing plants may require potting on twice each year. They

Ensete ventricosum

rarely bloom in containers or in cooler conditions and can therefore be quite long lived, but be aware that they do become very large.

Hedychium
(ginger lily).
Zingiberaceae
(ginger family)

    some

Hedychium species vary in their requirements but are all moisture-loving ginger relatives with spikes of colourful flowers that may be strongly scented. Leaves are broad and are borne alternately up the tall stems. *Hedychium densiflorum* and its varieties are the hardiest and should be planted as tubers at around 15cm (6in) depth at the base of a sunny, south-facing wall or similar situation. A mulch of straw is helpful in avoiding excessive cold. Plants in such a situation will, however, require abundant watering during growth in summer. *H. gardnerianum* is almost hardy and may survive in a similar situation if given ample winter protection. This species is probably better in a container that can be kept dry and frost-free during winter, chiefly because this species is less amenable to the loss of its abundant foliage, which will last until replaced by the new shoots the following year. Other species such as *H. coronarium* and *H. greenei* require a little more warmth and are less likely to thrive outside. To bloom well, *Hedychium*

Hedychium gardnerianum

species require a long growing season and are best started early, in much the same way as *Canna* at the beginning of spring. Their growing requirements are also similar, but stand containers in a dish of water to maintain the wet soil conditions that these plants enjoy when in growth.

Musa
(banana, plantain).
Musaceae
(banana family)

One species of banana, *Musa basjoo*, is sufficiently hardy to survive with protection out of doors the whole year round. Like its more tender relatives, however, it will fare better in a container with winter protection. Whether in the open ground or in containers, bananas are an important element in the exotic garden and cannot be bettered for that tropical effect, with smooth, arching grey-green leaves often 2m (6½ft) in length. Most bananas are dormant in winter and grow little. Some may even become leafless. With spring warmth, growth will begin. Pot on and feed if necessary, and stand out of doors as often as possible when the weather is dry and mild.

Do not subject bananas in growth to temperatures of less than 8°C (46°F), and avoid water collecting in the leaf bases in cold weather as this may cause rot. Ensure that they receive plenty of sunshine and plenty of water as growth begins. By late spring it is usually safe to leave them out permanently, but make sure to watch for cool nights.

Bananas suffer from wind damage in exposed positions, so stand them somewhere sheltered. Even then, leaves may split to the main vein.

Musa basjoo as subtropical bedding in Badenweiler, Germany

This does little harm to the plant, but detracts from its architectural value. More serious are snapped petioles that can result in the loss of a leaf. During the summer, expect a new leaf every two or three weeks and an associated increase in height of 2.5–4cm (1–1½in) per leaf. Tall stems may bloom, producing an arching, pendent spike with many large scales enclosing the flowers. You may even get fruit – but watch out for seeds and fibres. Flowered stems die, and can be cut back to the base when the leaves wither. Usually the plant will have produced suckers, and these may be left to form a clump of new stems, or severed with a sharp knife and potted up individually: provide bottom heat to help the divisions root rapidly. To keep them growing well, feed bananas frequently with a high nitrogen fertilizer and provide plenty of water. Bring all tender and pot-grown bananas under cover before night temperatures fall in autumn to 8°C (46°F) – 4°C (39°F) for M. *basjoo* – and maintain this minimum through

the winter. In the open ground remove any leaves from M. *basjoo* before the first frost, cutting with a sharp knife at the top of the pseudostem. Surround the plant stem with bales of straw, old carpets, or a wide drain pipe packed with straw, bracken or shredded newspaper. Cover the top of the severed stem with similar packing and cover the whole with a plastic sheet (preferably a double layer) to keep out moisture. Peg or weigh down the edges to prevent wind penetration.

Without doubt, the best banana for the exotic garden is *Musa basjoo* with its much greater tolerance of cold temperatures. However, its leaves are relatively narrow and the slender trunk is black-purple and commonly obscured by dead leaf bases. M. *acuminata* 'Dwarf Cavendish' 6°C is tender but stands up well to adverse conditions, provided that it is not allowed to get too cold or wet in winter. The mottled leaves are broader and more robust than those of M. *basjoo*, and the trunk is pink.

Musa basjoo

Roscoea
(hardy ginger).
Zingiberaceae
(ginger family)

These diminutive Himalayan gingers are of use in ground cover and in providing exotic flowers at low level. They are hardy if planted 10cm (4in) deep in a humus-rich soil. They prefer some shade. In late spring the shoots emerge above ground and expand rapidly into a stem which bears alternate, oval, keeled leaves. Flowers are produced at the top of the stem in mid-summer.

Roscoea plants die back rapidly in autumn when the remains of the foliage can be removed (check for seed capsules and save any seed for sowing in spring). *Roscoea* can be divided in early spring before growth begins or raised from seed sown on soil-less compost at 15C (42°).

Roscoea cautleyoides in the rock garden at Kew

The flowers of *Roscoea* are orchid-like in that they have a petal-like hood. *Roscoea purpurea* (R. *procera*) has purple flowers and grows around 30cm (12in) tall. R. *cautleyoides* is pale yellow and of similar dimensions. R. x 'Beesiana' is taller with yellow and purple flowers.

Strelitzia
(bird of paradise).
Strelitziaceae
(bird of paradise family)

The bird of paradise is well known as a florist's flower and is an attractive plant in its own right. Although not hardy, it will flourish in large pots or tubs that can be given winter protection. The paddle-like leaves of *Strelitzia reginae* are blue-green and waxy and reach 1.2m (4ft) in height on mature plants. The flower spikes arise from among the leaves and when mature produce a few horizontal green bracts from which the blue and orange flowers unfurl in sequence. Flowers are produced only on mature plants, and usually only when these are potbound. These plants enjoy sunshine and a well-drained compost of JI3 and sharp sand. They like ample water in summer when the temperatures are warm, but very little water in winter when they can be kept cool. There are other species of Strelitzia which are larger and more tropical in their requirements.

Thalia dealbata

Thalia
(water canna).
Marantaceae
(Arrowroot family)

 some

These are remarkably hardy *Canna* relatives which enjoy growing with their rhizomes in deep mud in 20cm (8in) depth of water, where they will survive most winters. The paddle-like grey-green leaves are borne on long petioles and have a narrow purple margin. Leaves may emerge from the water to a height of 2m (6½ft) in ideal conditions. When frosted, new shoots will replace dead stems in spring, although in mild areas leaves may remain through the winter. *Thalia dealbata* from the USA is the most common form. In late summer it produces wand-like spikes that bear small purple flowers in clusters toward the tip. Although a little tender, this plant is well worth obtaining for its excellent tropical appearance at the edge of a sunny pond. It can also be grown in tubs of water stood outside during summer, but moved undercover in winter where the leaves will be retained.

Aroids

Aroids are familiar to everyone in the form of our native 'lords and ladies' or 'cookoo pint' (*Arum*), the 'Swiss cheese plant' (*Monstera*) with its wonderfully architectural leaves, and the now frequently grown 'peace plant' or 'snail flower' (*Spathiphyllum*). Aroids constitute a large family with many species, most of which are tropical herbaceous perennials and climbers. As one might imagine, those with tuberous or rhizomatous storage organs and the ability to become dormant in winter are somewhat tougher, and a number of these can be cultivated outside in most parts of Britain. Others make spectacular foliage plants used for outdoor summer decoration in tubs or large pots.

The aroid 'flower' consists of a cowl-like spathe that surrounds the rod or club-shaped spadix, at the base of which are the true, very small flowers. Many aroids employ flies of various types for pollination, and one of the bi-products of this association is a tendency to have a slightly alarming odour. Tuberous aroids bear some of the most fascinating flowers of any plant group, and as architectural foliage plants they are difficult to beat. Admittedly, varieties with evil-smelling flowers will not appeal to those with sensitive noses, but all will appreciate the spectacular leaves which are produced either with or after the flowers. Most parts of most aroids are poisonous.

A typical aroid flower with the cowl-like spathe surrounding the true spike of tiny flowers, the spadix

Lysichiton americanus near Windsor Great Park, Berkshire, UK

Alocasia
(elephant's ear).
Araceae
(Arum family)

These are truly tropical aroids from Indonesia and surrounding areas with immense heart-shaped leaves to 1m (3¼ft) or more, borne on petioles of a similar length. They require warm conditions and a moist, rich soil to thrive. They are best grown in large tubs of JI3 with extra peat substitute. Feed regularly when in growth, and make sure to provide a very sheltered location for the large leaves. *Alocasia macrorrhiza* is becoming common and is probably the best species with which to begin, as it is more tolerant of short periods of neglect. Propagate by division of the rhizomes in late spring.

Amorphophallus
(konjaku).
Araceae
(Arum family)

Although mostly tropical, these tuberous plants are more amenable than some in having a distinct dry resting period that can correspond nicely with winter in more temperate climates. This genus contains the world's largest flowering structure, a gigantic, red, evil-smelling trumpet to 1.5m (5ft). It also contains some useful plants for tropical foliage

Amorphophallus konjac

effects on the summer patio. There are two reasonably tough species, of which *Amorphophallus konjac* (*A. rivieri*) is the most elegant. Each tuber sends up but a single leaf each year that is like an enormous shredded green umbrella supported by a mottled green and grey stalk to 1.2m (4ft) in height. Leaves arise in early summer, but if the tuber is to bloom it will produce its brown smelly flower spike in late spring, before the leaf. The individual leaflets of the umbrella are around 6cm (2⅜in) in length and broadly lance-shaped. Also sometimes available is A. *bulbifer* that is similar in dimensions but has much less divided leaves and correspondingly larger leaflets. You should plant tubers of both species in late spring, with their indented surfaces uppermost and with about 8cm (3in) of compost above them. Water well and keep them warm until mid-summer when they can

go outside to enjoy a semi-shaded position. The leaves will probably die back in a collapsed yellow heap before the first frosts. Bring them under cover and allow the pots to dry out through the autumn. Keep them cool and dry until growth resumes. The tubers grow best in a rich compost of equal parts JI3 and peat substitute. Feed them amply when in leaf. Propagation is achieved simply by the removal of the numerous young tubers that form around the parent. The big tubers will rot very quickly if too damp and cold in winter, leaving you with obvious subsidence in your pots.

Arisaema
(Jack-in-the-pulpit, cobra lily).
Araceae
(Arum family)

Arisaema plants have leaves that are variously divided into leaflets, commonly three in the Asian species but sometimes many more. The large leaves may be patterned with red or white veining and are usually supported on long petioles arising from the basal tuber. There are many species, most of them rare in cultivation, and all thrive in a lime-free humus-rich compost in semi-full shade with plenty of moisture while in leaf. Most species will stand some frost when dormant and a few of them, such as the North American *Arisaema triphyllum* (Jack in the pulpit) are fully hardy. They can be prone to the ravages of slugs, especially when the young leaves are emerging. The green-brown striped or marbled spathes are like those of *Arum* but more tubular, such that they may resemble the trumpets of the pitcher plant *Sarracenia*. They are often contorted into unlikely, gaping 'mouths' at the top, from which emerge the usually wiry spadix (e.g. *Arisaema tortuosa*, *A. costatum*). Some are less alarming but no less exotic. *A. candidum* is white with pink and brown-striped markings, while *A. sikokianum* is brown on the outside with a white interior and a rounded white spadix. These species, and the more tender *A. griffithii* and *A. speciosum* are worth growing for their large trifoliate leaves which are variously marked and born on spotty petioles. Most species are best

Arum italicum 'Marmoratum'

propagated from small offsets from the tubers: these can be dug up and separated shortly after the plants die back in autumn.

Arum
(lords and ladies,
cuckoo pint).
Araceae
(Arum family)

The genus *Arum* is generally of European and Western Asian distribution and contains a number of plants relevant to the tropical-style garden. The common *Arum maculatum* has robust heart-shaped to arrow-shaped leaves of a bright glossy green. Forms with prominent black markings on the leaves are the most interesting. The pale green spathes enclose a brown-purple spadix and are produced in early spring along with

the leaves. The bright orange fruits develop in summer after the leaves have died away. *Arum italicum* is similar with a yellow spadix and leaves that emerge in autumn. This species is more commonly encountered in the form *A. italicum* 'Marmoratum' which has leaves marked with yellow variegation. *Arum pictum* is also colourful with dark glossy leaves with lighter veining and brown spathes. *Arum creticum* is less hardy than these species, but has a more decorative flower consisting of a yellow or white recurved spathe and bold yellow spadix. Also available is *A. dioscoridis* with a green-yellow and purple spotted spathe. Similar in form to *Arum* but altogether smaller is *Arisarum proboscideum*, bearing its glossy elongate heart-shaped leaves in early spring, with strange purple and white striped spathes concealed beneath them. These have a long

Arisaema griffitthii

thread-like extension which is fancifully likened to a mouse tail.

Grow all of these aroids in a humus-rich compost in partial shade and provide shelter from strong winds. They like abundant moisture when in leaf, but prefer a drier period in late summer and early autumn when they rest. All can be propagated by removal of rhizome offsets when replanting, and most can be raised from stratified seed that will germinate in spring. All parts of all species are toxic.

Colocasia
(taro).
Araceae
(Arum family)

These are tuberous plants with large 50–80 cm (20–32in) heart-shaped leaves that like wet conditions. *Colocasia esculenta* can be grown as pond marginal plants

Xanthosoma violaceum

through the summer months, when active, but will require protection from frost during the winter, when they may go dormant. They should be kept dry and cool in the winter but will need triggering into growth in spring with some high temperatures and ample water. They can be grown in pots of JI2 stood in trays of water, but wherever they are placed they will require protection from wind. Similar in appearance but more tender is *Xanthosoma violaceum*, which requires drier conditions but is more decorative with purple leaf stalks and sometimes purple leaves. The tubers can be divided in spring just before planting. It is useful to cover the cut surfaces in green sulphur or some other fungicide. The best source of tubers can often be the local supermarket, where you should ensure that the produce has adequate growing points.

Dracunculus
(dragon arum).
Araceae
(Arum family)

All three species of these plants are fascinating but only *Dracunculus vulgaris* is hardy. This is a fearsome tuberous aroid which erupts from the ground in late winter, when it may require an inverted bucket to protect it from frost. The resulting stem produces alternate palmate compound leaves and is mottled with

Dracunculus vulgaris in Tenerife

purple. At around 1m (3¼ft) or so it may produce a flower that consists of a large 30cm (12in) brown-purple spathe and a thick black spadix. This is more interesting than pretty, but you will have to hold your nose while investigating as it is probably the smelliest hardy aroid. Grow *Dracunculus* in a well-drained soil (JI and extra sharp sand if grown in pots) in full sun. The tubers should be planted at least 10cm (4in) beneath soil level. The stems may need some support in windy sites. After flowering in summer, the plants die away rapidly and in mild areas will happily survive the winter where they have grown. pot-grown plants should be given some protection to prevent the tubers freezing. In contrast to *D. vulgaris*, *D. canariensis* is a charmer with narrow white spathes borne in early spring. It is not reliably hardy and is perhaps best grown in a pot in well-drained but fertile compost. The leaves of this species appear in autumn and last through the winter, which is one of the reasons why it requires winter protection. Propagate both species from seed sown in spring or from small tubers produced around the parent.

Lysichiton americanus foliage at Wisley, Surrey, UK

Lysichiton
(skunk cabbage).
Araceae
(Arum family)

These are excellent tropical-looking plants for boggy ground or the margins of ponds and slow streams in a sheltered, partly shaded site where they may be seen to good effect in the company of *Gunnera*. They need a good depth of nutritious soil to produce the biggest leaves and flowers. It is the slightly glossy leaves, rather than the flowers, that you can smell – and these only when bruised, so you don't need to worry about possible offence to the neighbours. Emerging in spring, the oval leaves expand until up to 1m (3¼ft) in length and are of a bright green colour. They tend to stay upright, forming a shuttlecock shape. Flowers just precede the leaves. In *Lysichiton americanus* the spathes are bright greenish-yellow and have a strange luminous quality. They surround a club-shaped green spadix. In the slightly smaller *Lysichiton camtcshatcensis* the spathes are white.

Also known as skunk cabbage is the more diminutive *Symplocarpus foetidus* from the USA, which has brownish egg-shaped spathes at ground level in early spring. It requires similar conditions to the other species. Propagate by division in spring or from seed sown on wet compost in early spring.

Lysichiton americanus

Symplocarpus foetidus

Orontium aquaticum

Orontium
(golden club).
Araceae
(Arum family)

The North American *Orontium aquaticum* is, as its name suggests, a true water plant, but I describe it here because it is an aroid – although one might not guess this from the flowers. The plant needs around 20–30cm (8–12in) water depth and a good depth of mud beneath this in which to spread. The leaves, which are produced in spring from the underwater rhizome, are simple floating ovals of a bright green colour. They may form quite dense clumps. In late spring emergent narrow yellow spikes are produced with a very reduced white spathe. These plants can also be grown in tubs or half barrels, where they can be viewed more closely than at the waterside. They like a sunny site but will tolerate a little shade. Propagate by division in spring.

Sauromatum
(voodoo lily).
Araceae
(Arum family)

This wonderful tuberous aroid is almost hardy and will survive outside with a little protection in most places. Young tubers appear to be hardier than the large older tubers and this tends to restrict their flowering outside. This can be an advantage as the 40cm (16in) tall mottled yellow and purple brown spathes and brown spadix emit a truly disgusting odour when they open in late spring. Plants will flower directly from dry tubers placed on a saucer but should be planted immediately after. The leaves, which emerge shortly after any flowers, are very architectural, consisting of a tall 50–80cm (20–32in) mottled stalk supporting a palmate compound leaf. The leaflets become successively smaller the further away they are from the stalk.

In pots, grow *Sauromatum venosum* in equal parts JI3 and peat substitute in a sunny position. Note that they need ample water and feeding when in growth. When the leaves die down in autumn, dry the pots off and store in a cool frost-free place such as a garage. Propagate the plants from the numerous tiny tubers produced around the parent.

Sauromatum venosum

Sauromatum venosum foliage

Zantedeschia
(arum lily).
Araceae
(Arum family)

The well-known arum lilies are of variable hardiness. The toughest are those derived from, and variants of, *Zantedeschia aethiopica* from southern Africa. This is the familiar white arum lily with tall flower stems supporting a pure white spathe surrounding a yellow spadix. The leaves are mid to dark green and elongate heart-shaped. They may reach 30cm (12in) or more in length and are borne on 40cm (16in) petioles from a tuberous rootstock. It is the rootstock that requires winter protection from severe frosts, since in most cases the leaves will be lost in winter. In frost-free areas growth continues throughout the year. Flowers are produced in mid-spring, along with a flush of new leaves. Generally arum lilies enjoy abundant moisture, and *Z. aethiopica* can be grown in ponds as a deep marginal where the rootstock will not freeze. Plants grow best in full sun or with a little shade and produce the biggest leaves in a rich soil (JI3 with extra peat substitute in pots). The hardiest form is *Z. aethiopica* 'Crowborough' but there are some newer forms such as *Z.* 'Kiwi Blush' with pinkish flowers that are just as hardy. A little more tender but more imposing is *Z.* 'Green Godess', which has tall flowers marked with green as though they are not sure whether they should actually be leaves. The more tender forms with yellow, red and pink flowers should be treated in much the same way as *Canna* plants, with which they combine well to produce wonderful foliage and flower effects. Propagate *Zantedeschia* by dividing the large tuberous rootstocks in spring as growth starts. The tubers rot easily, so coat the cut surfaces in a fungicide and leave them to dry for a few days before replanting.

Zantedeschia aethiopica 'Crowborough'

141

Tender perennials and annuals

Tender perennials have become very popular recently as their cultivation has been shown to be relatively undemanding. Many of the plants already described in previous sections fall comfortably into the category of tender perennials (e.g. *Fuchsia, Canna, Leonotis* and *Gladiolus*). For those with a more adventurous nature and plenty of winter protection space there are books devoted entirely to the diversity of tender perennials and their culture. Those featured below are probably the most commonly available but are none the less worth a mention. In addition, many of the plants often grown as annuals are short-lived perennials in their native habitat. These are usually raised from seed sown in warmth in spring and given protection from frost until such time as they can be planted outside in the border or containers. True annuals will bloom enthusiastically the year they are sown and will die once they have set seed. To prolong their duration of bloom and the life of the plant, remove faded flowers before the seeds begin to develop. Most annuals enjoy a sunny situation, plenty of moisture, and a moderately fertile soil (JI1 or 2 in containers). Climbing annuals can be found with the perennial climbers elsewhere in this work. Because of their deserved popularity, many of the plants in this section are available in a diversity of forms as hybrids and cultivars. A few of these I mention individually but, because of the rapid development of new forms, I generally refrain from a commentary on particular strains.

A display of summer bedding using a variety of tropical annuals and tender perennials

Amaranthus
(cat tail).
Amaranthaceae
(cat tail family)

 -

Species of *Amaranthus* are leafy short-lived shrubs or annuals from South America cultivated in some tropical areas for their cereal-like seeds. They have heart-shaped to arrow-shaped leaves with slightly indented margin. The most spectacular species is probably *Amaranthus caudatus* (love lies bleeding) which is shrubby (to 1m; 3¼ft or more), with rounded leaves that are generally green but may be red or purplish in certain forms. The flowers are tiny, borne in long hanging tassels, and may be of red, purple or green. Also splendid is the tall *A. tricolor* which has more elongate leaves that come in a range of colours from green to gold, red, pink and purple. The flowers are insignificant. *A. hypochondriacus* is similar with some good colour variants. All of these species are quite tender, and seedlings sown in spring should be protected from frost. They are both tolerant of poor soils and often colour better in these. However, for leaf size and luxuriant growth, plant in a fertile compost with abundant water and sunshine.

Atriplex hortensis form

Atriplex
(orache).
Chenopodiaceae
(goosefoot family)

 -

Many species of *Atriplex* are coarse weeds, but one is an excellent bold annual for the wilder part of the tropical-style garden. *Atriplex hortensis* from Asia is a slim, tall plant reaching 1m (3¼ft) or more in height and bearing elongate arrow-shaped leaves to 15cm (6in) in length. The relatively insignificant flowers are produced in terminal tassels. There are a number of named variants with leaves of gold, pink, green and red and with terminal flower clusters in the same colour. Young seedlings need protection from frost but are otherwise happy in a well-drained, moderately fertile soil in full sun with protection from wind.

Amaranthus caudatus

Begonia 'Semperflorens' form

Begonia
(begonia).
Begoniaceae
(begonia family)

  some

Tuberous *Begonia* plants are generally hybrids and can sometimes be found under the category name of *Begonia* x *tuberhybrida*. They come in a wide range of forms from upright to cascading, and the flower colours encompass everything from white, pink, orange, yellow, red and purple. Some produce enormous double flowers, while others have quite small, simple blooms with few petals, often of different sizes. These plants are easily grown in a humus-rich compost in pots or as bedding. They enjoy some shade and plenty of moisture when in growth. Start the tubers individually in pots in a warm place (around 15°C; 59°F) in early or mid-spring. They should be placed concave side uppermost, with the top of the tuber barely covered. All of these tuberous forms can be placed outside once all risk of frost is passed. The same is true of the 'Semperflorens' fibrous-rooted species

Begonia sutherlandii

usually grown as annuals and raised from seed (sown in early spring in a warm place) each year. These forms have small flowers in pinks and reds and succulent glossy leaves, often with red or purple tints. They will tolerate sun or shade.

Tuberous forms should be taken inside in autumn and allowed to dry off gradually. Old stems and leaves will shrivel and will eventually detach cleanly from the tubers, which can then be stored dry and frost-free in string bags or trays of dry peat substitute for the winter. Good forms of 'Semperflorens' *Begonia* can be potted in containers and over-wintered in a frost-free position.

Other interesting *Begonia* species include the relatively tough *B. fuchsioides* and *B.* x *argentioguttata* which form upright stems. *B. fuchsioides* has small red, pink or white flowers which, as the name suggests, are rather *Fuchsia*-like. The leaves of this species are tiny and a bright glossy green but, like all leaves of *Begonia* plants, they are asymmetrical, one half of the leaf being smaller than the other. *B.* x *argentioguttata* is commonly grown as a houseplant but will enjoy a shady spot outside in summer. Both of these species require warm conditions in the winter 8°C when they continue to grow. Much hardier is *Begonia grandis* subsp. *evansiana*, which is a small tuberous species that bears pink or white flowers in late summer. The leaves are a bright, almost yellow-green with a dark purple-red underside. The plant is herbaceous and will stand light frosts . Also relatively hardy is *B. sutherlandii,* with more linear leaves and orange flowers. Like other Begonia species, these require a semi-shaded position in a humus-rich compost. Most *Begonia* forms can be propagated from cuttings of the succulent stems rooted in early summer. Slugs may be a problem for most types outside.

Beta
(chard).
Chenopodiaceae
(goosefoot family)

The beetroots and chards (*Beta vulgaris* subsp. *cicla*) have spectacular large leaves, often with purple shading, and although usually

Beta vulgaris subsp. *cicla* (rhubarb chard)

considered vegetables, they certainly warrant a position in the exotic-style garden on account of their foliage. The flowers are insignificant, tiny and borne on branching spikes. All chards are easily raised from seed sown in mid-spring. Seedlings can be potted individually into small pots and planted out once frosts have passed. They are hardy, but this treatment gives them a good start. Alternatively, seeds can be sown where they are to grow in late spring. The plants enjoy a reasonably moist, sunny situation and a moderately fertile soil. There are a number of named forms of which the rhubarb chards, with purple 40cm (16in) leaves, are particularly good. There is also a variety ('Bright Lights') in which the stalks and main veins of the leaves are yellow, red or pink. Although popular with slugs, the plants seem to survive despite developing ragged leaves.

Cleome
(spider flower).
Capparidaceae
(caper family)

Cleome hassleriana is large South American annual (to 1.2m; 4ft) that needs to be sown early and in warmth for it to achieve its full potential. The plant produces robust stems bearing compound leaves and conspicuous spine-like stipules. Rounded flower clusters develop at the top of the stems in late summer.

The individual flowers have extremely long stamens, giving the plant its vernacular name. The flowers are scented, and range from purple to white (mixtures and pure colours are available). They require a well-drained compost of moderate fertility and a warm sunny position to flourish. They can be grown in large containers of JI2 and will need to be potted into this medium before transferral to the garden once all risk of frost has passed.

Clianthus
(glory pea).
Fabaceae
(pea family)

There are two species of these scrambling shrubs. *Clianthus formosus* from Australia is a spreading short-lived shrub with silvery ferny

Cleome hassleriana, white form

145

Clianthus puniceus

foliage and curiously curved brilliant red pea flowers with a black marking toward the centre. *C. puniceus* from New Zealand is larger and will climb a support to a height of 2.5m (8ft). It has darker, larger, pinnate compound leaves and flowers that lack the black spot, but it has the advantage of a number of named colour variants in pink and white. It is also hardier and will withstand a light frost, often by regrowing from the base. Both species require full sun and a well-drained compost of JI3 with extra sand and grit. If growing in containers, water well but allow them to dry between waterings and try to avoid wetting the foliage. In winter keep cool and only just moist. Both species are best if raised from seed sown in spring and watered very judiciously.

Gazania
(gazania).
Asteraceae
(daisy family)

These wonderful South African daisies are sprawling perennials often grown as annuals, but where frosts are light they will survive for a number of years. The variously cut foliage is either bright green and glossy or silvery and covered in fine hairs. Most garden forms are hybrids obtained by crossing *Gazania krebsiana* with other related plants. The flowers come in a wide range of yellows, reds, white, pink and orange and the best forms have a peacock feather-like 'eye' marking at the base. The plants rarely reach more then 40cm (16in) in height and the flowers, which open fully only in bright sunshine, are held above the foliage. These plants are generally raised from seed each year, but basal cuttings can also be taken in late summer. *Gazania* hybrids like a well-drained soil in a sunny situation.

Helianthus
(sunflower).
Asteraceae
(daisy family)

These large-leaved daisies are useful as foliage components in the tropical-style garden. *Helianthus annuus* is the well-known sunflower which is probably among the tallest of annuals. Competitions for the tallest

Gazania hybrid

are regularly held, and winners can be as much as 4m (13ft) in height. Natives of southern North America, they are moderately hardy and need to be sown under glass in early spring to attain large proportions. They should be potted on in JI2 and planted outside once frosts have passed. The leaves are often around 25cm (10in) long and spade-shaped, dark green and hairy. The large disc-like flower heads contain hundreds of tiny flowers surrounded by yellow to russet large-petalled blooms, the resulting daisy reaching 30cm (12in) in diameter.

There are dwarf forms of sunflower but, for me, they rather miss the point. *H. tuberosus*, the fully hardy Jerusalem artichoke, is a herbaceous perennial with leaves and a growth rate similar to that of *H. annuus*. The flower heads are much smaller, and in poor years they may not be produced. The plant is, however, excellent as a foliage screen and is easily available in large quantities from supermarkets in the autumn (the forms with smooth tubers having darker green leaves). Grow *Helianthus* in a sunny position, possibly with support and certainly with protection from strong winds. They enjoy a well-drained, fertile soil.

Tithonia rotundifolia is the Mexican sunflower and is another huge annual, to 2m (6½ft) in height. It has lobed bright green leaves and very bright orange flowers around 6cm (2½in) in diameter. It requires similar cultivation to *Helianthus annuus*.

Impatiens walleriana form

Impatiens
(busy Lizzie).
Balsaminaceae
(busy Lizzie family)

   mostly

Most of these are fleshy tropical short-lived shrubs and perennials, but some are annual and provide some good contributions to

Impatiens

the tropical-style garden. The common bedding busy Lizzie is derived from the perennial *Impatiens walleriana* from Africa and is available in a wide range of colours, some stripy and some double, mostly in reds, orange, pink and purple. They do well in shade and are moderately easy from seed sown in spring and planted out only after all risk of frost has passed, flowering generously by mid-summer. The 'New Guinea' hybrids are derived from *I. hawkeri* and are taller, more robust-growing plants with dark, sometimes bronzed, lance-shaped leaves and larger flowers. They can be over-wintered with care on a warm windowsill as can the exotic Congo cockatoo (*Impatiens naimnaimensis*), which has hooded and strongly spurred red and yellow flowers. Other interesting Impatiens include the tall, hardy annual *I. glandulifera* (policeman's helmet) from the Himalayas. This can reach

147

Isoplexis canariensis

2m (6½ft) in height, whereupon it bears the hooded flowers in shades of pink that confer its common name. This species and the shorter *I. balfourii* have explosive seed pods which can be most entertaining.

Isoplexis
(Canary Island foxglove).
Scrophulariaceae
(foxglove family)

soplexis canariensis is a small shrub with tough, toothed lance-shaped leaves around 12cm (5in) in length. Its main attraction is the 20cm (8in) spikes of pale orange foxglove-like flowers which are usually produced in summer. The blooms have an extended hood much like that of the tropical *Columnea*, and are quite exotic in appearance. Plants are easily grown in a sunny position in containers of JI2 compost. They need plenty of water when in growth, but little water in winter when they rest. Cuttings of new shoots can be taken in spring, and rooted with just a little bottom heat.

Lycopersicon
(tomato).
Solanaceae
(tomato family)

Yes, I really do mean tomatoes (*Lycopersicon esculentum*). So often we segregate plants into the flower garden and the vegetable patch that we tend to ignore the possibility of using vegetables as decorative items. Both gourds (*Cucurbita*) and ornamental corn (*Zea*) seem to have made this transition comfortably, so why not tomatoes? With renewed interest in some of the older varieties with variously coloured fruits, there is an abundance to choose from. Tomatoes require a fertile soil in a sunny site to thrive. They also need warmth and abundant moisture. Although yields may be less than we may reasonably expect from the pampered individuals whose fruits are destined for culinary use, tomatoes in the border can still add interest with what fruits they do manage to produce.

Try some of the small fruited cherry tomatoes in groups, where their shorter, bushy stature makes them less inclined to collapse. Leave their side shoots on (ignoring, in other words, the normal horticultural advice) and let them do their own thing. They will reward with lush green, much-cut foliage, small yellow flowers and, ultimately, coloured fruits. Much the same can be said for the related aubergines, peppers and chillies, all of which would not look out of place in the exotic border. Sow seed of tomatoes in early spring and pot on the plants in an equal mixture of JI2 and a peat substitute compost. They can be planted outside once all risk of frost has passed.

Tomatoes growing on an obelisk

Mimulus aurantiacus

Mimulus
(monkey flower).
Scrophulariaceae
(foxglove family)

These plants fall into two distinct categories with respect to their requirements. Most forms enjoy cool, moist conditions and will tolerate some shade, while *Mimulus aurantiacus* 'California' prefers full sun and a well-drained position. The monkey flowers all have bright, colourful trumpet-shaped flowers in reds, yellows and pinks. *Mimulus* x *hybridus* encompasses the many forms often derived from the North American *Mimulus guttatus*, a splendid herbaceous plant in its own right for a damp pond margin. Newer hybrids tend to be shorter and have larger flowers, many of which have a red or maroon spotted throat or petals. They are easily raised from seed sown in spring and protected from frost after which they will form rapidly spreading patches, blooming in summer. The leaves and flowers are much loved by slugs.

M. *aurantiacus* is a more upright, shrubby plant reaching almost 1m (3¼ft). The flowers are borne throughout the summer above the sticky lance-shaped bright green leaves and are usually in shades of orange. Most *Mimulus* are short-lived.

Nicotiana
(tobacco flower).
Solanaceae
(tomato family)

To me, the point of growing *Nicotiana* is for its scent, but in the drive to produce shorter plants with a wider range of colours for bedding purposes, much of the scent has unfortunately been lost. For the exotic garden then, species are perhaps better than the newer hybrids. *Nicotiana alata* is usually grown as an annual but, like other species, it may over-winter in very mild areas, behaving as a herbaceous perennial. It has large oval leaves and may reach 1m (3¼ft) in height. Its trumpet blooms are green-white and very fragrant in the evening. Taller still (to 2m; 6½ft) is N. *sylvestris* which may need some support because of its height. It forms almost cabbage-like rosettes of oval leaves, from which arise spikes surmounted by clusters of long tubular white flowers that flare at the mouth. Grow these rather sticky South American delights in a rich, moist compost in partial shade or sun. Sow seed in early spring and transplant to pots of JI2 and peat substitute before planting out after all risk of frost has passed.

Nicotiana sylvestris

Osteospermum
(Vanstadens River daisy).
Asteraceae
(daisy family)

Forms of *Osteospermum* have become increasingly common in recent years as it is realised that with a little winter protection many are relatively hardy. Like many South African daisies they require a warm, sunny position and good drainage in order to flourish.

To keep them through the winter outside they will require protection from winter rain and cold. They can, however, easily be potted up and bought under cover, where they should be watered sparingly and kept just frost-free.

The foliage of most forms is dark to grey green, the leaves being elongate with variously toothed margins. On older plants, the leaves may become somewhat scruffy.

Flowers are borne in summer individually above the foliage on short or long stalks and in varying shades of pink, purple, white and, more recently, yellow. Many have a darker eye in purple-blue, and commonly the underside of the petals has a blue metallic sheen.

In my view, the dark purple-flowered forms such as *O. jucundum* are probably the best for the tropical-style garden, and these have the advantage of being the more hardy. Most are easily propagated from cuttings taken in summer.

Osteospermum form

Pelargonium
(geranium).
Geraniaceae
(geranium family)

 mostly

The various forms of *Pelargonium* are stalwarts of the summer garden and are familiar to everyone. The zonal types are probably most commonly grown. They are upright shrubby plants with rounded, scented leaves variously marked in concentric bands and thick succulent stems. The flowers range from purple to pink, red and orange and may be single or double. They are borne in large clusters supported on a strong upright stem. Generally I prefer the single flowered forms with a strong red or purple colour, but there are some good pastel shades if you prefer these. There are variegated leaf forms too, of which *P.* 'Contrast' (with yellow, green and maroon leaves) is particularly eye-catching and has the advantage of well-structured flowers in orange-red.

Also familiar are the ivy-leaved forms of *Pelargonium*. These naturally have a trailing habit and, as the name suggests, have leaves that are lobed much like those of *Hedera helix*. The flowers of the ivy-leaved forms tend to have more narrow petals but are available in a similar range of colours to the zonal types. Particularly good are the 'Decora' forms with bright foliage and abundant strong-coloured flowers. Also good is 'Mexicana' with bicoloured pink and purple flowers and strong, succulent growth.

Pelargonium 'Contrast'

flowering and makes them more susceptible to winter rot. They are all excellent container plants, and the ivy-leaved forms perform well as hanging basket subjects, where they will be more tolerant of dry spells than many other plants. Some zonal forms can be raised from seed sown in early spring and are available as mixtures that will flower in their first year. Named forms must, however, be raised from cuttings of soft shoots taken in summer and rooted in a very well-drained medium such as pearlite. In winter, all forms will rest and require a cool (but frost-free), dry environment with adequate light. In early spring they can be started into growth with a light watering and a little more warmth. Once underway, they can be pruned and repotted as necessary. *Pelargonium* plants can suffer from all manner of pests and diseases, but few seem to be fatal.

The regal forms of *Pelargonium* are shrubby and have bright green finely lobed or toothed leaves and are less succulent than the above types. They bear large, often slightly frilled, flowers in clusters in summer. The flowers frequently have darker stripes and spots within the throat and come in a range of pinks, reds and even dark purple-reds. Angel forms are similar to the regals but smaller. Their flowers have a comparable range of colours, but often the upper two petals are of a different colour and may be strongly marked with purple veining. *P.* 'Tip Top Duet' is particularly fetching. *P.* 'Black Knight' is an old variety midway between a regal and an angel. It has eye-catching dark mauve flowers outlined in white.

Lastly there is a range of scented-leaved forms that are often true species or closely related to these. Most have variously lobed leaves that smell of peppermint, lemon, mothballs and creosote, to name but a few. Most have quite small flowers in pink or lavender. I particularly like *Pelargonium* 'Graveolens' which has deeply lobed, crinkly leaves with a lemony scent, and 'Lady Plymouth' which seems to be a variegated form of this. 'Graveolens' is remarkably hardy and will survive most winters in a sheltered sunny spot if planted with plenty of stem below ground.

All *Pelargonium* forms like a sunny situation and good drainage. They will cope well on poor dry soils: indeed, overfeeding can reduce

Pelargonium 'Mexicana'

Pelargonium 'Black Knight'

151

Ricinus
(caster oil plant).
Euphorbiaceae
(spurge family)

These very poisonous shrubs are such fast growers that they can be used as annuals in summer bedding and indeed they may flower in their first year. The colourful seeds should be sown in early spring and the resulting plants kept warm and potted up in JI2 until they can be transferred to their summer positions. They must be kept free of frost. The plants have robust stems and large palmate leaves with toothed edges and prominent veins. The leaves may reach 50cm (20in) across and plants may grow up to 2m (6½ft) in their first season. Flower clusters are small and yellowish, but they are soon followed

Ricinus communis

by 2cm (¾in) diameter spiny red seed pods which are most attractive in their own right.

Various forms are available with red or purple leaf colouration and some, such as *Ricinus communis* 'Zanzibarensis' have white, rather than the usual red, leaf veins. Needless to say, if you have greenhouse space to spare you can pot up your shrubs at the end of the season before frosts occur and keep them warm and just a little moist until it is safe to return them to the garden.

Salvia
(sage).
Lamiaceae
(mint family)

  -  some

Salvia species have recently become very popular as it is realised what a wealth of interesting forms occur within the genus. Beyond *Salvia officinalis* (common sage) and its various forms are a number of interesting and pretty plants with luxuriant scented foliage and bright tubular hooded flowers. *Salvia splendens* is the well-known annual scarlet sage raised from seed and much used in bedding, but it, too, is a perennial and will survive the winter in a frost-free site. More interesting are the larger semi-herbaceous species such as *S. patens* and *S. cacaliifolia* with flowers in a range of named blues and *S. elegans* with scarlet flowers. Very unusual is *Salvia discolor*,

Salvia officinalis 'Purpurea' with other Mediterranean plants

with greyish foliage, grey-green bracts and extremely dark purple-blue flowers. All of these forms are of a delicate disposition and, although they may survive a winter below ground, they are probably best lifted and stored in pots under cover where they will require less water and frost-free conditions.

Revive them in spring with a good watering and a rise in temperature. They can then be tidied up by the removal of dead portions. This is also the time to divide clumps. Cuttings may also be taken of non-flowering shoots in summer.

Solenostemon
(coleus).
Lamiaceae
(mint family)

Long known as *Coleus*, these mint relatives lack scented leaves but have spikes of mint-like flowers which are probably best removed as these plants are principally grown for their foliage colour. The diversity of *Solenostemon* leaf colouration is well known and includes an almost indescribable range of green, red, pink, dark purple brown, white and yellow, sometimes all on the same leaf. There are forms with twisted and curled leaves as well as ones with deeply lobed or cut foliage. They are easily raised from seed sown in spring and grow quickly to produce small plants that can be encouraged to bush by the removal of the growing tips at intervals. All forms like warm conditions and should only be put outside once all risk of frost has passed. Even then they will not grow vigorously until the nights warm up. They are worth the effort if you can keep the slugs away from them. Good seed-raised forms or named varieties can be propagated from soft cuttings taken in summer and rooted in warmth. The related plant *Perilla*

Verbena x *hybrida*

Salvia patens

frutescens var. *crispa* is similar but much more resilient and is somewhat hardier. It is a true annual and should be raised from seed in spring. Sadly it usually comes only as the purple-leaved form, but this can be an effective contrast to plants such as *Hosta* and grasses.

Verbena
(verbena).
Verbenaceae
(verbena family)

   some

The bedding varieties of South American *Verbena* are colourful perennials that succeed as annuals when sown in early spring in warmth. They can be planted out once all risk of frost has passed. The common varieties are forms of *Verbena* x

hybrida, many of which have been bred for pastel shades, but for the exotic-style garden there are some good strong colours, particularly dark purples and reds. The leaves of *Verbena* plants are rough and bristly and usually lance-shaped to linear. The flowers are borne in rounded heads on sprawling stems. *Verbena bonariensis* is something of a weed, but its tall, almost leafless branching stems (to 1m; 3¼ft or more) and its clusters of lavender-purple flowers have an odd luminance at dusk, providing an unusual structural element in a planting. It is a moderately hardy herbaceous perennial . All *Verbena* species require moist but well-drained soil in full sun. They can be propagated from non-flowering shoots taken as soft cuttings in summer and then rooted in warmth.

Succulents

Some of the most striking plants seen in the warmer, drier places of the world are the succulents. These are all plants which are able to store water in their fleshy tissues (usually leaves or stems) to tide them over periods of drought. Unfortunately for the gardener seeking this particular aspect of the tropical-style, the large water content of these plants usually means that they are unable to survive frosts. Surprisingly, some from the harshest of deserts, where temperatures fall rapidly at night, can survive a light frost provided that its duration is short and the plant is relatively dry. This includes many *Agave* and *Opuntia* cactus species from the American deserts. Avoiding excess watering is the key to success with succulents which are superb as specimen pot plants for the patio, wall tops, steps or even on the roof. In general, tender succulents should be potted in a gritty mixture (try 4 parts JI2, one part pearlite, one part peat substitute and two parts grit) to ensure good drainage. Most succulents do better in terracotta pots rather than in plastic as the compost dries faster in porous clay. Fortunately though, there are some succulent plants that are fully hardy, and these can be exploited to the full in drier garden soils and sites. All succulents also need plenty of sunshine as this keeps them tough, robust and colourful, so stand them in the sunniest place when you bring your tender succulents out for the summer. Water them if they get very dry during summer, but bring them in again before they get too soggy in the autumn rains and keep them cool, dry and frost-free for the winter. They will not need much water until early spring if you keep them at around 4°C (40°F). Most succulents are easy to propagate, so there is no excuse for not trying a few of the more tender types in a dry, sheltered site outside. Many have fierce, potentially dangerous spines: in places where children and animals have access, do be careful where you use spiny plants.

Various barrel cacti in Gran Canaria

Aeonium used in the border at Tresco, Isles of Scilly, UK

Aeonium
(tree houseleek).
Crassulaceae
(stonecrop family)

These are very amenable plants that consist of concentrated rosettes of usually spoon-shaped leaves borne to varying degrees on stems. Most commonly available is *Aeonium arboreum* f. *atropurpureum* which has a 4–12cm (1½–5in) diameter, flattened, plate-like rosette of tightly-packed leaves – in this form, with a maroon blush. The colour becomes more intense in bright sunshine. As the plants grow, they produce subsidiary rosettes, these too developing stems until the plants gradually become sparsely shrubby. A. 'Schwarzkopf' is a particularly good, very dark form. The purple-leaved variants rarely flower, but the green form will produce terminal branching clusters of small, star-shaped, yellow flowers. *Aeonium balsamiferum* is similar, but has more cup-shaped rosettes and broader, pale green to olive green sticky leaves.

Aeonium arboreum f. *atropurpureum*

Aeonium tabuliforme in Tenerife

Smaller and more readily branching is *Aeonium haworthii*, which has thicker blue-green leaves with a more triangular tip and reddish margin. The rosettes are more lax and rarely exceed 8cm (3in) in diameter. There is a pretty variegated form. Both flower freely, producing terminal clusters of pale yellow or creamy star-like blooms. A. *sedifolium* is very small, with rosettes of club-shaped 1cm (⅜in) leaves. These are bright green and marked with purple. The flower clusters consist of a few bright yellow blooms.

Some species of *Aeonium* produce solitary stemless rosettes. The most beautiful of these is possibly A. *tabuliforme*, which gradually produces a completely flat rosette of hundreds of pale green, long, spoon-like leaves reaching up to 20cm (8in) in diameter. Eventually a large flower cluster will emerge from the centre of the rosette and will produce numerous yellow flowers. Individual

rosettes die after blooming (true of all species of *Aeonium*) but will commonly set seed. This can be sown as soon as ripe in late summer on moist compost. Seedlings should develop rapidly and will require a little moisture and warmth to keep them active through their first winter.

Aeonium species are excellent in pots stood outside in a sunny place in summer. From the Canary Islands, they are essentially winter-growing, but they readily adapt to a winter rest and summer growth. Naturally growing in rock crevices, these plants need relatively small pots filled with JI2 and extra grit. In winter, keep them cool and relatively dry, when the rosettes will shrink in size and tighten. Cuttings of *Aeonium* rosettes with around 5cm (2in) of stem beneath root readily, but should be left in a semi-shaded dry place for at least two weeks before insertion into potting mixture. Under cover, *Aeonium* species are prone to attack from mealy bug.

155

Various *Agave* species at the Botanical Gardens, Gran Canaria

Agave
(century plant).
Agavaceae
(century plant family)

These are possibly the best rosette succulents for outdoor summer containers. They are robust plants and usually very large at maturity. Rosettes die after flowering but this is rare when they are confined to containers and they usually leave behind a plethora of offsets so total loss is unlikely. *Agave americana* is the

Potted *Agave americana* 'Mediopicta' as part of the summer bedding at Hidcote Manor, Gloucestershire, UK

biggest and boldest commonly encountered. Widespread in the Mediterranean it, like other of the genus, is a native of North America. The leaves of this species are grey-green, tough, thick and fiercely edged with spines. They may reach up to 1.5m (5ft) or more in length on mature specimens but rarely exceed 1m (3¼ft) on containerised plants. The leaves end in a very sharp brown terminal spine. On more mature specimens, the leaves curve upward and away from the centre of the rosette in a particularly graceful manner for such a ferocious plant. The flower spikes resemble telegraph poles. There are several forms of this species with variegated leaves margined, or with the centre marked with creamy yellow or silvery white, and these make striking focal points when grown in containers.

Other smaller species of *Agave* worth trying are *A. filifera*, which has

numerous upward-curving narrow bright green leaves from which wispy strands peel along the margin. These, too, are viciously spine-tipped. The rosettes reach around 70cm (28in) in diameter but are usually smaller. *A. attenuata* is a softer individual with pale green leaves borne in large rosettes which develop a stem over time. The leaves usually lack spines. There are many other species of *Agave*, all of which will enjoy the same free-draining JI3 and extra grit soil mixture. They need moderate watering in summer and require none at all in winter, when they should be kept cool and in a dry atmosphere. Like most succulents, *Agave* species require full sun and will grow weak and spindly in shade, when they will become susceptible to rot. Propagate in spring from the offsets that are produced in abundance at the base of most species.

Flowering *Agave* at Tresco, Isles of Scilly

Aloe
(aloe).
Asphodelaceae
(asphodel family)

From Africa, species of *Aloe* are rosette plants that may form woody stems or remain stemless. The sap of *Aloe vera* is widely known as a cosmetic ingredient with soothing properties and has been used to treat radiation burns. The plants are moderately attractive, with thick juicy grey-green leaves sparsely rising from a short-stemmed rosette. These cluster in time to form clumps. *Aloe aristata* is a small stemless species with a rosette consisting of numerous white- spotted dark green tapering leaves. The edges of the leaves have small white spines and the tip of the leaf ends in a white whisker. The clustering rosettes may reach 20cm (8in) and consist of numerous tightly-packed leaves. In summer an occasionally branched flower spike emerges from the centre of large rosettes and will elongate to as much as 40cm (16in). Pinkish-orange tubular flowers are produced toward the top of the spike. This species is remarkably hardy if reasonably dry and well-drained in winter.

For dramatic effect in containers, *Aloe arborescens* is difficult to beat. Ultimately forming a small thicket, the rosettes both cluster and extend on woody stems. The leaves are grey green and sharply toothed along the margins. Large rosettes reach around

Aloe marlothii

40cm (16in) or more in diameter, and may produce branched spikes of tubular red flowers in spring. In dry sunny situations, the leaves can take on red tints.

Even bigger is the solitary *A. marlothii* which forms a gigantic blue-green rosette of toothy leaves to over 1m (3¼ft) in diameter. It has branching clusters of brown-yellow flowers, but they are produced only on very large plants. Younger plants nonetheless look very dramatic.

All *Aloe* species need a well-drained gritty compost and lots of sunshine. (*A. aristata* will tolerate a little shade.) They like a regular soaking when in growth during the summer, but let them dry out between waterings. In autumn bring them under cover and cease watering. Keep them cool and dry until spring, when they can be revived with a little warmth and water. Many *Aloe* species

produce offsets that can easily be removed (often with roots attached) and potted separately. Others have to be raised from seed sown in spring in warm, moist conditions.

Cacti
(prickly pear, barrel cacti).
Cactaceae
(cactus family)

There are a wide variety of cacti available, most of which are only suitable for cultivation under glass. However, some of the more robust kinds can be given a 'summer holiday' outside while the weather is warm, and a few may even be grown outside in a dry, sheltered site. The toughest cacti have got to be the various forms of *Opuntia,* many of which are frost hardy if dry. They mostly have flattened oval or cylindrical stem segments which branch to form a bushy structure. From various points over the stem segments, needle-like

Opuntia with *Yucca* at Kew

157

Opuntia santa-rita

spines emerge – many species also possess almost microscopic bristly spines which readily become detached and can be quite dangerous. Many *Opuntia* species take on purple hues to the pads during the dry winter period and can be very decorative. *O. santa-rita* is one such with (on large plants) wonderful rose-like orange-yellow flowers. Other relatively hardy

Opuntia tunicata

Opuntia species include O. *ficus-indica*, which has large, elongate blueish pads with few if any spines, and O. *erinacea* and O. *phaeacantha* that are very spiny. These mostly produce yellow flowers, but again, only on mature plants. Of the cylindrical stemmed forms, O. *tunicata* is unbelievably prickly but very decorative, as each spine is enclosed in a papery sheath. The hardiest *Opuntia* is said to be the diminutive O. *compressa*. This and other species may succeed outside if they have near perfect drainage, a sunny site, perhaps at the base of a south-facing wall, and some protection from winter rains, such as a plastic cloche or sheet.

Other forms of cacti that will do well with abundant fresh air and sun in summer include *Echinocactus grusonii*, an eventually 50–60cm (20–24in) barrel cactus with golden yellow spines, various forms of the

robust spined genus *Ferocactus* and the tall, columnar *Cleistocactus* with fine silvery spines. These are less tolerant of cold and wet than *Opuntia*, so stand them out only once all possibility of frost has passed, and ensure that they do not become excessively wet due to over-watering or heavy rainfall. All cacti need to be moved to a frost-free place for the winter in the autumn so that they dry out thoroughly before the colder weather arrives. During winter, keep them cool and dry. In spring give small amounts of water and raise the temperature a little. Growth usually starts in earnest in late spring and once summer is underway the plants can again be stood outside. Grow cacti in a well-drained compost as described for succulents in general. *Opuntia* can be propagated in spring from detached stem segments that must be allowed to dry thoroughly for at least two weeks before planting to

Cleistocactus brookei

half their depth in compost. Other species produce offsets that may be potted up separately, but many are best raised from seed sown in early spring in warm, moist conditions. Cacti can suffer from mealy bug, and the young pads of *Opuntia* may be damaged by slugs. Rotting of plants may occur in damp situations.

Carpobrotus
(Hottentot fig).
Aizoaceae
(vygie family)

A number of species in the large South African vygie family have escaped into southern coastal areas of Britain and thrive there, such is their relative hardiness. Inland, where conditions are usually colder, they may need some protection, but they will often flourish in sheltered sites in a well-drained soil in full sun. The largest of these escaped species are *Carpobrotus edulis* and C.

Naturalized vygies at Lizard Point, Cornwall, UK

acinaciformis. These are spreading sub-shrubs with dark green, three-angled finger-like leaves born at intervals on what become rather woody stems. When not in flower they are virtually indistinguishable. The former has 10cm (4in) diameter bright pink, daisy-like blooms and the latter pale yellow. Also vigorously spreading is

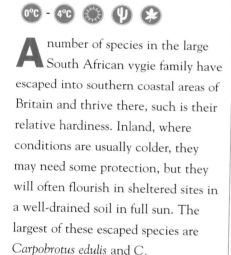

Carpobrotus edulis

Aptenia cordifolia, which has long trailing stems with small, light green fleshy heart-shaped leaves. The flowers are small and a purplish red. Various species and forms of *Lampranthus* are also sometimes available. These are shrubby plants with small greyish cylindrical leaves and very bright daisy flowers that come in pinks, oranges, reds and yellows. They are a little less hardy than their escapee relatives and require some winter protection. The bright flower colours of vygies (see also *Dorotheanthus*) make them well worth the effort to cultivate them, even if this means giving them winter protection in the greenhouse with other succulents. Most can be propagated from seed if this is available, or from cuttings of trailing stems rooted in early summer.

Crassula
(money plant).
Crassulaceae
(stonecrop family)

Crassula sarcocaulis is more or less hardy ❄ but is not especially inspiring. It forms a small, upright, much-branched shrub to 25cm (10in) which bears small cylindrical mid-green leaves and, in spring and summer, numerous tiny pinkish flowers barely 3mm (⅛in) in diameter. Much more interesting are the tender forms which come in all shapes and sizes. Best known is

Crassula ovata

Crassula ovata, commonly known as the money plant. This ultimately forms a shrub to 1.2m (4ft), but is usually smaller in containers. It has thick stems which bear pairs of oval leaves around 3cm (1⅛in) in length which are a glossy dark green with a red margin. On older specimens, sprays of small white star-like flowers may be produced in winter. *Crassula arborescens* is of similar habit, but the leaves are more circular in outline, grey-blue and around 4cm (1½in) in diameter. A hybrid, C. 'Blue Bird', also has blueish leaves with a red margin, but in this form they are long and narrow. It is however free-flowering, with clusters of pinkish stars in winter. These large bush *Crassula* species are easy to care for, enjoying full sun (although they will tolerate a little shade) and good drainage. Keep them frost-free and dry in winter. All are easily propagated from detached leaves (sending out roots if simply laid on moist compost), and by short cuttings (left for a week to dry before insertion into compost). The plants may suffer from mealy bug in dry conditions.

Dorotheanthus
(Livingstone daisy, vygie).
Aizoaceae
(vygie family)

These are pretty annual vygies that need protection from frost. They have spoon-shaped leaves which appear to have a fine crystalline, sugar-like coating. Being desert succulents, they grow rapidly from seed sown in spring in moist conditions and can be in bloom a month after sowing. Although they are usually available in mixed colours of pink, white, yellow, buff orange and purple, it is now possible to get single colour variants of *Dorotheanthus bellidiformis* such as 'Lunette' – yellow with a red centre. Other spreading daisy-like annuals include *D. gramineus*, with narrow leaves and bicoloured pink and white flowers. The flowers of these, like other vygies, open fully only in bright sunshine.

Similar in habit, but unrelated, are the various forms of *Portulaca grandiflora* (Portulacaceae) with their variously coloured 3cm (1in) blooms in red, yellow, white and purple. All of these plants will succeed in poor, dry, sunny conditions where other annuals might struggle.

Echeveria
(echeveria).
Crassulaceae
(stonecrop family)

Species of North American and Mexican *Echeveria* are small rosette plants with often tightly-packed grey-green or grey-blue leaves which individually are spoon-shaped, often ending in a pointed tip. *Echeveria secunda* var. *glauca* is commonly encountered as a carpet bedding plant. It has neat rosettes up to 15cm (6in) diameter of a powdery blue-grey. In summer, flower spikes are produced from within the rosette, and these terminate in small urn-shaped red and yellow flowers. Similar but smaller is *E. derenbergii* with pale grey-green and much shorter flower spikes. There are many other species, all with interesting leaf colours and shapes. Very powdery indeed is the closely related *Dudleya farinosa* with almost pure white leaves when happy. This has rather less interesting flower

Dudleya farinosa

spikes. All *Echeveria* species require a largely dry winter rest with a little warmth (6–8°C; 42–48°F) and good light. They need good drainage and should be planted in a mixture of JI3, sharp sand and grit. In summer they are happy in the open air in full sun, where they will develop their wonderful leaf colours to the full. They may suffer from mealy bug among the old dried-up leaves and vine weevils that eat out the centres of the soft stems.

Euphorbia,

see Hardy trees and shrubs (p. 28).

Sedum
(stonecrop).
Crassulaceae
(stonecrop family)

 mostly

Sedum species are most commonly encountered as 'alpines', and there are many that fall into this category. For the exotic garden we are generally looking for something slightly larger, and there are some species that are suitable. To begin with there are ground-cover species which tend to be quite invasive. The best of these is *Sedum spurium* 'Purpurteppich', which has rosettes of wedge-shaped leaves borne on leafless, spreading, wiry stems. The leaves are a burgundy purple colour and the flowers, borne in mid-summer, are clusters of small red-pink

Sedum aizoides

stars. *Sedum stoloniferum* is similar but has bright green leaves, red stems and very pink flower clusters.

Sedum album is taller and has stems fully clothed with short, bright green, club-shaped leaves. Its flowers are white. S. 'Coral Carpet' has leaves that redden in full sunshine.

An important group of *Sedum* species are those that behave as herbaceous perennials, dying back to basal shoots each autumn. Many of

these are sometimes known as *Hylotelephium*. *Sedum spectabile* is one of the more familiar, the form usually grown being S. 'Brilliant'. This has 3cm(1¼in) long, broad grey-green leaves borne on upright stems to 50cm (20in) which terminate in late summer with spreading clusters of bright pink flowers much loved by butterflies. S. 'Autumn Joy' is similar, but the leaves are a darker green and slightly more toothed, and the flowers are a darker pink. S. 'Iceberg' has grey white flowers. *Sedum telephium* 'Atropurpurium' is a more robust plant, with large purple-green leaves borne in opposite pairs on red-purple stems and with cream-pink flower clusters. *Sedum* 'Matrona' is similar and very robust. Smaller herbaceous forms include S. *aizoides* (30cm; 12in) with bright green narrow leaves and clusters of yellow flowers, and S. *cauticola* 'Bertrand Anderson' with small grey-purple leaves and similar coloured flowers on trailing stems.

Sedum 'Matrona'

Rather different is *Sedum dendroideum* subsp. *prealtum* . This is a vigorous shrubby sedum that seems to be remarkably hardy, surviving quite hard frosts if dry at the roots. It thrives at the base of south-facing walls and can become quite large (up to 60cm; 2ft). The whole plant is bright green with glossy lance-shaped leaves. Occasionally it will produce loose clusters of small yellow star-like flowers. Another small *Sedum*-like plant is *Chiastophyllum oppositifolium*. This has rounded dark green leaves with a scalloped edge. In late spring it produces arching spikes to 10cm (4in) covered in bright yellow tiny bell-like flowers It is happier with some shade. There is a number of non-hardy species of *Sedum* with colourful leaves, such as the blue *Sedum pachyphyllum* and pink *S. rubrotinctum* 'Aurora', which are very pretty if grown in clay pots and allowed to hang over the sides as they grow. All of the tender species can be over-wintered in a cold, dry but frost-free place and stood outside in summer in a sunny place to enjoy the warmth.

Propagation of *Sedum* is especially easy as most parts that break off will root – in some cases even individual leaves. *Sedum album* and *S. spurium* may seed around, and birds will happily distribute bits for you, so keep a check on their spread. Divide the herbaceous species in spring as growth begins or root cuttings of non-flowering stems in summer. The larger herbaceous *Sedum* species may suffer from botrytis in a wet winter and can also be attacked by vine weevil. Tender *Sedum* species may become infested with mealy bug.

Sempervivum
(houseleek).
Crassulaceae
(stonecrop family)

Houseleek is but one of an enormous number of vernacular names applied to the genus *Sempervivum*, which in Latin means 'living for ever'. These plants all form tight rosettes of triangular fleshy leaves up to 12cm (5in) in diameter, each leaf often with bristly margins and a terminal bristle. Daisy-like flowers in pale pink or yellow are borne in clusters produced on a spike formed by the upward extension of a rosette, mostly in summer. A flowered rosette usually dies, but most houseleeks produce abundant offsets, so an entire colony is rarely lost to bloom. *Sempervivum tectorum* is one of the more common species, with light green leaves, often with a purple tint. *S. calcaratum* has blueish leaves with maroon tips. *S. arachnoideum* is small, with rosettes only 2–5cm (¾–2in) in diameter. It has very long leaf bristles which become entangled in a cobweb-like surface covering to each rosette. There are numerous named forms and hybrids, of which 'Commander Hay' is one of the best. This is a large rosette type, its reddish leaves having green tips. All species and forms like full sun in a well-drained but reasonably fertile soil. The addition of a little peat substitute helps their fine roots penetrate the soil and retains enough moisture to keep the rosettes large. They need little protection in winter but may suffer in wet and icy winters, when a protective sheet of polythene will help to keep them dry. Propagate by detaching rooted offsets. They can be prone to attack from vine weevil.

Sempervivum calcaratum

Ferns

Ferns are essential in the tropical-style garden where their large fronds consisting of numerous leaflets are evocative of warm, moist jungles. Fortunately there is a number of large-leaved hardy ferns available, as well as the semi-hardy tree ferns, and these have the advantage of being evergreen in sheltered areas. Most ferns require shady sites and a moist, humus-rich soil. Some forms will grow in full sun, provided that they have ample watering and protection from drying winds. Most forms have wiry roots that emerge from robust rhizomes, but in tree ferns these roots emerge from just below the growing point and head straight down through the mass of former leaf bases toward the soil. Over time these roots form the bulk of a tree fern trunk. Such trunks are therefore living structures and, in order to flourish, both they and the soil in which they are growing need to be kept moist. Other ferns, such as *Osmunda*, enjoy quite wet soils, and some are floating aquatics. Ferns are largely foliage plants since they do not produce flowers. Instead they produce spores from various parts of their leaves – commonly the undersides of fronds, but occasionally on modified leaves, as in *Matteuccia*, the ostrich fern.

Unfurling fronds of *Dicksonia antarctica*, a moderately hardy tree fern

Asplenium
(spleenwort).
Aspleniaceae
(spleenwort family)

 some

This is a large genus of ferns with a great diversity of foliage forms. *Asplenium bulbiferum* from Australia and New Zealand is a large, mound-forming species with leaves to over 1m (3¼ft) in length. They consist of thousands of small leaflets of a mid-to dark green colour. Small plantlets develop from the main veins of the fronds. Once of a reasonable size, these can be detached and provide a good method of propagation. The plants require a sheltered position in humus-rich soil, preferably of a neutral or acid nature. *Asplenium scolopendrium* is a widespread, smaller fern that could

Asplenium scolopendrium

hardly be more different in appearance, since the deciduous leaves are solid and do not consist of leaflets as in most ferns. Formerly known as *Phyllitis scolopendrium*, this hardy species resembles to some extent the tropical birds-nest ferns (e.g. *Asplenium nidus*) that live on tree branches. It is, however, a terrestrial fern which enjoys a slightly alkaline soil and will thrive in moist cracks in walls and on damp, shady banks. The leaves are tongue-shaped and elongate, reaching up to 30cm (12in). There are numerous forms, some of which have divided leaves while others have strongly undulating margins. A. *trichomanes* is a smaller, mostly evergreen species which enjoys shady sites amongst rocks. It has branched, dark green, lacy fronds with the leaflets borne on thin stalks. Most species of *Asplenium* can be propagated by division of the rhizomes in spring.

Asplenium bulbiferum

Athyrium
(lady ferns).
Athyriaceae
(lady fern family)

These are all lovely, easily grown deciduous ferns tolerant of many situations: indeed, most will tolerate sunny, periodically dry sites. The cosmopolitan *Athyrium felix-femina*

Athyrium felix-femina form

Athyrium niponicum 'Pictum'

a pond surface. In autumn and winter the plants take on a red/bronze colour, after which you will find that they begin to die away.

Usually some parts will survive the winter, and in warm areas they will also regenerate from spores. Where winters are cold, small quantities can be over-wintered in a frost-free place, in a plastic bucket full of water.

produces pale, yellow-green arching leaves in a tight shuttlecock shape. They have a strong 'ferny' smell if brushed. There are variously plumed and crested forms of this species, most of which, to my mind, resemble parsley. Very good for leaf colour is A. *niponicum* 'Pictum' from Japan, its small, beautifully marbled leaves having silvery grey and sometimes purple hints. All grow happily in a humus-rich soil and can be propagated from portions of detached rhizome, each with a crown.

of branching stems clothed on the upper surface with tiny (1–2mm; $\frac{1}{32}$–$\frac{5}{64}$in) wedge-shaped leaves of a grey-green colour. Hair-like structures hang from beneath, supplying nutrients from the water. As the clusters enlarge they break up, forming new clusters, and in this way they can rapidly and densely colonise

Azolla
(fairy moss).
Salviniaceae
(Kariba weed family)

Azolla filiculoides

Blechnum
(hard fern).
Blechnaceae
(hard fern family)

 mostly

There are two species of these acid-loving ferns suitable for the exotic garden. *Blechnum spicant* (hard fern) is a widespread temperate species that is fully hardy. It forms small spreading clumps of fronds. The

Certainly one of the strangest of all ferns is *Azolla*. The principal species is the North American *Azolla filiculoides*, which forms small clusters

Blechnum tabulare

leaves are simple, with the leaflets borne along a single midrib. They are robust, dark green in colour, and can reach 0.5m (1½ft) on large plants. Much bigger is *B. tabulare*, with broad pinnate fronds to 75cm (30in) in length, of a dark green colour and a very leathery texture. It is widespread in the southern hemisphere. It gradually forms large clumps spreading by underground rhizomes. This species will tolerate some sunshine provided that it is in a deep, moist soil, perhaps by water where it looks well with *Osmunda* and *Lysichiton*. *B. gibbum* is a tender species sometimes available. It is a short-stemmed tree fern with long, pinnate, mid-green leaves. It can comfortably occupy a shady place in the garden in the summer months. All species of *Blechnum* produce their spores on leaves that have been modified purely for this purpose. Generally, spore-bearing leaves (which usually have

little green material) are produced after the main flush of new leaves, and they are commonly more erect than the normal foliage.

Cyathea
(tree fern).
Cyatheaceae
(tree fern family)

These tree ferns are generally not as hardy as *Dicksonia*, but some can survive in sheltered sites and all are suitable for cultivation in containers of humus-rich compost. Most spectacular is the black tree fern. This has enormous branched fronds to 5m (16ft) – usually much less in containers – of a mid-green colour and consisting of thousands of small, pointed leaflets. The leaves are supported on massive petioles that are black and scaly. *C. brownii* is said to

be slightly more hardy. It has brown, scaly petioles and light green leaves. Although ultimately reaching 5m (16ft) or more in height, these tree ferns are very slow-growing. They produce less rooting structures around their stems than other tree ferns, but still appreciate moist trunks and humidity at all times. They are best propagated from spores, but this is a slow process, taking many years to produce a specimen plant.

Dicksonia
(woolly tree fern).
Dicksoniaceae
(woolly tree fern family).

Dicksonia antarctica is the toughest of tree ferns and will survive most winters outside, requiring protection only in the colder sites in Britain. However, in

Cyathea medullaris

Dicksonia antarctica at Heligan, Cornwall, UK

view of the value of larger specimens, you may wish to lavish a little extra winter protection on these spectacular plants. They require some shade and a moist, fertile soil but also (and of more importance) a sheltered site in which the local humidity tends to be high. This means avoiding windy or very sunny positions. Planting them on a slope helps to protect them from frosts in winter, when they should have their crowns protected by wrapping in straw or dead fronds, perhaps also covered with a plastic sheet. If grown in containers (of JI2 and peat substitute) it is best to take them under cover where they can be kept just frost-free. In summer, water and feed the plants regularly but ensure that the soil does not become waterlogged. Spray the trunks frequently with soft water, especially

in dry and windy weather. *D. squarrosa* is also quite hardy and may be worth trying in sheltered localities, but it is so similar to *D. antarctica* that there seems little point. The plants can be propagated from very occasional offsets or spores.

Dryopteris
(buckler fern).
Aspleniaceae
(spleenwort family)

 -

A large genus of more or less hardy ferns with large, decorative leaves. Probably the most robust of all garden ferns is *Dryopteris felix-mas* (male fern) which is extremely tolerant of all manner of conditions, including relatively dry and sunny sites. It forms a large upright dark green cluster of leaves arising from the base in the form of a shuttlecock. The thick rhizomes are creeping at, or just below, soil level. New, bright green fronds emerge in late spring, unfurling from rust-brown hairy crosiers. The leaves remain green well into autumn in sheltered sites.

Dryopteris wallichiana is a large fern with leaves somewhat similar to those of *D. felix-mas*, although they tend to remain a more olive green in colour. This is a most attractive fern in late spring, as the crosiers are covered in abundant long black hairs. This almost evergreen fern requires a more sheltered position than its relatives and is less tolerant of bright sunshine.

Dryopteris felix-mas at How Caple Manor, Herefordshire, UK

Dryopteris erythrosora is smaller. Its leaves unfurl an interesting copper-bronze in colour and gradually turn green as the summer progresses. Other species worth acquiring are *D. affinis*, *D. dilitata* and the many variants of these, and *D. felix-mas*. Generally, *Dryopteris* prefer semi-shade and loamy soil with some extra leaf mould and moderate drainage. They can be divided when overcrowded by separation of the branching rhizomes.

Equisetum
(horsetail).
Eqisetaceae
(horsetail family)

These are pernicious deciduous weeds and can be a major problem if allowed to escape. Some species, however, are reasonably well behaved and find a place in the tropical-style garden for their upright reedy stems. *Equisetum telmateia* is a widespread horsetail which grows

Equisetum telmateia

happily in moist soils in semi-shade or sun. The stems may reach 1m (3¼ft) in height. At intervals they produce encircling rings of wiry green stems. These plants are only distantly related to ferns and produce spores in cone like structures rather than on leaves. The cones of *E. telmateia* are borne on short stems in early spring. *E. telmateia* can be difficult to establish, as it tends to grow close to natural springs but not actually in water. If you can recreate these conditions it should be happy. Also of interest is *E. hyemale* which is a good plant for wet soils or at the margins of ponds. The stems reach 1m (3¼ft) or more in height and have very little in the way of subsidiary rings of stems. The cones are borne terminally on stems in summer. There are several smaller species that are perhaps best contained in pots from which escape can be prevented.

Matteuccia
(ostrich fern).
Aspleniaceae
(spleenwort family)

The widespread *Matteuccia struthiopteris* forms spectacular bright green shuttlecocks in spring, composed of erect fronds reaching

Matteuccia struthiopteris

Osmunda regalis with brown spore-producing fronds

over 1m (3¼ft) in length in favourable conditions. These gradually arch as they mature and as the brown spore-bearing fronds emerge from the centre of the structure. *Matteuccia* can be quite invasive when happy, as the plants readily spread by underground runners. They like semi-shade or full shade and do not like drying wind, so put them where they will receive some shelter. In winter the spore-bearing leaves remain but the others will wither. Propagate from the young plants formed at the end of runners in early spring.

Osmunda
(royal fern).
Osmundaceae
(royal fern family)

These large ferns are essentials for moist or wet, neutral or acidic areas of the exotic garden as they alone come close to the size of some of the tropical ferns. The widespread *Osmunda regalis* is the most common species. This produces erect to arching leaves that can reach 2m (6½ft) in length and are moderately branched. The more or less linear leaflets are large (up to 4cm; 1½in long) and are a light to mid-green in colour. The plants gradually form tight, raised clumps from which small portions can be removed in early spring for propagation. Spores – produced on modified (brownish) upper parts of normal leaves or on purely spore-bearing leaves – are interesting in being bright green. O. *regalis* 'Purpurascens' has purple tints to the foliage in spring. O. *cinnamomea* from North America is similar to O. *regalis* but is generally smaller with more blue-green leaves.

Phanerophlebia
(large-leaved holly fern).
Aspleniaceae
(spleenwort family)

From Japan, *Phanerophlebia falcatum* (also known as *Cyrtomium falcatum*) is a small fern with a spread of about 0.5m (1½ft), and less than this in height, but it is worthy of a place because of its large, holly-like leaflets arranged along the midrib of each arching leaf. Leaves are borne in clusters from an underground rhizome and are more or less evergreen in sheltered areas. This fern is a slightly more tender

Polypodium vulgare

Polystichum setiferum form

than some and it certainly requires a little winter protection – perhaps nothing more than a bracken covering directly over the rhizome. Divide the clumps in early spring.

Polypodium
(polypody).
Polypodiaceae
(polypody family)

This is a very widespread group of small spreading ferns, many of which are able to grow on tree trunks and rocks where they are subject to short periods of drought. As a result they make good plants for hanging baskets and other similar containers. The cosmopolitan *Polypodium vulgare* is readily available and has many subspecies, forms and close relatives which are difficult to distinguish (e.g. *P. cambricum*, *P. interjectum* and *P. australe*). The species has a simple,

somewhat leathery pinnate leaf with leaflets reaching around 3cm (1in). They are a bright to dark green. The plant is winter evergreen but may become leafless for a short time in summer. The North American *P. glycyrrhiza* is similar but with more pointed leaflets. Easily grown in moist soils in shade or part shade. Propagate from portions of rhizome with roots and shoots in early summer.

Polystichum
(shield fern).
Aspleniaceae
(spleenwort family)

There are a number of species of *Polystichum*, all of which are splendid ferns, but my favourite is *P. setiferum* and, in particular, the forms with very finely divided leaflets. These are wonderful soft, lacy ferns that also have a robust but airy quality and the advantage of complete hardiness. *P. setiferum* Divisilobum Group have pointed, highly divided leaves consisting of thousands of tiny pointed leaflets while the Plumosodivisilobum and Plumosomultilobum Groups have a further division of the leaflets which tends to give a three-dimensional, mossy appearance to the leaves. In my view both these latter forms have excessively complicated leaves and names. The best advice is probably to try them and see if you like them. Some of these plants can produce quite large leaves, up to 0.5m (1½ft) and will form good shuttlecock shapes if the branching rhizomes are not too crowded. Even larger is *P. munitum* from North America, which in

favourable conditions will produce less complicated leaves of nearly 1m (3¼ft) in length. Grow these lovely semi-evergreen plants in semi-shade in moist soil in a reasonably sheltered site, and avoid excessive wet in winter. Divide established clumps in spring or peg down older leaves that show bulbils or young plantlets so that they can root.

Salvinia
(Kariba weed).
Salviniaceae
(Kariba weed family)

These tender floating aquatic ferns are pretty colonizers of the water surface in the summer months but

will be killed by winter ice and frosts. They form spreading patches of floating stems clothed with oval grey-green or yellow-green leaves apparently folded down the middle and covered in curved, water-repellent hairs. Root-like modified leaves hang beneath. There are two species: *Salvinia auriculata* with 4cm (1½in) leaves and *S. natans* with 2cm (¾in) leaves. Both can easily be over-wintered in a frost-free greenhouse in shallow trays of water with a little sandy soil at the base.

Woodwardia
(chain fern).
Blechnaceae
(hard fern family)

There are several species of these big, more or less evergreen, arching ferns, all of which are best in mild areas and in shade in a humus-rich, neutral soil.

Woodwardia radicans from Madeira and other Atlantic islands bears large branching fronds to 2m (6½ft) in length which are a pleasing dark green in colour. *W. unigemmata* is similar, but has reddish young fronds. These are large ferns that need room to spread but are excellent beneath trees as ground cover. Sometimes they produce young plants towards the tips of the leaves that can be used for propagation. Otherwise, clumps may be divided in spring.

Woodwardia radicans

Water plants and lovers of wet soils

The majority of water plants are herbaceous perennials that may live in deep water with surface floating leaves, shallow water with emergent foliage, or damp marginal soils. A few plants are poorly rooted or are entirely floating at the surface or just beneath. The diversity of plant types is such that these specialists present as much architectural variety as their drier relatives. Some plants that are often included as water plants have been described elsewhere in this work and include *Azolla, Cyperus, Glyceria, Gunnera, Houttuynia, Iris, Juncus, Ligularia, Lysichiton, Orontium, Osmunda, Petasites, Rumex, Salvinia, Thalia* and *Zantedeschia*. What remains, however, is a selection of marginal plants and aquatics with bold leaves and sometimes exotic flowers. Water is, in my view, essential to the tropical-style garden, and it matters not whether this is a still pond or a trickling stream. Water brings life into a garden and not just in terms of its ambience. Many additional kinds of insect and animal will frequent your garden if it contains accessible water. Dragonflies, for example, are as exotic as humming birds, while frogs, especially at night, can even add tropical sounds. Marginal vegetation is naturally lush as a result of abundant soil moisture and consists of plants with some of the largest leaves we can produce in temperate climes. Don't miss out on this luxuriant display.

Water in a garden is certain to attract a diversity of wildlife

Tree ferns by water at Heligan, Cornwall, UK

Aponogeton
(water hawthorn).
Aponogetonaceae
(water hawthorn family)

Aponogeton distachyos is a lovely plant from southern Africa and is hardy if it is planted in mud in around 80cm (30in) depth of water. The 25cm (10in) elongate, oval, mid-green leaves are reddish as they emerge through the water surface and uncurl to lie flat. The flowers are particularly unusual in being borne on a pair of unfurling spikes that may reach 6cm (2½in) in length: the pair are joined at the water surface where they float. Each spike produces a series of white, sometimes pink-tinged, flowers with no particular form to them. They do, however, have a strong scent so try to grow the plant where its perfume can reach a seating area or path. The flowers are borne in early spring to early summer and the leaves appear at around the same time but tend to diminish for the remainder of the year. The plants are vigorous and in warm places will seed abundantly-and may therefore become a problem.

Caltha
(kingcup).
Ranunculaceae
(buttercup family)

Caltha palustris is a pretty plant for the margins of a pond or for very shallow water. It has rounded dark green leaves of about 15cm (6in) diameter borne on 30cm (12in) petioles from mid-spring to late summer. In early to mid-spring branching clusters of yellow, buttercup-like flowers expand above the developing foliage. There is a double-flowered form with the sole advantage of having longer-lasting blooms. Best of all is the North American C. palustris var. palustris (C. polypetala) which is larger in all its parts and can have purple tints to the older leaves, especially in full sun – which all forms of the plant enjoy. Easily grown and valuable for their early flowers, Caltha species are propagated by rhizome division in early spring, or from seed sown on moist soil as soon as available.

Caltha palustris

Aponogeton distachyos

Eichhornia
(water hyacinth).
Pontederiaceae
(pickerel weed family)

One of the worst tropical weeds, this floating aquatic can have a truly alarming growth rate, and its cultivation in many places is illegal. In temperate climates it is safe, as our cooler temperatures reduce its growth rate, while frosts in winter kill the plants. *Eichhornia crassipes* is a floating plant that achieves this by means of its inflated petioles upon which are borne large bright green kidney-shaped leaves around 10cm (4in) wide. When growing very rapidly or in shade, the leaves may become more elongate. Greyish rooting filaments hang from beneath the plant, and these may become anchored in shallow water. In warm areas, hyacinth-like flower spikes are produced consisting of lavender-blue short-lived blooms. The flowers have a yellow eye and markings on the upper petals. Once all frosts have passed, plants can be simply floated on sunny ponds, where they will spread across the surface during the summer by means of the numerous offsets they produce. A few plants can be kept through the winter in a container of wet mud or shallow water (6–10cm; 2½–4in depth) over mud in a bright, warm place.

A plant of similar requirements and similar invasiveness is the water lettuce (*Pistia stratiotes*, Araceae), which is a floating rosette aroid with broad velvety pale green (15cm; 6in) leaves that have strong radial veins. It has insignificant flowers, but is a better choice for a slightly shaded pond.

Hippuris
(mare's tail)
Hippuridaceae
(mare's tail family)

An elegant shallow water plant rather like a horse-tail (*Equisetum*) but much less invasive. *Hippuris vulgaris* is a cosmopolitan hardy plant that produces annual erect, hollow stems clothed in rings of dark green linear leaves. The flowers are inconspicuous. Stems arise from rhizomes or runners and many will grow submerged where they produce larger, paler leaves.

The plant provides an excellent contrast to the upright linear stems of *Iris* or *Typha* and against the bold foliage of *Lysichiton* or *Pontederia*. Propagation is easy from fragments of rhizome rooted in water.

Myriophyllum
(parrot's feather).
Haloragidaceae
(water milfoil family)

The various species of *Myriophyllum* are mostly submerged aquatics with rings of ferny foliage. Many are fully hardy and make good oxygenating plants where fish are kept. One species, however, is an emergent plant, often supported purely by its highly water-repellent grey-green ferny foliage borne in rings along sparsely-branched stems. The South American *Myriophyllum aquaticum* (*M. proserpinacoides*), may in time creep onto dry land. Flowers are inconspicuous, but this is of no consequence against the wonderful silvery shoots. The plant will survive

Myriophyllum aquaticum

173

most winters, especially as submerged portions, so ensure that plenty of rooted shoots exist well down in the water before the onset of winter. Exposed and creeping shoots rarely survive except in mild climates. Propagation is by rooting of lengths of shoot in water.

Nymphaea
(water lily).
Nymphaeaceae
(water lily family)

No area of still water would be complete without water lilies. They come in all sizes and virtually all colours, especially if you can find the space to over-winter some of the tender varieties. Most hardy water lilies have almost circular floating leaves that range from a few centimetres to half a metre or more. They may be reddish or marked with various red or purple spots. The generally floating flowers are also

Nymphaea odorata 'Minor'

Nymphaea 'James Brydon'

varied in size but are usually in proportion to the leaf. They consist of numerous rounded or pointed petals surrounding a central mass of stamens and stigmas. Most last for 3–4 days and close at night. Flowers are produced on mature plants from early summer to autumn, although some forms have a more restricted flowering period. All water lilies need abundant sunshine to flower well, but many will produce exuberant foliage in part shade. Water lilies need a good depth of mud in which to grow well and need to be planted at the right depth for the size of plant. Generally, the smaller the leaf, the shallower the water depth required: between 4 and 6 times the leaf diameter is usually a rough guide to depth. If you purchase a more or less leafless water lily (usually in spring), plant it in a basket at a shallow depth until its size becomes clear during the first summer. Reposition when necessary.

Remember, too, that most water lilies spread their leaves over the surface and need an area of clear water of a diameter roughly equivalent to twice the depth at which they are planted. Most forms lose most of their leaves in winter and are often late to surface in spring if the water is cold. Mature plants can be propagated by removal of rooted parts of the large rhizomes, each with an active growing point. This is best achieved in early summer.

There are hundreds of varieties of water lily, and listing all but a few is impossible. Small water lilies make good water-filled tub plants providing these are deep enough and have some protection in winter. *Nymphaea tetragonal* 'Helvola' is a dwarf, pale yellow-flowered form, with leaves of around 10cm (4in) diameter. It is happy in shallow water but is not as hardy as the slightly larger, white, scented-flowered *N. odorata* 'Minor'. This latter form can be shy-flowering until established. Larger are 'Chromatella' (pale lemon yellow), 'Escarboucle' (pink-red) and 'James Brydon' (deep pink), all with leaves around 20cm (8in) in diameter. They are all good for the smaller pond or pool. For large areas, try the giants such as 'Attraction' (purple-red flowers and bronzed leaves) or *Nymphaea alba*, with creamy white flowers and green leaves to 30cm (12in). You could also try the related genus *Nuphar lutea* and *N. advena* (brandy bottles) that have leaves to 40cm (16in) but smaller, buttercup-like flowers of orange-yellow.

Pontederia
(pickerel weed).
Pontederiaceae
(pickerel weed family)

Pontederia cordata is an essential for any tropical effect. The plant bears paddle-shaped leathery leaves around 15cm (6in) in length held vertically on broad, succulent stems around 40cm (16in) in length which arise from underwater rhizomes. Leaves and stems are bright, glossy green with paler veining. Short flower spikes emerge from the junction of leaf and stem on leaves produced later in the year. The small blue flowers (with yellow centres) are borne tightly within the spike, and although they only last a day many open in succession over a week or so.

Pontederia cordata

white-flowered and dwarf forms occur. Plants require water above the rhizomes and grow best at a depth of 10–15 cm (4–6in). Being particularly hardy, *Pontederia* will thrive in tubs of water provided that the rhizomes remain submerged in winter when all top growth is lost.

To flower well *Pontederia* requires full sun and warm summer water, and for the latter reason it often blooms well in containers. Propagate them by division of the rhizomes in spring as growth begins. Slugs, alas, may be troublesome if they are able to reach the leaves.

Sagittaria
(arrowhead).
Alismataceae
(water plantain family)

Sagittaria latifolia (from North America) and *S. sagittifolia* (from Europe and Asia) are hardy herbaceous plants which tend to spread around a pond area by means of floating spongy tubers, most commonly seen in early spring. They are the inevitable method of propagation for gardeners, too. Plants will grow in shallow water or as marginals in wet ground. The arrow-shaped leaves arise on petioles to around 70cm (28in), and from a cluster of these leaves a taller spike of small white flowers is produced in summer. The flowers are in sparsely distributed clusters that open for at

most a few days. These plants are well worth cultivating for their minimal requirements and for their lush foliage of an exotic shape.

Sparganium
(bur reed).
Sparganiaceae
(bur reed family)

The bur reeds are hardy, vigorous marginal plants that will happily grow in shallow water in a sunny position. *Sparganium erectum* is the largest, and produces tall, linear keeled leaves to 1.5m (5ft) from a spreading basal rhizome. The leaves are mid-green in colour and similar to those of *Typha*. The flower spikes branch and bear green-brown rounded flower clusters followed by prickly fruits. Although relatively

Sparganium erectum

175

subdued, they are interesting plants that are not often seen. They combine well with *Osmunda* and larger plants such as *Gunnera*. Propagate them by division of the rhizomes in spring as soon as growth starts.

Stratiotes
(water soldier).
Hydrocharitaceae
(frogbit family)

Stratiotes aloides is a strange plant, looking much like a bromeliad but mostly submerged. The linear leaves form brittle olive green or reddish rosettes. Each leaf is strongly veined and bears remarkably prickly spines along the edge. The rosettes produce a few insignificant roots but are mostly floating plants. In early summer they tend to rise to the surface where white, three-petalled flowers are borne just above the water surface. Each lasts only a couple of days. Rosettes produce basal offsets on short stalks that readily snap off to form new plants. In this way they may quickly colonise a small volume of water. *Stratiotes* likes a good depth of water, as it over-winters at the bottom beneath any ice that may form.

Typha
(reedmace).
Typhaceae
(reedmace family)

The reedmace is sometimes wrongly called bulrush (probably a species of *Scirpus*). There are three species commonly available, all of which like plenty of sunshine. *Typha minima* is a delicate, spreading grassy plant only 30–40cm (12–16in) in height and bearing spherical brown flower heads 1–2cm (⅜–¾in) in length in summer. It likes very shallow water or even wet soil, where it can be invasive. It is probably a little insignificant for the tropical-style, but grow it if you like it. Much better is

Typha latifolia

Typha angustifolia, which has tape-like leaves to 1m (3¼ft) in length. In summer it produces narrow (15cm; 6in) spikes of brown flowers, often with a yellowish tip. The arching leaves are particularly effective against large leaves such as *Gunnera* or *Lysichiton*. It will grow in wet soil or in water of up to 10cm (4in) depth. It is a rampant spreader, producing branching rhizomes from which it may be propagated as growth begins in spring. A variegated form is very decorative and a little less vigorous. *Typha latifolia* is bigger still, reaching 2m (6½ft) in height when in flower. It is very grand, with broader, iris-like leaves, but is probably too big and invasive for most gardens. However, if you have room, why not try it? *T. latifolia* prefers a depth of water over the rhizomes, and 15cm (6in) is quite adequate. To be at its best it requires quite a depth of soil beneath the water, largely for roots to support the top growth.

Stratiotes aloides

Glossary

Bract: A leaf-like structure found adjacent to flowers. It is usually green, but in some plants (such as *Bougainvillea*) the bracts are coloured and they can be brighter than the actual flowers.

Compound leaves: Leaves made up of a number of separate leaflets. The leaflets may all link to a single point (compound palmate) or may arise along a stem-like petiole (pinnate compound). *Fraxinus* (ash) leaves are a typical example of pinnate compound leaves, while the leaves of *Aesculus* (horse chestnut) are palmate compound.

Epiphyte: A plant that grows entirely supported by another plant without harming the host. Epiphytes are not rooted in the soil, but gain their nutrients from decomposing leaf material and rain water that collects in their immediate vicinity. Many of the bromeliads, ferns and orchids are epiphytes.

Palmate: An arrangement of leaves or leaf parts in which the component parts radiate from a single point. A typical palmate leaf is that of *Trachycarpus*, the Chusan palm, although the term is not restricted solely to palms.

Peltate: Leaves that are attached to their petioles in the centre of the leaf rather than at one end, somewhat like an umbrella. A typical example would be *Tropaeolum majus*.

Petioles: The stem-like structure that links a leaf to the main stem or branch. Petioles may support numerous leaflets in a compound leaf (e.g. in *Juglans*). In some cases petioles clasp the stems forming a sheath as in the grasses.

Photosynthesis: The process by which plants use water, carbon dioxide and light energy to make sugars.

Bougainvillea is typical of plants with colourful bracts

The leaves of *Phoenix* palms and cycads are pinnate

Stratification: Some seeds will not germinate unless they have been exposed to a period of cold. Stratification is the process by which seeds are exposed to cold winter weather (or two months in the fridge!) and then given warmth to encourage germination.

Symbiont: An organism that lives in close association with another such that both gain a benefit from the relationship. Some *Yucca* species are symbiotic with certain bats. The *Yucca* is pollinated by the bats and the bats feed on nectar from the *Yucca* flowers.

Trifoliate: Compound leaves with only three leaflets, two at the sides and one at the end. Clover (*Trifolium*) is a typical example. **Ternate** is a comparable term.

Pinnate: An arrangement of leaves or leaf parts in which the component parts occur along a main vein, midrib or stem-like petiole. A typical example of a pinnate leaf is that of *Sophora* or *Galega*.

Sepals: Often enclosing the petals when in bud, sepals are the outer or lower part of a flower, commonly green, but sometimes coloured as in buttercups (*Ranunculus*)

Stamens: The male parts of a flower. They usually consist of the anther (the part that produces pollen) and a stalk-like filament upon which the anthers are borne.

Stigma: Part of the female component of a flower adapted for the collection of pollen. It usually occurs in the centre of a flower and it may be variously feathered or lobed.

The flowers of *Cleome* have prominent stamens

Acknowledgements

Thanks are due to my many friends in Cardiff and elsewhere who have encouraged me to complete this book. Thanks especially to Philip Bidwell and Angela Hort for reading the drafts, to my parents for continuing support, and to all those who have taught me the botany that I know and now have the privilege of passing on to others. Thanks must also go to Ina Stradins for my training in plant photography and to staff at GMC Publications for having confidence in my ability to produce what I hope is an interesting and useful book.

About the Author

Born in 1963, Alan Hemsley developed a fascination for plants at an early age, and his passion for collecting British species of grasses had to be deterred by his parents to avoid conflict with his early education. Through school in Quorn, Leicestershire, he specialized in science, with an emphasis on biology, but it was at London University that he discovered a predisposition for systematic botany and plant taxonomy. As part of his degree studies he was introduced to the fossil history of plants and the evolution of their reproductive mechanisms, a subject in which he was later to become an authority.

Following his first degree, Alan took up the position of garden centre manager with a local DIY superstore, where he became aware of a public interest in exotic and architectural plants, but his interest in systematic botany led him back to university after only a year in retailing. After taking a masters degree in plant taxonomy at Reading University and a doctorate at London University (studying fossil spores from ferns and related plants) Alan moved to Montepellier in France to undertake further research into fern reproduction. Here he also found

many exotic plants growing in exposed and relatively cold places, and it was this that led him to the view that many of them should also be hardy in Britain. While abroad he left his collection of weird and wonderful plants, including some awful-smelling aroids, with his long-suffering parents, eventually finding room for them all in his garden when he took up his present position at Cardiff University, South Wales.

In both his academic work and his gardening Alan is an experimenter, and he firmly believes in testing ideas about his extinct fossil and living exotic plants, so that many of his comments about plant hardiness are derived from personal experience.

His aim is to have a garden large enough to experiment with even more exotic-looking species, with room to propagate them such that these often rare plants can become more widely available.

Index

Pages highlighted in **bold** include illustrations of plants.

A SELECTION OF PUBLICATIONS FROM
GMC Publications
BOOKS

GARDENING

Alpine Gardening	*Chris & Valerie Wheeler*
Auriculas for Everyone: How to Grow and Show Perfect Plants	
	Mary Robinson
Beginners' Guide to Herb Gardening	*Yvonne Cuthbertson*
Beginners' Guide to Water Gardening	*Graham Clarke*
Big Leaves for Exotic Effect	*Stephen Griffith*
The Birdwatcher's Garden	*Hazel & Pamela Johnson*
Companions to Clematis: Growing Clematis with Other Plants	
	Marigold Badcock
Creating Contrast with Dark Plants	*Freya Martin*
Creating Small Habitats for Wildlife in your Garden	*Josie Briggs*
Exotics are Easy	*GMC Publications*
Gardening with Hebes	*Chris & Valerie Wheeler*
Gardening with Shrubs	*Eric Sawford*
Gardening with Wild Plants	*Julian Slatcher*
Growing Cacti and Other Succulents in the Conservatory and Indoors	*Shirley-Anne Bell*
Growing Cacti and Other Succulents in the Garden	*Shirley-Anne Bell*
Growing Successful Orchids in the Greenhouse and Conservatory	
	Mark Isaac-Williams
Hardy Palms and Palm-Like Plants	*Martyn Graham*
Hardy Perennials: A Beginner's Guide	*Eric Sawford*
Hedges: Creating Screens and Edges	*Averil Bedrich*
How to Attract Butterflies to your Garden	*John & Maureen Tampion*
Marginal Plants	*Bernard Sleeman*
Orchids are Easy: A Beginner's Guide to their Care and Cultivation	*Tom Gilland*
Plant Alert: A Garden Guide for Parents	*Catherine Collins*
Planting Plans for Your Garden	*Jenny Shukman*
Sink and Container Gardening Using Dwarf Hardy Plants	
	Chris & Valerie Wheeler
The Successful Conservatory and Growing Exotic Plants	*Joan Phelan*
Success with Cuttings	*Chris & Valerie Wheeler*
Success with Seeds	*Chris & Valerie Wheeler*
Tropical Garden Style with Hardy Plants	*Alan Hemsley*
Water Garden Projects: From Groundwork to Planting	
	Roger Sweetinburgh

PHOTOGRAPHY

Close-Up on Insects	*Robert Thompson*
Digital Enhancement for Landscape Photographers	
	Arjan Hoogendam & Herb Parkin
Double Vision	*Chris Weston & Nigel Hicks*
An Essential Guide to Bird Photography	*Steve Young*
Field Guide to Bird Photography	*Steve Young*
Field Guide to Landscape Photography	*Peter Watson*
How to Photograph Pets	*Nick Ridley*
In my Mind's Eye: Seeing in Black and White	*Charlie Waite*
Life in the Wild: A Photographer's Year	*Andy Rouse*
Light in the Landscape: A Photographer's Year	*Peter Watson*
Outdoor Photography Portfolio	*GMC Publications*
Photographers on Location with Charlie Waite	*Charlie Waite*
Photographing Fungi in the Field	*George McCarthy*
Photography for the Naturalist	*Mark Lucock*
Photojournalism: An Essential Guide	*David Herrod*
Professional Landscape and Environmental Photography: From 35mm to Large Format	*Mark Lucock*

Rangefinder	*Roger Hicks & Frances Schultz*
Underwater Photography	*Paul Kay*
Viewpoints from *Outdoor Photography*	*GMC Publications*
Where and How to Photograph Wildlife	*Peter Evans*
Wildlife Photography Workshops	*Steve & Ann Toon*

CRAFTS

Bargello: A Fresh Approach to Florentine Embroidery	*Brenda Day*
Beginning Picture Marquetry	*Lawrence Threadgold*
Blackwork: A New Approach	*Brenda Day*
Celtic Cross Stitch Designs	*Carol Phillipson*
Celtic Knotwork Designs	*Sheila Sturrock*
Celtic Knotwork Handbook	*Sheila Sturrock*
Celtic Spirals and Other Designs	*Sheila Sturrock*
Celtic Spirals Handbook	*Sheila Sturrock*
Complete Pyrography	*Stephen Poole*
Creating Made-to-Measure Knitwear: A Revolutionary Approach to Knitwear Design	*Sylvia Wynn*
Creative Backstitch	*Helen Hall*
Creative Log-Cabin Patchwork	*Pauline Brown*
Creative Machine Knitting	*GMC Publications*
The Creative Quilter: Techniques and Projects	*Pauline Brown*
Cross-Stitch Designs from China	*Carol Phillipson*
Cross-Stitch Floral Designs	*Joanne Sanderson*
Decoration on Fabric: A Sourcebook of Ideas	*Pauline Brown*
Decorative Beaded Purses	*Enid Taylor*
Designing and Making Cards	*Glennis Gilruth*
Designs for Pyrography and Other Crafts	*Norma Gregory*
Dried Flowers: A Complete Guide	*Lindy Bird*
Exotic Textiles in Needlepoint	*Stella Knight*
Glass Engraving Pattern Book	*John Everett*
Glass Painting	*Emma Sedman*
Handcrafted Rugs	*Sandra Hardy*
Hobby Ceramics: Techniques and Projects for Beginners	
	Patricia A. Waller
How to Arrange Flowers: A Japanese Approach to English Design	*Taeko Marvelly*
How to Make First-Class Cards	*Debbie Brown*
An Introduction to Crewel Embroidery	*Mave Glenny*
Machine-Knitted Babywear	*Christine Eames*
Making Decorative Screens	*Amanda Howes*
Making Fabergé-Style Eggs	*Denise Hopper*
Making Fairies and Fantastical Creatures	*Julie Sharp*
Making Hand-Sewn Boxes: Techniques and Projects	*Jackie Woolsey*
Making Mini Cards, Gift Tags & Invitations	*Glennis Gilruth*
Native American Bead Weaving	*Lynne Garner*
New Ideas for Crochet: Stylish Projects for the Home	*Darsha Capaldi*
Papercraft Projects for Special Occasions	*Sine Chesterman*
Papermaking and Bookbinding: Coastal Inspirations	*Joanne Kaar*
Patchwork for Beginners	*Pauline Brown*
Pyrography Designs	*Norma Gregory*
Rose Windows for Quilters	*Angela Besley*
Silk Painting for Beginners	*Jill Clay*
Sponge Painting	*Ann Rooney*
Stained Glass: Techniques and Projects	*Mary Shanahan*
Step-by-Step Pyrography Projects for the Solid Point Machine	*Norma Gregory*
Stitched Cards and Gift Tags for Special Occasions	*Carol Phillipson*
Tassel Making for Beginners	*Enid Taylor*

Tatting Collage — *Lindsay Rogers*
Tatting Patterns — *Lyn Morton*
Temari: A Traditional Japanese Embroidery Technique — *Margaret Ludlow*
Three-Dimensional Découpage: Innovative Projects for Beginners — *Hilda Stokes*
Trompe l'Oeil: Techniques and Projects — *Jan Lee Johnson*
Tudor Treasures to Embroider — *Pamela Warner*
Wax Art — *Hazel Marsh*

DOLLS' HOUSES AND MINIATURES

1/12 Scale Character Figures for the Dolls' House — *James Carrington*
Americana in 1/12 Scale: 50 Authentic Projects — *Joanne Ogreenc & Mary Lou Santovec*
The Authentic Georgian Dolls' House — *Brian Long*
A Beginners' Guide to the Dolls' House Hobby — *Jean Nisbett*
Celtic, Medieval and Tudor Wall Hangings in 1/12 Scale Needlepoint — *Sandra Whitehead*
Creating Decorative Fabrics: Projects in 1/12 Scale — *Janet Storey*
Dolls' House Accessories, Fixtures and Fittings — *Andrea Barham*
Dolls' House Furniture: Easy-to-Make Projects in 1/12 Scale — *Freida Gray*
Dolls' House Makeovers — *Jean Nisbett*
Dolls' House Window Treatments — *Eve Harwood*
Edwardian-Style Hand-Knitted Fashion for 1/12 Scale Dolls — *Yvonne Wakefield*
How to Make Your Dolls' House Special: Fresh Ideas for Decorating — *Beryl Armstrong*
Making 1/12 Scale Wicker Furniture for the Dolls' House — *Sheila Smith*
Making Miniature Chinese Rugs and Carpets — *Carol Phillipson*
Making Miniature Food and Market Stalls — *Angie Scarr*
Making Miniature Gardens — *Freida Gray*
Making Miniature Oriental Rugs & Carpets — *Meik & Ian McNaughton*
Making Miniatures: Projects for the 1/12 Scale Dolls' House — *Christiane Berridge*
Making Period Dolls' House Accessories — *Andrea Barham*
Making Tudor Dolls' Houses — *Derek Rowbottom*
Making Upholstered Furniture in 1/12 Scale — *Janet Storey*
Making Victorian Dolls' House Furniture — *Patricia King*
Medieval and Tudor Needlecraft: Knights and Ladies in 1/12 Scale — *Sandra Whitehead*
Miniature Bobbin Lace — *Roz Snowden*
Miniature Crochet: Projects in 1/12 Scale — *Roz Walters*
Miniature Embroidery for the Georgian Dolls' House — *Pamela Warner*
Miniature Embroidery for the Tudor and Stuart Dolls' House — *Pamela Warner*
Miniature Embroidery for the 20th-Century Dolls' House — *Pamela Warner*
Miniature Embroidery for the Victorian Dolls' House — *Pamela Warner*
Miniature Needlepoint Carpets — *Janet Granger*
More Miniature Oriental Rugs & Carpets — *Meik & Ian McNaughton*

Needlepoint 1/12 Scale: Design Collections for the Dolls' House — *Felicity Price*
New Ideas for Miniature Bobbin Lace — *Roz Snowden*
Patchwork Quilts for the Dolls' House: 20 Projects in 1/12 Scale — *Sarah Williams*
Simple Country Furniture Projects in 1/12 Scale — *Alison J. White*

WOODWORKING

Beginning Picture Marquetry — *Lawrence Threadgold*
Celtic Carved Lovespoons: 30 Patterns — *Sharon Littley & Clive Griffin*
Celtic Woodcraft — *Glenda Bennett*
Complete Woodfinishing (Revised Edition) — *Ian Hosker*
David Charlesworth's Furniture-Making Techniques — *David Charlesworth*
David Charlesworth's Furniture-Making Techniques – Volume 2 — *David Charlesworth*
Furniture-Making Projects for the Wood Craftsman — *GMC Publications*
Furniture-Making Techniques for the Wood Craftsman — *GMC Publications*
Furniture Projects with the Router — *Kevin Ley*
Furniture Restoration (Practical Crafts) — *Kevin Jan Bonner*
Furniture Restoration: A Professional at Work — *John Lloyd*
Furniture Restoration and Repair for Beginners — *Kevin Jan Bonner*
Furniture Restoration Workshop — *Kevin Jan Bonner*
Green Woodwork — *Mike Abbott*
Intarsia: 30 Patterns for the Scrollsaw — *John Everett*
Kevin Ley's Furniture Projects — *Kevin Ley*
Making Chairs and Tables – Volume 2 — *GMC Publications*
Making Classic English Furniture — *Paul Richardson*
Making Heirloom Boxes — *Peter Lloyd*
Making Screw Threads in Wood — *Fred Holder*
Making Woodwork Aids and Devices — *Robert Wearing*
Mastering the Router — *Ron Fox*
Pine Furniture Projects for the Home — *Dave Mackenzie*
Router Magic: Jigs, Fixtures and Tricks to Unleash your Router's Full Potential — *Bill Hylton*
Router Projects for the Home — *GMC Publications*
Router Tips & Techniques — *Robert Wearing*
Routing: A Workshop Handbook — *Anthony Bailey*
Routing for Beginners — *Anthony Bailey*
Sharpening: The Complete Guide — *Jim Kingshott*
Space-Saving Furniture Projects — *Dave Mackenzie*
Stickmaking: A Complete Course — *Andrew Jones & Clive George*
Stickmaking Handbook — *Andrew Jones & Clive George*
Storage Projects for the Router — *GMC Publications*
Veneering: A Complete Course — *Ian Hosker*
Veneering Handbook — *Ian Hosker*
Woodworking Techniques and Projects — *Anthony Bailey*
Woodworking with the Router: Professional Router Techniques any Woodworker can Use — *Bill Hylton & Fred Matlack*

MAGAZINES

WOODTURNING ◆ WOODCARVING ◆ FURNITURE & CABINETMAKING ◆ THE ROUTER
NEW WOODWORKING ◆ THE DOLLS' HOUSE MAGAZINE ◆ OUTDOOR PHOTOGRAPHY
BLACK & WHITE PHOTOGRAPHY ◆ TRAVEL PHOTOGRAPHY ◆ MACHINE KNITTING NEWS
KNITTING ◆ GUILD OF MASTER CRAFTSMEN NEWS

The above represents titles currently published or scheduled to be published. All are available direct from the Publishers or through bookshops, newsagents and specialist retailers. To place an order, or to obtain a complete catalogue, contact:

**GMC Publications 166 High Street Lewes East Sussex BN7 1XU United Kingdom
Tel: 01273 488005 Fax: 01273 478606 E-mail: pubs@thegmcgroup.com**

Orders by credit card are accepted